STUDY GUIDE
FOR
FIRE INSPECTION AND CODE ENFORCEMENT

FIFTH EDITION

DEVELOPED BY
ROBERT P. FLEISCHNER
PUBLICATIONS SPECIALIST

PUBLISHED BY
FIRE PROTECTION PUBLICATIONS
OKLAHOMA STATE UNIVERSITY

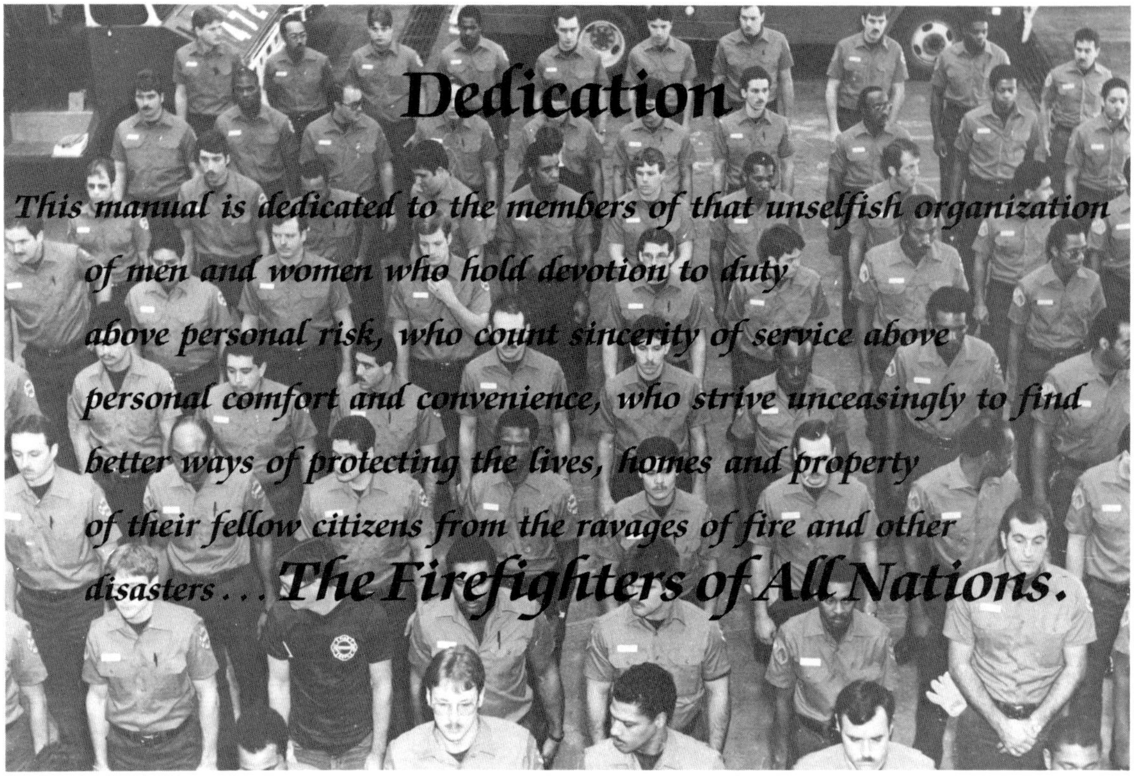

Dear Firefighter:

The International Fire Service Training Association (IFSTA) is an organization that exists for the purpose of serving firefighters' training needs. Fire Protection Publications is the publisher of IFSTA materials. Fire Protection Publications staff members participate in the National Fire Protection Association, International Association of Fire Chiefs, and the International Society of Fire Service Instructors.

If you need additional information concerning our organization or assistance with manual orders, contact:

Customer Services
Fire Protection Publications
Oklahoma State University
Stillwater, OK 74078-0118
1-(800) 654-4055

For assistance with training materials, recommended material for inclusion in a manual or questions on manual content, contact:

Technical Services
Fire Protection Publications
Oklahoma State University
Stillwater, OK 74078-0118
(405) 744-5723

First Printing, March 1989
Second Printing, June May 1994

ISBN 0-87939-080-8
Library of Congress 87-82661
First Edition
Printed in the United States of America

TABLE OF CONTENTS

CASE STUDIES

PREFACE

5/94 Special acknowledgement and thanks are extended to Pat Brock of the Oklahoma State University School of Fire Protection and Safety Technology and Gary Courtney of Oklahoma State University Fire Service Training for their comments on the case studies presented in this edition. The time and effort of James Sipes for the artwork in the case study section is also greatly appreciated.

Gratitude is also extended to the following members of the Fire Protection Publications staff whose contributions made the final publication of this study guide possible.

Michael Wieder, Associate Editor
Carol Smith, Associate Editor
Bob Fleischner, Publications Specialist
Cynthia Brakhage, Publications Specialist
Rhonda Wiley-Jones, Instructional Development Coordinator
Don Davis, Production Coordinator
Ann Moffat, Graphic Designer
Lori Schoonover, Graphic Designer
Karen Murphy, Phototypesetter Operator II
Desa Porter, Phototypesetter Operator II
Terry Jo Gaines, Senior Clerk Typist

Gene P. Carlson
Managing Editor

INTRODUCTION

This study guide is written at various levels of learning. Each chapter is designed to test knowledge and comprehension, application and analysis, and synthesis and evaluation; furthermore, it is designed to be used in conjunction with and as a supplement to the Fifth Edition of **Fire Inspection and Code Enforcement**. To receive the maximum learning experience from this study guide, it is recommended the student use the following procedure:

1. Read each chapter in the **Fire Inspection and Code Enforcement** manual. After reading the chapter, underline or highlight important topics and subject matter in that chapter.

2. Open the study guide to the corresponding chapter and answer all the questions in the study guide. **DO NOT** answer each question and immediately check that answer. Answer *all* the questions; then, check *all* the answers. If your answer is incorrect, the answer section contains the page number where the correct answer is located in the manual.

3. After checking and correcting your answers, complete the case studies located at the back of the book for that chapter. The case studies may require personal experience or material not necessarily presented in the manual. For example, you may need to reference NFPA or BOCA codes to provide an answer. Since regulations and standard operating procedures vary within jurisdictions, the answers to the case studies in this study guide may not always agree with your answers. The answers provided are a suggested possible consideration. Discuss your answers with your chief or training officer if they disagree with the ones written in the book.

1

Authority, Responsibility, and Organization

This chapter provides information that addresses performance objectives described in NFPA 1031, *Standard for Professional Qualifications for Fire Inspector* (1987), particularly those referenced in the following sections:

Fire Inspector I

3-1 General.

3-1.7

3-1.9

3-1.10

3-20 Inspection and Code Enforcement Procedures.

3-20.2.2

Authority, Responsibility, and Organization

1

TRUE/FALSE

Mark each statement true or false.

1. ☐ T ☐ F The fire inspector's responsibilities and legal authority are basically the same from area to area.

2. ☐ T ☐ F Statutes include federal regulations, state laws, and municipal ordinances.

3. ☐ T ☐ F Court decisions further affect authority and liability.

4. ☐ T ☐ F Jurisdictions are unable to give limited police power to fire inspectors.

5. ☐ T ☐ F In many jurisdictions, fire inspectors are considered to be public officers and therefore immune from liability.

6. ☐ T ☐ F Generally, fire inspectors are not held liable for discretionary acts.

7. ☐ T ☐ F Fire inspectors *cannot* be held liable for the manner in which they carry out or perform an act or policy.

8. ☐ T ☐ F Communities normally indemnify their officers.

9. ☐ T ☐ F The "Duty to Inspect" clauses are significant for inspectors because they normally prevent selective enforcement.

10. ☐ T ☐ F A liability area fire inspectors need to be aware of is violations of civil rights laws.

11. ☐ T ☐ F While researching the extent of authority, fire inspectors should determine if there is a right to enter into contracts with outside agencies.

12. ☐ T ☐ F Inspectors must request permission to inspect premises.

13. ☐ T ☐ F Fire inspectors will, from time to time, be asked to accept alternate materials, products, or systems as "equivalent" for code compliance.

14. ☐ T ☐ F Most codes establish an appeal procedure with a Board of Appeals that allows them to petition the legislature.

15. ☐ T ☐ F Fire inspectors need to know how a Board of Appeals functions.

16. ☐ T ☐ F An exchange of information with other agencies can help inspectors stay current.

1

17. ☐ T ☐ F Fire codes and standards that include fire-related considerations must vary to avoid confusion and duplication of effort.

18. ☐ T ☐ F The enforcement of various codes is often assigned to different agencies.

19. ☐ T ☐ F Within the structure of the local department, fire inspectors should know who their counterpart is (in terms of equivalent authority).

20. ☐ T ☐ F It is common for laws or ordinances to assign responsibilities to an agency, but not to provide the appropriate enforcement powers.

21. ☐ T ☐ F The local fire inspector is responsible for enforcing federal regulations.

22. ☐ T ☐ F Federal laws define and specify the powers and responsibilities of the state fire marshal.

23. ☐ T ☐ F Local laws are more specific and more personal in order to address the specific needs of a county, municipality, or a fire protection district.

24. ☐ T ☐ F Fire inspectors can use the model codes to help structure more adequate and effective fire prevention and inspection requirements.

MULTIPLE CHOICE

Circle the letter corresponding to the most appropriate response.

25. Which of the following is **NOT** required for inspectors to understand.

    A. The statutes that create the position, and how to change them
    B. Legal basis and limits of authority
    C. Laws, codes, and ordinances
    D. History of the laws and statutes they enforce

26. It is extremely important fire inspectors obtain a clear understanding of the statutes. To obtain an understanding of the statutes inspectors are responsible for enforcing, inspectors should contact the city or county ______.

    A. zoning commission
    B. attorney
    C. municipal court
    D. building commission

27. In general, inspectors should begin investigating legal status at the ______ level.

    A. local
    B. county
    C. federal
    D. state

28. It is better to conduct ______ inspections.
    A. fewer but more thorough
    B. many but less thorough
    C. random
    D. surprise

29. When violations are discovered, the owners are normally notified. They are ______.
    A. fined according to local laws
    B. given time to comply with the code
    C. ordered to appear in municipal court
    D. issued a "cease to operate" order

30. If fire inspectors find that the statutes in the local jurisdiction do not provide for adequate legal process to ensure code compliance, they should ______.
    A. consult an attorney to waiver the inadequate statute
    B. report the inadequate statute to a model code organization
    C. initiate action aimed at revising the statute to make it more effective
    D. seek a federal statute that supersedes the local statute

31. Inspectors may find laws at the federal, state, and local level. Which law usually applies?
    A. federal
    B. local
    C. state
    D. most stringent

32. Gaining compliance before a structure is occupied requires a close working relationship with the members of the local building department, planning department, and the ______.
    A. Federal Building Authority (FBA)
    B. zoning department
    C. contractor office
    D. utilities department

33. If the Board of Appeals rules that the code is too vague for enforcement, fire inspectors must ______.
    A. enforce the current code as is
    B. file a "Temporary Appeal Code" form
    C. consult a federal agency
    D. remove the vagueness in the code

SHORT ANSWER

Briefly answer each question in your own words.

34. Inspectors authority falls into two key areas. Name the two areas.
    A. ______________________________
    B. ______________________________

1

35. In assessing the statutes of the local jurisdiction dealing with code compliance, the inspector should know the answers to the following questions:

    A. Is noncompliance a __________ or __________ violation?

    B. What have been the major methods of achieving __________?

    C. What __________ are applied for voluntary action for compliance?

    D. What is the nature of the __________ applied to ensure compliance?

36. The constitution guarantees the owner of property the right to refuse entry to fire inspectors unless the inspector has

    ____

    ____

    ____

37. Warrantless entry violates the owners rights under which two Amendments?

    A. ____

    B. ____

38. If the owner does not comply with your recommendations, inspectors should decide upon three basic options.

    A. ____

    B. ____

    C. ____

39. There are two kinds of organizational structures that may affect the inspection activities of fire inspectors. Name them.

    A. ____

    B. ____

40. Many federal agencies have set forth many regulations designed to ensure the safety of the public. Name at least three regulations.

    A. ____

    B. ____

    C. ____

41. Fire safety regulations generally fall into two categories. Name these two categories.

    A. ____

    B. ____

2

Inspection Procedures

This chapter provides information that addresses performance objectives described in NFPA 1031, *Standard for Professional Qualifications for Fire Inspector* (1987), particularly those referenced in the following sections:

Fire Inspector I

3-1 General.

3-1.8

3-19 General Fire Safety.

3-19.1.3

3-19.3 Fire Drills.

3-19.3.1

3-19.3.2

3-20 Inspection and Code Enforcement Procedures.

3-20.1

3-20.2.2

3-20.2.3

3-20.2.4

3-20.2.5

3-20.2.6

3-20.2.7

3-20.2.8

3-20.2.10

3-20.3 Report Preparation.

3-20.3.1

3-20.3.2

3-20.4 Code Enforcement Equipment.

Fire Inspector II

4-10 Emergency Evacuation Plans.

4-10.1

4-10.2

Inspection Procedures 2

TRUE/FALSE

Mark each statement true or false.

1. ☐ T ☐ F One of the most important aspects of NFPA 101, *Life Safety Code®* is that it outlines standards and special considerations needed to build fire-resistant construction.
2. ☐ T ☐ F The inspector's manner of dress is a factor that may have a bearing on the amount of cooperation that can be expected.
3. ☐ T ☐ F A positive attitude will usually encourage a positive reaction from the management.
4. ☐ T ☐ F Upon arrival at the inspection site, inspectors should first inspect the outside premise for possible clues to inside violations.
5. ☐ T ☐ F Inspectors must have good listening skills.
6. ☐ T ☐ F It is common to begin an inspection with the exterior of the building.
7. ☐ T ☐ F Interior inspections should be conducted from top to bottom.
8. ☐ T ☐ F Diagrams provide an exact record of conditions at the time of inspection.
9. ☐ T ☐ F For every film, negative, print, or transparency, a record must be kept of any transfer to anyone other than the photographer.
10. ☐ T ☐ F The field sketch used to make the final inspection drawing should include all the necessary building information.
11. ☐ T ☐ F Written reports can be used as a basis for legal action.
12. ☐ T ☐ F Fire inspectors must record every fire inspection and file a formal report.
13. ☐ T ☐ F In an inspection report, inspectors should be opinionated when adding their personal comments.
14. ☐ T ☐ F Follow-up inspections are made to ensure that the recommendations made in the inspection report have been followed.
15. ☐ T ☐ F Many municipalities allow the jurisdiction's attorney to modify various provisions of the respective code.

2

16. ☐ T ☐ F Applications for appeal must normally be submitted to the Board of Appeals for review within 30 days of the notice from the inspecting official.

17. ☐ T ☐ F The Board of Appeals usually consists of five to seven members.

18. ☐ T ☐ F Questions regarding the admissibility of photographs in evidence should be cleared in advance with legal counsel.

19. ☐ T ☐ F As a witness, fire inspectors should confine their testimony to the facts, avoid "hearsay" and irrelevant statements.

20. ☐ T ☐ F Public involvement is an essential factor in a successful fire prevention program.

21. ☐ T ☐ F When investigating a complaint, fire inspectors should give the owner/tenant advance notice.

22. ☐ T ☐ F Fire drills should be conducted in all types of occupancies.

23. ☐ T ☐ F The responsibility for planning and executing fire drills lies with the occupancy's fire loss prevention and control management staff.

24. ☐ T ☐ F Plans for drills need to be discussed with both middle and line management.

25. ☐ T ☐ F Exit drills should be conducted at least yearly and at different times of the day.

26. ☐ T ☐ F In occupancies such as nursing homes, hospitals, hotels, and stores, fire drills usually involve staff personnel only to avoid alarming patients, guests, or customers.

27. ☐ T ☐ F Drills in educational occupancies should ensure that all persons in the building actually participate.

28. ☐ T ☐ F The lives of inmates, visitors, and security personnel in correctional facilities depend upon the quick and effective actions of the fire department.

29. ☐ T ☐ F The vast majority of fires in correctional facilities are caused due to the age of the facility and limited inspection practices.

30. ☐ T ☐ F In hotels and motels, management should post evacuation procedures in all rooms, at all fire alarm stations, and by exits.

31. ☐ T ☐ F Inspectors should identify and implement home fire safety programs.

32. ☐ T ☐ F Home fire safety programs are designed to instruct the public in emergency procedures to follow if they are involved in a fire.

MULTIPLE CHOICE

Circle the letter corresponding to the most appropriate response.

33. Which of the following is **NOT** usual human behavior during a fire?

    A. Detection of the fire
    B. Definition of the situation
    C. Save important items
    D. Cope with the incident

34. It is helpful to review previous inspection reports for a particular occupancy in order to become familiar with the ______.

    A. hazards that are likely to be found
    B. personnel in charge of the occupancy
    C. layout of the building
    D. hydrant locations around the premises

35. Fire inspectors should make prior contact with the property owner to ______.

    A. announce the inspection time
    B. request an inspection date and time
    C. allow "pre-compliance" time
    D. ensure the property owner is present

36. The fundamentals of effective oral communication are enthusiasm, confidence, preparation and ______.

    A. strength
    B. presentation
    C. diction
    D. voice inflection

37. The purpose of the closing interview is to note the good conditions and discuss the ______.

    A. date and time of the next inspection
    B. fire drill procedures for that occupancy
    C. conditions that need correcting
    D. ways he/she could extinguish a small fire

38. There are three general types of drawings used to show building information: the plot plan, the floor plan, and the ______ plan.

    A. electrical
    B. mechanical
    C. sprinkler
    D. elevation

39. After completing the final inspection drawing, fire inspectors should attach ______.

    A. clear legible notes
    B. the previous inspection drawing
    C. the next tentative inspection date
    D. none of the above

2

40. In the contents of the formal report, fire inspectors should ______.

A. illustrate, compile, and analyze
B. critique, analyze, and compile
C. inform, analyze, and recommend
D. analyze, warn, and authorize

41. During a follow-up inspection, if the hazards have not been corrected and it is apparent the owner is making no effort to correct them, then the inspector should ______.

A. issue a "cease to operate" order
B. consult the jurisdiction's attorney
C. issue a final notice
D. issue a citation

42. When taking cases to court, inspectors are sometimes called upon to be an advisor. Fire inspectors can assist the prosecuting attorney with information about the fire ordinances, technical terms, and ______.

A. angles of prosecution
B. personal experiences
C. Board of Appeals decisions
D. facts of the case

43. When responding to a complaint inspection, inspectors frequently encounter ______.

A. vacant premises
B. negative attitudes
C. life-threatening situations
D. cooperative tenants

44. In the event of a fire, one of the biggest decisions made by management, and perhaps the most difficult for some, is ______.

A. when to call the fire department
B. when to evacuate the building
C. when to save valuable documents
D. when to fight the fire with extinguishers

45. A Phase I procedure is explained by the acronym "REACT." The acronym "REACT" is:

A. R – Report the fire immediately.
E – Extinguish the fire if possible.
A – Allow other personnel to assist.
C – Cooperate in any way possible.
T – Try to evacuate any occupants.
B. R – Report the fire immediately.
E – Evacuate those in immediate danger.
A – Acquire a fire extinguisher.
C – Control the fire.
T – Team with other personnel.

2

C. R – Remove those in immediate danger.
   E – Ensure that the room door is closed.
   A – Activate the fire alarm if not activated.
   C – Call the fire department.
   T – Try to extinguish or control the fire.

D. R – Report the fire immediately.
   E – Evacuate those in immediate danger.
   A – Assist in locating extinguishers.
   C – Control the fire.
   T – Think rationally and intelligently.

46. Hotels and motels provide different problems for fire inspectors with regard to fire exit drills and evacuation procedures because of the ______.

   A. number of rooms usually found
   B. temporary nature of the occupancy
   C. high turn-over rate of personnel
   D. individual activities within the structure

MATCHING

Match the Standard Map Symbol with its correct name.

47. ___ Fire Department Connection
48. ___ Not Sprinklered
49. ___ Fire Alarm Box
50. ___ Single Hydrant
51. ___ Fire Escape
52. ___ Public Water Service
53. ___ Private Water Service
54. ___ Vertical Pipe or Standpipe
55. ___ Fire Detection System
56. ___ Sprinkler Riser (Size Indicated)
57. ___ Triple Hydrant
58. ___ Fire Pump
59. ___ Frame Enclosed Elevator
60. ___ Open Elevator

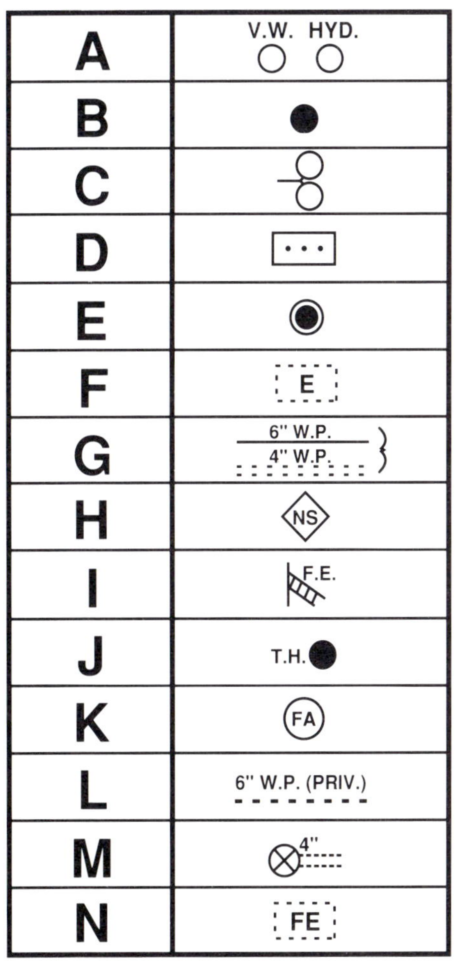

2

Match the correct color code with the description.

61. ___ Fire Resistive Protected Steel
62. ___ Brick, Hollow Tile
63. ___ Frame — Wood, Stucco
64. ___ Concrete, Stone or Hollow Concrete Block
65. ___ Noncombustible Unprotected Steel

A. Yellow
B. Gray
C. Blue
D. Red
E. Brown

SHORT ANSWER

Briefly answer each question in your own words.

66. What are three important actions fire departments consider before a fire?

A. ______________________________

B. ______________________________

C. ______________________________

67. Personal safety should always be considered. If an area is under construction, what two minimum items should fire inspectors always wear?

A. ______________________________

B. ______________________________

68. Name at least five pieces of information that is collected during the exterior inspection.

____

____

____

____

____

69. Name five pieces of general information a field sketch should show.

____

____

____

____

____

70. During the closing interview, some individuals will display hostility toward the inspector's remarks and recommendation. In these instances, what should you do?

____

____

____

____

71. If voluntary compliance is not gained after reinspection, most jurisdictions issue some type of sanction. Name three sanctions.

72. In preparation for court, fire inspectors should gather all pertinent information used for prosecution. Name three items used as evidence.

A.

B.

C.

73. In 1981, Lee M. Feldstein prepared a publication for the Federal Emergency Management Agency that lists additional sources of code information. Name that publication.

74. The northwest section of a 10,000 square foot (9 290 m^2) industrial plant appears to be on fire. Although flames are not visible, there is thick black smoke, the employees evacuate the area. Should management order an evacuation of the entire building? It is raining outside. Why or why not?

75. Hospital and nursing homes require special evacuation procedures. Identify the following Phases:

A. Phase I

B. Phase II

C. Phase III

D. Phase IV

76. During a fire in a correctional facility, what is of primary importance?

2

77. Place a "X" by the equipment usually needed during a general inspection.

    ___ coveralls
    ___ clipboard
    ___ telephone book
    ___ paper and pencil
    ___ matches or lighter
    ___ small caliber handgun
    ___ safety hat and shoes
    ___ goggles
    ___ 50-foot measuring tape
    ___ flashlight
    ___ turnout gear
    ___ camera with strobe
    ___ pitot tube and gauges
    ___ ¼-inch socket set
    ___ reference books
    ___ atmospheric detection equipment

3

Principles of Combustion and Fire Cause Determination

This chapter provides information that addresses performance objectives described in NFPA 1031, *Standard for Professional Qualifications for Fire Inspector* (1987), particularly those referenced in the following sections:

Fire Inspector I

3-9 Fire Behavior

3-9.9

3-12 Flammable and Combustible Liquids.
(see NFPA 30, *Flammable and Combustible Liquids Code.***)**

3-12.1.5

3-20.6 Fire Cause Determination.

Fire Inspector II

4-11 Fire Cause Determination.

Principles of Combustion and Fire Cause Determination

3

TRUE/FALSE

Mark each statement true or false.

1. ☐ T ☐ F Fire is a chemical process known as combustion.
2. ☐ T ☐ F Atmospheric air contains 78% oxygen, 21% nitrogen, and 1% other gases.
3. ☐ T ☐ F One of the characteristics of chemical heat energy is spontaneous heating.
4. ☐ T ☐ F One of the characteristics of electrical heat energy is frictional sparks.
5. ☐ T ☐ F One of the characteristics of mechanical heat energy is heat of compression.
6. ☐ T ☐ F The characteristics of nuclear heat energy are nuclear fission and fusion.
7. ☐ T ☐ F Pyrolysis is defined as the chemical decomposition of a liquid through the action of heat.
8. ☐ T ☐ F The larger the surface area of a solid object, the faster the material will heat.
9. ☐ T ☐ F The density of liquids in relation to water is known as the specific gravity.
10. ☐ T ☐ F Liquids with a specific gravity greater than one are lighter than water.
11. ☐ T ☐ F Most flammable liquids have a specific gravity of less than one.
12. ☐ T ☐ F The scales of temperature are based on the freezing and boiling points of pure water.
13. ☐ T ☐ F When matter (fuel) burns, it undergoes molecular change.
14. ☐ T ☐ F A backdraft explosion occurs when stalled combustion is resumed by instantaneous combustion of oxygen and carbon particles when air is introduced to the combustion zone.

3

15. ☐ T ☐ F Ventilation is the systematic removal of heated air, smoke, water, and gases from a structure.

16. ☐ T ☐ F Flameover and flashover mean the same thing.

17. ☐ T ☐ F A fire hazard may be defined as any material, condition, or act that contributes to the start of a fire or that increases the extent and severity of a fire.

18. ☐ T ☐ F Fire hazards can be considered a cause-effect phenomena that cannot usually be prevented.

19. ☐ T ☐ F Fire can start by a hazardous act, an accident, or arson.

20. ☐ T ☐ F The terms "fire cause" and "fire hazard" mean the same thing and are used interchangeably to describe the reason for the incident.

21. ☐ T ☐ F The primary objective of fire cause determination is discovering who is responsible for setting the fire.

22. ☐ T ☐ F The chief has the legal responsibility for fire cause determination.

23. ☐ T ☐ F Calling for a fire investigator means arson is the cause of the fire.

MULTIPLE CHOICE

Circle the letter corresponding to the most appropriate response.

24. Heat is a form of energy caused by ______.

    A. the movement of molecules
    B. the transfer of protons
    C. the rapid expansion of atoms
    D. none of the above

25. When a body of matter is heated, and the temperature increases, the speed of ______.

    A. decomposition multiplies inversely
    B. the protons increase activity
    C. the molecules increase activity
    D. all of the above

26. Fuels must be converted to gas before ______ occurs.

    A. pyrolysis
    B. vaporization
    C. combustion
    D. all of the above

27. Converting fuel to a gaseous state is the ______ phase of combustion.

    A. first
    B. second
    C. third
    D. fourth

28. A vertically shaped solid fuel will spread fire more rapidly than a horizontally shaped solid fuel due to the increased heat transfer through ______.

A. collection
B. constriction
C. convection
D. conduction

29. Volatile liquids have a ______.

A. low flash point
B. high specific gravity
C. high flash index
D. low flash index

30. A gas is a liquid that tends to assume the shape of its container, has no specific volume, and is ______.

A. always lighter than air
B. always heavier than air
C. always flammable
D. always compressible

31. The mixture of the fuel vapor with an oxidizer (air) within the flammable range is the ______ phase of combustion.

A. first
B. second
C. third
D. fourth

32. The four products of combustion are ______.

A. heat, flame, ash, and gas
B. heat, gas, light, and smoke
C. fuel, heat, flame, and gas
D. carbon, flame, smoke, and gas

33. The missing element(s) of combustion in the smoldering phase of burning is/are ______.

A. oxygen
B. fuel
C. heat
D. A and B

34. The level of hazard present in an occupancy or structure is determined by the authority having jurisdiction, such as the ______.

A. fire chief
B. fire marshal
C. fire inspector
D. any of the above

3

35. When firefighters discover possible physical evidence, they should report everything to a superior officer and ______.

A. gather samples of what was reported
B. photograph everything they reported
C. do not disturb anything needlessly
D. begin salvage and overhaul

MATCHING

Match the term with the correct description.

36. ___ Flash Point
37. ___ Fire Point
38. ___ Flameover
39. ___ Flashover
40. ___ Conduction
41. ___ Convection
42. ___ Radiation
43. ___ Rollover
44. ___ Ignition Temperature
45. ___ Fire Hazard

A. The temperature at which liquids vaporize.
B. The temperature at which liquids will continue to burn.
C. The minimum temperature at which a solid fuel emits sufficient vapor to form an ignitable mixture.
D. The temperature at which the fuel will continue to burn.
E. A condition when a portion of heated gases trapped around a ceiling burst into flame and spreads across the ceiling until all heated gas has ignited.
F. When the entire contents of the fire area become heated to their ignition temperature. Simultaneous ignition occurs and the area becomes engulfed in flames.
G. The transfer of heat from one body to another body by direct contact of two bodies or by an intervening heat-conducting medium.
H. The transfer of heat by the movement of air or liquid.
I. The transmission of heat waves through air.
J. Any action, whether accidental or deliberate, that joins a fuel supply with a heat source at sufficient temperature to sustain combustion.
K. Contents of low combustibility in which no self-propagating fire is likely to occur.
L. The fire consumes the free oxygen until there is insufficient oxygen to react with the fuel.
M. The systematic removal of heated air, smoke, water, and gases from a structure.
N. Means the same as flameover.

SHORT ANSWER

Briefly answer each question in your own words.

46. The same elements that are necessary for fire to exist are also necessary for animal life to exist. Name those three elements.

    A. ______________________________

    B. ______________________________

    C. ______________________________

47. There are four general categories of heat energy. Name those four categories.

    A. ______________________________

    B. ______________________________

    C. ______________________________

    D. ______________________________

48. Fuel may be found in any of three states of matter. Name those three states.

    A. ______________________________

    B. ______________________________

    C. ______________________________

49. What three elements does the fire triangle illustrate?

    A. ______________________________

    B. ______________________________

    C. ______________________________

50. What does the fourth side of the fire tetrahedron represent?

    ____

51. Heat and temperature are not the same. What is the difference between the two?

    ____

    ____

    ____

52. Fire itself has three progressive phases: incipient, free burning, and smoldering. Define these three phases.

    A. Incipient ______________________________

    ____

    ____

    ____

    B. Free burning ______________________________

    ____

    ____

    ____

3

C. Hot smoldering

53. In what terms do fire inspectors often measure fire hazards?

54. Describe how the following fuel hazards are measured?

A. Flammable Gases

B. Flammable Liquids

C. Solids

55. Name five examples of common fire hazards and five examples of special fire hazards within your jurisdiction.

Common fire hazards:

Special fire hazards:

56. There are three classifications of hazards: Low Hazards, Ordinary Hazards, and High Hazards. Define these classifications.

A. Low Hazard

B. Ordinary Hazard ______________________________

____

____

C. High Hazard ______________________________

____

____

57. The reasons for fire cause determination are numerous. Name five.

____

____

____

____

____

58. Evidence that is moved must be handled carefully. Briefly explain how to handle the following evidence.

A. Glass or bottles for fingerprints

____

____

B. Ash and most fire debris

____

____

C. Flammable liquid containers

____

____

D. Flammable liquid samples

____

____

E. Charred documents

____

____

F. Tire tracks or footprints

____

____

4

General Fire Safety

This chapter provides information that addresses performance objectives described in NFPA 1031, *Standard for Professional Qualifications for Fire Inspector* (1987), particularly those referenced in the following sections:

Fire Inspector I

3-18 Principles of Electricity.

3-18.1

3-18.2

3-18.3

3-18.4

3-19 General Fire Safety.

3-19.1.2

3-19.1.4

General Fire Safety 4

TRUE/FALSE

Mark each statement true or false.

1. ☐ T ☐ F Inspectors will encounter some general fire safety matters that apply to **ALL** occupancies.

2. ☐ T ☐ F Trash containers should be constructed of a noncombustible material and should not tip over.

3. ☐ T ☐ F Building inspectors consider how many waste containers are needed and where they should be placed.

4. ☐ T ☐ F Inspection of exterior trash disposal for fire safety are part of the duties of the county health department.

5. ☐ T ☐ F Fire inspectors should check individual work areas and operations within an industrial occupancy.

6. ☐ T ☐ F Operations using flammable or combustible liquids should have 5-gallon (2 kg) metal buckets to catch any drippings.

7. ☐ T ☐ F Ashtrays (for cigarette and cigar smokers) should **NOT** be placed near ventilation equipment.

8. ☐ T ☐ F After receiving a permit for open burning, trash or rubbish may be burned only between 7:30 a.m. and 4:30 p.m.

9. ☐ T ☐ F In occupancies where flammable decorations are used, fire inspectors must make sure that highly flammable materials are treated with a fire-retardant substance.

10. ☐ T ☐ F Electrical energy can produce unwanted and unexpected fires because of the by-product of electrical energy: heat.

11. ☐ T ☐ F Basically, electricity involves the transfer or movement of protons between atoms.

12. ☐ T ☐ F Glass, dry wood, or rubber impede the flow of electrical energy.

13. ☐ T ☐ F The flow of electricity through a wiring system is like the flow of water through a water distribution system.

14. ☐ T ☐ F If an electrical circuit or switch is closed, the resistance is infinite.

15. ☐ T ☐ F As a general rule, the greatest threat of electricity involves the possibility of electrical fires.

16. ☐ T ☐ F Currents of 100 milliamperes may cause ventricular fibrillation of the heart.

4

17. ☐ T ☐ F After being exposed to 200 milliamperes or more, people may lose consciousness and suffer severe burns.

18. ☐ T ☐ F The majority of accidents that result in injury, fires, or damaged machinery occur during maintenance and repair operations.

19. ☐ T ☐ F If an electrical fire should occur, occupants should first be instructed to deenergize the circuit.

20. ☐ T ☐ F Deenergizing the main supply of current to circuits will make the circuits safe for personnel and inspectors.

21. ☐ T ☐ F In order to inspect electrical equipment and installations properly, inspectors must be allowed to activate switches under the supervision of trained personnel.

22. ☐ T ☐ F Fire inspectors can prevent static electricity from being generated.

23. ☐ T ☐ F Bonding involves connecting two objects that conduct electricity with something that is also a conductor.

24. ☐ T ☐ F Grounding involves connecting an object that conducts electricity to the ground with something that is a conductor.

25. ☐ T ☐ F Another acceptable means of dissipating static charges is to ionize the air in the immediate area where the charges accumulate.

MULTIPLE CHOICE

Circle the letter corresponding to the most appropriate response.

26. The storage and disposal of trash and debris often present serious problems in terms of fire hazards because of ______.

    A. bacteria, flammability, and apathy
    B. storage, quantity, and flammability
    C. ignorance, negligence, and apathy
    D. storage, flammability, and apathy

27. Where smoking is permitted, fire inspectors must make sure an adequate number of ______.

    A. "smoking area" signs are posted
    B. ashtrays are conveniently located
    C. portable extinguishers are available
    D. ventilation devices are installed

28. Open burning of trash and rubbish should be controlled by the ______.

    A. Environmental Protection Agency (EPA)
    B. state health department
    C. local ordinances
    D. Department of Sanitation

29. Fire inspectors should make sure that the incinerators are in good shape and ______.

    A. its spark arresters are in place
    B. the fire department is notified
    C. a garden hose is charged
    D. explosive materials will not be incinerated

30. The distance from any structure when using approved incinerators is at least ______.

    A. 10 feet (3 m)
    B. 15 feet (5 m)
    C. 20 feet (6 m)
    D. 25 feet (8 m)

31. The distance from all structures during open burning (fire) is at least ______.

    A. 20 feet (6 m)
    B. 30 feet (10 m)
    C. 40 feet (13 m)
    D. 50 feet (15 m)

32. When considering the flammability of decorations with regard to fire safety, fire inspectors must remember that the degree of hazard involved depends upon ______.

    A. the availability of egress versus occupancy
    B. the design of the automatic sprinkler system
    C. the ease with which the decoration can be ignited
    D. precautionary measures initiated by occupants

33. Materials that allow a free movement of large numbers of electrons are referred to as ______.

    A. conductors
    B. semiconductors
    C. resistors
    D. capacitors

34. Copper, gold, silver, and aluminum are among the more common materials used in ______.

    A. controllers
    B. wiring
    C. nodes
    D. diodes

35. Materials that are neither good conductors nor good insulators are ______.

    A. hemiconductors
    B. semiconductors
    C. demiconductors
    D. none of the above

4

36. Electrical flow (current) is measured in units of ______.

    A. voltage (volts)
    B. amperes (amps)
    C. ohms
    D. watts

37. Electrical pressure is measured in units of ______.

    A. voltage (volts)
    B. amperes (amps)
    C. ohms
    D. watts

38. Resistance in an electrical circuit is measured in units of ______.

    A. voltage (volts)
    B. amperes (amps)
    C. ohms
    D. watts

39. The damage produced by an electrical shock depends upon ______.

    A. the number of vital organs affected
    B. the ambient temperature and weather
    C. the number of ohms passed through the body
    D. if rubber boots and gloves were worn

40. A lethal current to humans is from ______.

    A. 100 to 200 milliamperes
    B. 200 to 300 milliamperes
    C. 300 to 400 milliamperes
    D. 400 milliamperes or greater

41. Rectifiers introduce an additional problem into the fire situation; when they burn, they produce poisonous fumes of ______.

    A. carbon monoxide
    B. trimenthenol chloride
    C. selenium dioxide
    D. sulfur dioxide

42. When an inspector must evaluate an electrical installation in a damp or wet location, he or she should have ______.

    A. full turnout gear
    B. day boots
    C. a rubber mat to walk on
    D. rubber gloves (minimum ⅛-inch thick)

43. One of the best methods of controlling static electricity associated with the manufacturing of paper, cloth, and fiber involves controlling the ______.

    A. temperature
    B. rag content
    C. ventilation
    D. humidity

SHORT ANSWER

Briefly answer each question in your own words.

44. Containers should be available for specific types of waste. Name three waste materials requiring special waste containers.

45. Flammable industrial waste, such as oil or greasy materials, should be discarded in special containers. Briefly describe these containers.

46. When observing general housekeeping practices, fire inspectors should check the basic structural components of the occupancy. List what components this includes, and what inspectors should be looking for.

47. Mops used to clean up hazardous drippings should have detachable handles and should be stored in special containers. Briefly describe these containers.

48. Commercially designed ashtrays have certain requirements. Briefly describe the design.

49. Why should fire inspectors evaluate the location selected for open burning?

4

50. Flame tests should be performed in such a way that they cannot result in a fire that can get out of control. Briefly explain the procedure for testing decorations and identify what should not occur.

____

____

____

____

____

51. Define static electricity.

____

____

____

____

52. Water flow has three major components: quantity, pressure, and resistance. Electrical flow is also measured by quantity, pressure, and resistance. Show the analogy between water and electricity by identifying the units of measurements of each in the table below.

Relationship Between Water and Electrons

Measurement	*Water*	*Electricity*
Quantity	______	______
Pressure	______	______
Resistance	______	______

53. The seriousness of an electrical shock depends on four conditions. Name those conditions.

A. ____

B. ____

C. ____

D. ____

54. Why is proper grounding of electrical equipment so important to the user?

____

____

____

____

55. What happens to the shell of an appliance if it is incorrectly grounded?

____

____

____

56. What are the two major hazards associated with using batteries other than the possibility of a person being shocked?

A. ______________________________

____

B. ______________________________

____

57. Many common processes generate static charges. List four examples.

____

____

____

____

58. Fire inspectors must answer four questions concerning static electricity as an ignition source. Identify those four questions.

A. ______________________________

____

B. ______________________________

____

C. ______________________________

____

D. ______________________________

____

59. Every inspector should be able to define the procedure that citizens should take to report fires and other emergencies correctly. Explain the procedures for citizens to notify the fire department by telephone, fire alarm box, and fire alarm station.

Telephone: ______________________________

____

____

____

____

Fire Alarm Box: ______________________________

____

____

Fire Alarm Station: ______________________________

____

____

5

Building Construction for Fire and Life Safety

This chapter provides information that addresses performance objectives described in NFPA 1031, *Standard for Professional Qualifications for Fire Inspector* (1987), particularly those referenced in the following sections:

Fire Inspector I

3-17 Heating and Cooking Equipment.

3-17.1

3-17.2

3-17.3

3-17.4

3-19.1.6 Interior Finishes.
(See NFPA 101, *Life Safety Code®* **and NFPA 220,** *Standard on Types of Building Construction.***)**

3-19.1.6.1

3-19.1.6.2

3-19.1.6.3

3-19.1.7 Building Construction.

3-19.1.7.1

3-19.1.7.2

3-19.1.7.3

3-19.1.7.4

3-19.1.7.6

3-19.1.7.7

3-19.1.7.8

3-19.1.7.9

3-19.1.7.10

3-19.1.8 Building Equipment.

3-19.1.8.1

3-19.1.8.2

3-19.1.8.3

3-19.2 Decorations, Decorative Materials, and Furnishings.

3-19.2.1

3-19.2.2

Fire Inspector II

4-7 Heating and Cooking Equipment.

4-7.1

4-7.2

4-7.3

4-7.4 Industrial Ovens and Furnaces.

4-7.4.1

4-7.4.2

4-8 Safety to Life.
(See NFPA 101, *Life Safety Code.***)**

4-8.2.1

4-8.2 Interior Finishes.

4-8.2.2

Building Construction For Fire and Life Safety

5

TRUE/FALSE

Mark each statement true or false.

1. ☐ T ☐ F Fire can alter the structural systems of a building.

2. ☐ T ☐ F Steel beams are the only part of a building that fire does not affect.

3. ☐ T ☐ F Roofs that can be easily ignited by flaming brands have **NOT** been a frequent cause of *major* fires.

4. ☐ T ☐ F In general, construction classifications are based upon materials used in construction and upon hourly fire-resistance ratings of structural components.

5. ☐ T ☐ F NFPA 256, *Methods of Fire Tests of Roof Coverings* evaluates the flammability of the roof covering, the protection it provides to a combustible roof deck, and the potential for producing flaming brands.

6. ☐ T ☐ F No material is immune to damage from severe and prolonged exposure to fire temperatures.

7. ☐ T ☐ F It is necessary to specify the desired fire resistance of materials to be used in a building.

8. ☐ T ☐ F The burning brand test is used to determine whether burning brands are likely to ignite adjacent grasses and landscaping.

9. ☐ T ☐ F The rain test is used to determine if the fire-retardant abilities of the roof are adversely affected by rain.

10. ☐ T ☐ F When the rain test is complete, the testing is complete, and the roofing material is assigned a Class based on the cumulative test results.

11. ☐ T ☐ F Fire resistance is defined as the ability of a structural assembly to maintain its load-bearing ability under fire conditions.

12. ☐ T ☐ F Fire-resistance ratings are given for each individual structural element.

13. ☐ T ☐ F The fire-resistance ratings form the basis for the types of building construction that are recognized in building codes.

14. ☐ T ☐ F An important consideration in overall building fire safety is the combustibility of the materials used for interior finish.

5

15. ☐ T ☐ F The speed and extent to which flame travels over interior surfaces are primary concerns in evaluating occupancies for life safety.

16. ☐ T ☐ F A "Flame Spread Rating" is a numerical rating to designate the pattern a flame burns a material.

17. ☐ T ☐ F The fire wall should extend from the foundation of a structure through and above the roof.

18. ☐ T ☐ F Self-supporting fire walls are most often found in one- and two-story industrial occupancies and storage facilities that have unprotected steel frame construction.

19. ☐ T ☐ F A fire partition usually has a greater degree of fire resistivity than a fire wall.

20. ☐ T ☐ F Doorways in fire walls do not reduce the walls' effectiveness as fire barriers.

21. ☐ T ☐ F A fire door assembly is the special mounting brackets used to secure the fire door with interlocking bolts during a fire emergency.

22. ☐ T ☐ F Standard fire doors are always horizontal or vertical sliding doors.

23. ☐ T ☐ F Fire doors that serve as part of an exit should always be able to be opened from either direction.

24. ☐ T ☐ F Horizontal sliding fire doors are mounted close to the wall and require little floor space and room for operation.

25. ☐ T ☐ F Fire inspectors must make sure that rolling doors are checked regularly to ensure that objects do not prevent them from closing completely.

26. ☐ T ☐ F The windows used in stairwell fire doors must be wired glass and no longer than 100 square inches (65 416 mm^2).

27. ☐ T ☐ F Draft curtains prevent the mushrooming effect of heat and smoke as it settles within a large building.

28. ☐ T ☐ F Removal of the toxic gases produced in a fire situation has often been the determining factor in successful rescue and effective fire control.

29. ☐ T ☐ F Monitors are vents that resemble small buildings on the top of structures.

30. ☐ T ☐ F Continuous gravity vents consist of a continuous narrow slot opening protected by a weather hood.

31. ☐ T ☐ F Unit-type vents are usually large, with an effective venting area in excess of 100 square feet (9.29 m^2).

32. ☐ T ☐ F Roof skylights may be used as vents if the glass is of ordinary strength.

33. ☐ T ☐ F Power roof ventilators are activated by fire conditions and eliminate the need for large roof vents.

34. ☐ T ☐ F A fire damper is a device that automatically interrupts air flow.

35. ☐ T ☐ F Fire stopping is a means of limiting the spread of fire by the use of a solid wall.

36. ☐ T ☐ F A self-contained wall furnace, indirect fired gas or oil heater installed in or on a wall is considered a central heating appliance.

37. ☐ T ☐ F Filtering devices, used to particulate dust and pollens, are classified into three classes: Class I — does not contribute as fuel, Class II — burns moderately with no smoke, and Class III — burns moderately with moderate smoke.

38. ☐ T ☐ F In HVAC systems, crawl spaces are not considered fire hazards because they are used as plenums.

39. ☐ T ☐ F The duct work in HVAC systems may be combustible.

40. ☐ T ☐ F A smoke damper is a device that restricts the passage of smoke in an air handling system.

41. ☐ T ☐ F A fire inspector encountering instances of structural abuse during fire inspection should refer the matter to the local building department.

42. ☐ T ☐ F Exhaust systems for cooking equipment are a necessity as well as a major fire problem.

MULTIPLE CHOICE

Circle the letter corresponding to the most appropriate response.

43. Test methods have been developed to evaluate the fire hazards of roof coverings. Roof materials are classified as ______.

   A. Class A, Class B, and Class C
   B. Class 1, Class 2, and Class 3
   C. Class I, Class II, and Class III
   D. Class L, Class M, and Class H

44. During the intermittent flame exposure test, a gas flame of specified temperature is applied to the test deck in a/an ______ application.

   A. continuous
   B. random
   C. on/off
   D. low, medium, and high

5

45. During the spread of flame test, the gas flame is applied in a/an ______ application.

    A. continuous
    B. random
    C. on/off
    D. low, medium, and high

46. During the spread of flame test, the gas flame is applied for 10 minutes to ______ decks.

    A. Class A and Class B
    B. Class 1 and Class 2
    C. Class I and Class II
    D. Class L and Class M

47. During the spread of flame test, the gas flame is applied for 4 minutes to ______ decks.

    A. Class C
    B. Class 3
    C. Class III
    D. Class H

48. During the flying brand test, a flame is applied to the roof covering for a specified time with a ______ air current.

    A. 10-mph (16.1 km/h)
    B. 12-mph (19.3 km/h)
    C. 14-mph (22.5 km/h)
    D. 16-mph (25.7 km/h)

49. During the rain test, spray nozzles are mounted above the test decks, these nozzles deliver an average of ______ of water per hour.

    A. 0.5 inch (12.7 mm)
    B. 0.7 inch (17.8 mm)
    C. 0.9 inch (22.9 mm)
    D. 1.0 inch (25.4 mm)

50. The fire resistance of a structural component is a function of various properties of the materials used. This includes their combustibility, thermal conductivity, chemical composition, and ______.

    A. protective coating
    B. age
    C. NFC factors
    D. dimensions

51. The fire-resistance ratings of materials are determined by using the ______.

    A. standard time-temperature curve
    B. flame resistance ratio
    C. NFC Material Flame test
    D. Construction Assembly test

52. In the standard time-temperature curve, the temperature rises to 1,000°F (538°C) in 5 minutes, then to ______.

A. 1,700°F (927°C) in 30 minutes
B. 1,700°F (927°C) in 60 minutes
C. 2,000°F (1 093°C) in 30 minutes
D. 2,000°F (1 093°C) in 60 minutes

53. Although an assembly may fail at any time, fire resistance is expressed in certain standard intervals such as 15 minutes, 30 minutes, 45 minutes, 1 hour, 1.5 hours, 2 hours, 3 hours, and ______ hours.

A. 4
B. 5
C. 6
D. 9

54. The most widely used test for determining the surface burning characteristics of interior finishes is the ______ Tunnel Test.

A. Intermittent Flame
B. Flame-Resistance
C. UL Fire
D. Steiner

55. The numerical flame spread rating is compared to two standard materials: asbestos cement board and ______.

A. walnut
B. red oak
C. blond ash
D. northern pine

56. In addition to the flame spread rating, the tunnel test provides two other measures of combustibility. They are the ______.

A. rate-of-rise index and toxic by-products
B. fuel contributed and the smoke developed
C. toxic by-products and smoke developed
D. FNC factors and direction of burn probability

57. Fire doors designed to serve as exit enclosures, such as doors into stairwells, must be ______.

A. rated at 6 hours
B. windowless
C. side hinged
D. able to be opened from both directions

58. A major problem with a window in a fire door is that the window permits ______.

A. a passage for flame
B. a passage for radiant heat
C. a hazard from broken glass
D. a probable backdraft explosion

59. In the area being protected, the depth of a draft curtain should be at least _______ of the ceiling height.

    A. 20 percent
    B. 25 percent
    C. 30 percent
    D. 32 percent

60. Fire dampers are usually activated by _______.

    A. a 9-volt power source
    B. manual control
    C. fusible links
    D. the sprinkler system

61. Smoke dampers operate automatically upon activation of _______.

    A. the smoke detector
    B. the sprinkler system
    C. the fire alarm
    D. the fire damper

62. There are four basic types of central heating appliances. Boilers, warm air furnaces, floor furnaces, and wall furnaces are all _______ heating appliances.

    A. special
    B. central
    C. Class B
    D. Class 3

63. The problem(s) associated with boilers is/are _______.

    A. mounting and clearances from combustible materials
    B. the pressure in the system becomes too high
    C. both A and B
    D. neither A nor B

64. As a general rule, smoke detectors should be provided in all systems rated over _______.

    A. 1,500 CFM (708 L/sec)
    B. 1,800 CFM (850 L/sec)
    C. 2,000 CFM (944 L/sec)
    D. 4,000 CFM (1 888 L/sec)

65. Inspectors must be aware cooking equipment presents several fire hazards; the most common fire hazard is the _______.

    A. cooking equipment itself
    B. adjacent combustible materials
    C. fuel used to heat the cooking equipment
    D. method used to cook the food

66. Fire inspectors must be aware of structural abuse to buildings. Which one of the following is **NOT** considered structural abuse.

   A. Subjecting the structure to loads for which it was not designed.
   B. Structural modifications by unqualified workers or contractors.
   C. Deterioration of structural members due to age, weather, or lack of maintenance.
   D. All of the above is considered structural abuse.

MATCHING

Match the correct toxicity level for each refrigerant.

Group 1 (Nonflammable to weakly flammable)

67. ___ Carbon Dioxide (R-744)
68. ___ Monochlorodifluoromethane (R-22)
69. ___ Dichlorodifluoromethane (R-12)
70. ___ Dichlorofluoromethane (R-21)
71. ___ Dichlorotetrafluoromethane (R-114)
72. ___ Trichlorofluoromethane (R-11)
73. ___ Methylene Chloride (R-30)
74. ___ Monochlorotrifluoromethane (R-13)
75. ___ Trichlortrifluoromethane (R-113)

A. Nontoxic
B. Slightly Toxic
C. Moderately Toxic
D. Toxic
E. Very Toxic

Group 2 (Flammable, except sulfur dioxide)

76. ___ Ammonia (R-717)
77. ___ Methyl Chloride
78. ___ Methyl Formate (R-611)
79. ___ Sulfur Dioxide (R-764)

Group 3 (Highly Flammable)

80. ___ Butane (R-746)
81. ___ Ethane (R-170)
82. ___ Propane (R-290)
83. ___ Ethylene (R-1150)
84. ___ Isobutane (R-601)

5

Match the flame spread ratings with their material class.

85. ___ Flame spread 25
Smoke developed 10
Fuel contributed 5

86. ___ Flame spread 180
Smoke developed 50
Fuel contributed 25

87. ___ Flame spread 55
Smoke developed 100
Fuel contributed 35

88. ___ Flame spread 75
Smoke developed 30
Fuel contributed 35

89. ___ Flame spread 15
Smoke developed 10
Fuel contributed 10

A. Class A
B. Class B
C. Class C

SHORT ANSWER

Briefly answer each question in your own words.

90. NFPA 220, *Types of Building Construction,* divides construction types into five basic classifications: Type I through Type V. Each classification is further broken into subtypes by use of a three-digit Arabic number code or several letters (for example, Type I-443):

A. The first digit (Type I-**4**43) refers to

____

____

____

B. The second digit (Type I-4**4**3) refers to

____

____

____

C. The third digit (Type I-44**3**) refers to

____

____

____

91. Using the *Basic Building Code,* establish the single-story area limits for the following:

A. School with Type 3A construction.

____

B. One-story home of Type 5B construction.

C. One-story movie theater of Type 2C construction.

D. Department store of fire-resistive Type 1B construction.

E. Department store of fire-resistive Type 1A construction.

F. One-story industrial occupancy of Type 5B construction.

Using the *Basic Building Code*, establish the height limits for the following:

G. A department store of Type 2C construction.

H. An S-1 storage warehouse of Type 4 construction.

I. Hospital (I-2) of Type 5B construction.

92. Briefly explain how roof coverings are tested.

93. Identify and briefly describe the characteristics of the following types of construction:

A. Type I construction (443 or 332)

B. Type II construction (222, 111, or 000)

C. Type III construction (211 or 200)

5

D. Type IV construction (2HH)

E. Type V construction (111 or 000)

94. Which Class of roofing material possesses the best fire retardant properties and which Class possesses the least?

95. Failure of an occupancy is determined by one of several factors. Name the three factors.

A.

B.

C.

96. Name four laboratories that perform fire-resistive tests.

97. Name the two NFPA Standards for testing building construction techniques and materials.

A.

B.

98. Name the NFPA Standard for testing fire doors.

99. Name the NFPA Standard for testing windows.

100. Interior finish contributes to fire impact in four ways. Name those four ways.

A. ______________________________

B. ______________________________

C. ______________________________

D. ______________________________

101. Briefly describe the Steiner Tunnel and the Steiner Tunnel Test.

____

102. Building codes usually classify interior finish materials according to their flame spread rating. Identify the numerical flame spread rating of the following classes of materials as recommended in NFPA 101, *Life Safety Code®*.

Class of Material	Flame Spread
A	______
B	______
C	______

103. Flame spread rating cannot be accurately determined in the field, the inspector must research the ratings of materials noted during the inspection. What is the name of the publisher and publication that documents these ratings?

____

5

104. Briefly define a fire wall.

105. There are several important items that fire inspectors must check when performing an inspection in a structure with fire walls. Name five of these items.

106. Maintenance of fire doors is relatively simple, but necessary. List the four basic maintenance requirements.

A. ______

B. ______

C. ______

D. ______

107. Venting a building involved in fire maintains visibility longer; however, venting has a major drawback. Specify that drawback.

108. List five automatic features of venting systems.

109. The most common form of fire stopping for wood-frame construction involves using pieces of wood, 2 inches (51 mm) thick, placed in walls, partitions, and ceilings between the studs at each floor level and at the upper end of the stud channel in the attic. Explain how this method of fire stopping works.

110. List five acceptable noncombustible materials used for fire stopping.

111. List the four types of heating appliances fire inspectors will generally encounter.

A.

B.

C.

D.

112. Fire problems due to inadequate clearances, lack of proper limit controls, heat exchanger burnout, improper installation, or improper maintenance procedures are characteristic of what specific type of heating appliance?

113. Fire inspectors should warn individuals using this type of heater not to cover the register or place clothing over it for purposes of drying. What specific heating appliance is this type of unit.

114. Primary safety controls are a basic requirement on all fuel-burning heating units. These controls stop fuel from flowing to the unit in the event of an ignition or flame failure. Name five other common controls that fire inspectors may encounter.

115. Explain how air conditioning systems are a form of mechanical refrigeration.

5

116. List the three types of Classes for ducts in HVAC systems.

A. ______

B. ______

C. ______

117. Active smoke control systems are especially applicable in high-rise structures. Briefly state why.

______

118. List the two recommended NFPA Codes that address safe practices for cooking equipment.

A. ______

B. ______

119. When industrial ovens or furnaces are being installed, there are a number of safety factors that are of concern to the inspector. Name these concerns.

A. ______

B. ______

C. ______

D. ______

E. ______

120. There are several important fire safety practices for industrial ovens and furnaces. Name four.

______

121. Flammable and combustible liquids storage rooms should be designed and built to rigid specifications. Briefly explain how the walls, ceilings, floors, doorways, ventilation, electrical wiring, and aisles should be constructed.

6

Occupancy Classifications and Means of Egress

This chapter provides information that addresses performance objectives described in NFPA 1031, *Standard for Professional Qualifications for Fire Inspector* (1987), particularly those referenced in the following sections:

Fire Inspector I

3-19.1 General.

3-19.1.1

3-19.1.5 Means of Egress.
(See NFPA 101, ***Life Safety Code®*****)**

3-19.1.5.1

3-19.1.5.2

3-19.1.5.3

3-19.1.5.4

3-19.1.5.5

3-19.1.5.6

3-19.1.5.7

3-19.1.5.8

Fire Inspector II

4-8.1 Means of Egress.

4-8.1.1

4-8.1.2

4-8.1.3

4-8.7 Occupant Loads.

4-8.7.1

4-8.7.2

Occupancy Classifications and Means of Egress

6

TRUE/FALSE

Mark each statement true or false.

1. ☐ T ☐ F An important aspect of life safety is the ability to *evacuate* a structure *rapidly*.

2. ☐ T ☐ F Restaurants are governed by the regulations for business occupancies.

3. ☐ T ☐ F "Public way" is defined as the method or the usual procedure used by the general public that is approved at a national level.

4. ☐ T ☐ F NFPA 101, *Life Safety Code*®, defines a means of egress as "a continuous and unobstructed way of exit travel from any point in a building or structure to a public way."

5. ☐ T ☐ F Doors should always open out.

6. ☐ T ☐ F Panic hardware is **NOT** required for all exit doors.

7. ☐ T ☐ F If stair treads are used to give good footing, landings are not required.

8. ☐ T ☐ F Railings are recommended for both sides of the stairs, and stairs that are exceptionally wide should have one or more intermediate rails.

9. ☐ T ☐ F Fire escape stairs are the same as exterior stairs.

10. ☐ T ☐ F Smokeproof enclosures provide the highest degree of fire protection of stair enclosures recommended by NFPA 101.

11. ☐ T ☐ F All smokeproof enclosures must discharge into a public way, into a yard or court having direct access to a public way, or into exit passageway.

12. ☐ T ☐ F A ramp can be used as a component in a means of egress; in fact, ramps are preferable to stairs in certain occupancies, particularly schools and institutions.

13. ☐ T ☐ F In general, the most important use of an exit passageway is to satisfy the requirements that exit stairs shall discharge directly outside multistory buildings.

14. ☐ T ☐ F Escalators and moving walks are **NOT** allowed as part of a means of egress in new occupancies.

15. ☐ T ☐ F Fire escape stairs cannot be used as any part of a means of egress in new construction.

16. ☐ T ☐ F Escape slides may be used as a means of egress where they are specifically authorized.

17. ☐ T ☐ F Fire escape ladders cannot ordinarily constitute any portion of a means of egress.

18. ☐ T ☐ F Under certain circumstances, in assembly occupancies, the maximum density allowed is 3 square feet (0.26 m^2) per person; and is subject to approval by the authority having jurisdiction.

19. ☐ T ☐ F Means of egress is measured by units of exit width. A single unit of exit width is 22 inches (560 mm).

20. ☐ T ☐ F The *Life Safety Code®* also designates 12 inches (305 mm) as one-half unit of exit width.

21. ☐ T ☐ F When computing occupant load, always be aware that the occupant load determined by the units of exit width method should always be equal to, or greater than, the occupant load determined by the floor area method.

22. ☐ T ☐ F To determine the overall capacity of an exit, it is necessary to compute the exit capacity for each of the three components of a means of egress.

23. ☐ T ☐ F Exit capacity is based on units of exit width.

24. ☐ T ☐ F For nonlevel egress, the exiting capacity of the lower floors must be sufficient to accommodate the persons who may be arriving from upper floors.

25. ☐ T ☐ F The number of exits required for an occupancy is located and specified by each occupancy chapter of NFPA 101.

26. ☐ T ☐ F Maximum travel distance refers to the total length of travel necessary to reach all of the exits.

27. ☐ T ☐ F Proper exit illumination, when required, must be at least 10 footcandles (107.6 lumens) measured at the floor.

28. ☐ T ☐ F Generally, illuminated exit signs are required.

MULTIPLE CHOICE

Circle the letter corresponding to the most appropriate response.

29. The fire inspector must ensure that each occupancy is correctly designated and that the means of egress meet the specifications set forth by NFPA 101, *Life Safety Code*®, Chapters ______.

A. 1 – 30
B. 1 – 25
C. 5 – 30
D. 5 – 25

30. Doors used as a means of egress must be constructed so that the way of exit travel is ______.

A. obvious
B. natural
C. bi-directional
D. augmented

31. In new buildings, each door opening serving as a component in a means of egress must be at least ______ wide.

A. 28 inches (710 mm)
B. 30 inches (762 mm)
C. 32 inches (810 mm)
D. 34 inches (864 mm)

32. In existing buildings, each door opening must be at least ______ wide.

A. 28 inches (710 mm)
B. 30 inches (762 mm)
C. 32 inches (810 mm)
D. 34 inches (864 mm)

33. When panic hardware is required, occupants should be able to open the door by applying a force of not more than ______ pounds.

A. 12 (53.38 N)
B. 15 (66.72 N)
C. 18 (80.06 N)
D. 20 (88.06 N)

34. Exit stairs are a critical component of the means of egress in multistoried buildings. Stairways must be at least 44 inches wide (1 120 mm), unless the total occupant load of all the floors served by stairways is ______.

A. less than 50
B. greater than 50
C. less than 40
D. greater than 60

6

35. An interior stair construction that encloses an exit with at least a 1-hour minimum fire resistance rating is required for a maximum of ______ stories.

A. two
B. three
C. four
D. five

36. The interior stair construction that encloses an exit with at least a 2-hour fire resistance rating is required for ______ stories or more.

A. four
B. five
C. six
D. seven

37. The only permissible openings in an exit are those that allow people to enter the exit from the building and those that empty to the ______.

A. exterior stairs
B. level G access
C. exit discharge
D. atrium exits

38. Horizontal exits are becoming popular in high-rise and ______ buildings.

A. institutional-type
B. assembly-type
C. educational-type
D. industrial-type

39. Horizontal exits may be substituted for other exits if they *do not* make up more than ______ of the total exit capacity of the building.

A. 25%
B. 30%
C. 40%
D. 50%

40. An exit passageway serves as an access ______.

A. to an exit
B. from an exit
C. to or from an exit
D. to or from an exit access corridor

41. In assembly areas where people are admitted into the building for the purpose of waiting for seating, exits should be provided for each person waiting based on ______ per person waiting.

A. 2 square feet (0.019 m^2)
B. 3 square feet (0.027 m^2)
C. 4 square feet (0.037 m^2)
D. 5 square feet (0.046 m^2)

42. In order to compute the total exit capacity of an occupancy (for level egress), it is necessary to first determine the capacity of each exit and then ______.

A. total the figures from each exit
B. measure the distance from each exit
C. subtract ineffective exits
D. add 25% for an extra safety margin

43. Where there are similar adjacent doors that are not exits, they must be ______.

A. less than 1½ units wide
B. marked "No Exit"
C. rated 1-hour fire resistant
D. unlocked in case of an emergency

44. Occupancies are classified not only by the type of activities conducted within them, but also by fire load. The concept of fire loading is determined by the ______.

A. National Bureau of Standards
B. NFPA 101, *Life Safety Code®*
C. Department of Transportation
D. *National Building Code*

SHORT ANSWER

Briefly answer each question in your own words.

45. For the purpose of inspection and code enforcement, NFPA 101, *Life Safety Code®* classifies buildings according to the type of occupancy or intended end use. Name the 10 classifications and briefly describe each one.

A. ______________________________

B. ______________________________

6

C.

D.

E.

F.

G.

H. ____

I. ____

J. ____

46. A means of egress consists of three distinct components. List these components, briefly describe their function, and provide an example.

A. ____

B. ____

C. ____

47. Doors serve two important functions in terms of life safety. Name these functions.

A. ____

B. ____

6

48. Access to a smokeproof enclosure is made through a vestibule or outside balcony. How does this arrangement prevent smoke from entering the stairwell when corridor doors are opened?

49. There are two main classes of ramps: Class A and Class B. Briefly explain each class.

A. Class A:

B. Class B:

50. Are fire escape stairs considered to be reliable or unreliable exits? Why?

51. Define occupant load.

52. The *Life Safety Code®* recognizes two methods of determining the occupant load of a structure or parts of a structure. Explain how to use both of these methods.

A. Floor Area Method

Step 1:

Step 2:

Step 3:

B. Unit of Width Method

Step 1: ______

Step 2: ______

Step 3: ______

53. The unit of exit width method can determine if the floor area method may be exceeded *if* two conditions exist. Name those two conditions.

A. ______

B. ______

54. Explain how to determine total exit capacity for a **Level Egress** occupancy.

Step 1: ______

Step 2: ______

Step 3: ______

55. Explain how to determine total exit capacity for a **Nonlevel Egress** occupancy.

Step 1: ______

Step 2: ______

Step 3: ______

56. Define fire load.

______

6

57. Provide examples for the following fire loads:

SLIGHT: TYPICAL FIRE LOAD 5 psf (Pounds per square foot) (24 kg/m^2)

MODERATE: TYPICAL FIRE LOAD 10 psf (49 kg/m^2)

MODERATELY SEVERE: TYPICAL FIRE LOAD 10 to 15 psf (49 kg/m^2 to 72 kg/m^2)

SEVERE: TYPICAL FIRE LOAD 15 to 20 psf (73 kg/m^2 to 93 kg/m^2)

VERY SEVERE: TYPICAL FIRE LOAD GREATER THAN 20 psf (93 kg/m^2)

58. If fire inspectors can estimate the fire load when conducting inspections of a building, they can subsequently estimate the loss potential. How and when can this information be extremely useful?

7

Fire Protection and Water Supply Systems

This chapter provides information that addresses performance objectives described in NFPA 1031, *Standard for Professional Qualifications for Fire Inspector* (1987), particularly those referenced in the following sections:

3-16.1 Portable Fire Extinguishers.

3-16.1.4

3-16.1.5

3-16.1.6

3-16.1.7

3-16.1.8

3-16.1.9

3-16.2 Fixed Fire Extinguishing Systems.

3-16.2.1

3-16.2.2

3-16.2.3

3-16.3 Sprinkler Systems.

3-16.3.1

3-16.3.9

3-16.3.10

3-16.4 Standpipe and Hose Systems.

3-16.4.1

3-16.4.2

3-16.4.3

3-16.4.4

3-16.5 Water Supply Systems.

3-16.5.2

3-16.5.9

3-16.6 Heat, Smoke, and Flame Detection Systems.
(See NFPA 72E, *Standard on Automatic Fire Detectors,* **and NFPA 74,** *Standard for the Installation, Maintenance, and Use of Household Fire Warning Equipment.***)**

3-16.6.1

3-16.6.2

3-16.6.3

3-16.7 Fire Alarm Systems and Devices.
(See NFPA 72A, 72B, 72C, 72D, and 72E.)

3-16.7.1

3-16.7.2

3-16.7.3

3-16.7.4

3-16.7.5

3-16.7.6

3-16.7.7

Fire Inspector II

4-6.4 Water Supply Systems.

4-6.4.1

4-6.4.2

4-6.4.3

4-8.4 Building Equipment.

Fire Protection and Water Supply Systems

7

TRUE/FALSE

Mark each statement true or false.

1. ☐ T ☐ F Extinguishing equipment provides a means of attacking fires during the steady-burning phase.

2. ☐ T ☐ F Standpipe systems permit either building occupants and/or firefighters to operate fire streams on different floors or in different areas of a building.

3. ☐ T ☐ F Fixed fire extinguishing systems can rapidly extinguish or control a fire before it reaches serious proportions.

4. ☐ T ☐ F Generally, separate water tanks are used to provide the water to standpipe and sprinkler systems and fire fighting operations.

5. ☐ T ☐ F All types of fire protection equipment must be installed, maintained, and tested in accordance with federal laws.

6. ☐ T ☐ F It is important that fire inspectors check equipment to be sure it has been tested, listed, and labeled by UL, FM, or another recognized national testing laboratory.

7. ☐ T ☐ F Multiple letters or numerical-letter ratings are used on portable fire extinguishers that are effective on more than one Class of fire.

8. ☐ T ☐ F Class A and Class B extinguishers also receive a numerical rating that precedes the letter.

9. ☐ T ☐ F It is better to use whatever fire extinguisher is available rather than not use any at all.

10. ☐ T ☐ F Extinguishers for Class C fires have no numerical rating and are tested only for electrical nonconductivity.

11. ☐ T ☐ F Extinguishers for Class D fires are rated from 1D-60D.

12. ☐ T ☐ F Carbon dioxide extinguishers are self-propelling.

13. ☐ T ☐ F Carbon dioxide extinguishers with metal horns are **NOT** considered safe for use on fires in energized electrical equipment.

14. ☐ T ☐ F Halogenated agent extinguishers (either Halon 1211 [bromochlorodifluoromethane] or Halon 1301 [bromotrifluoromethane]) operate on the principle of liquefied compressed gas, which will not support combustion, being discharged to smother and terminate flames.

15. ☐ T ☐ F Dry chemical extinguishers may be either stored pressure or *exterior* gas cartridge operated.

16. ☐ T ☐ F Dry powder extinguishers are used exclusively for Class C fires.

17. ☐ T ☐ F In 1969, American manufacturers stopped making all inverting-type extinguishers, except the soda-acid type extinguisher.

18. ☐ T ☐ F Inspectors should be familiar with all types of portable extinguishers and should be able to demonstrate the procedure for operating fire extinguishers.

19. ☐ T ☐ F Protection of a Class A hazard may use, upon approval of the authority having jurisdiction, several lower-rated extinguishers in place of one higher-rated extinguisher.

20. ☐ T ☐ F Protection of a Class B hazard can use two or more extinguishers of lower rating to replace one higher-rated extinguisher.

21. ☐ T ☐ F For Class B hazards, extinguisher placement must be based upon the depth of the fuel.

22. ☐ T ☐ F The distribution of Class B extinguishers is based solely on the size of the extinguisher and the maximum travel distance allowed.

23. ☐ T ☐ F Inspection of portable fire extinguishers is the responsibility of the fire department.

24. ☐ T ☐ F Enough Class III standpipes used in buildings of large area and height can take the place of an automatic extinguishing system.

25. ☐ T ☐ F The purpose of a standpipe is to provide a quick and convenient means for operating fire streams on different floors or in different areas of a building.

26. ☐ T ☐ F High-rise buildings having two or more zones require four fire department connections for each zone.

27. ☐ T ☐ F There must be **NO** shutoff valve between the FDC and the standpipe riser.

28. ☐ T ☐ F Most sprinklers (except deluge system sprinklers) are kept closed by fusible links or other heat-sensitive devices.

29. ☐ T ☐ F Every sprinkler system is equipped with a main water control valve.

30. ☐ T ☐ F All control valves are indicating valves.

31. ☐ T ☐ F The alarm test valve is located on a pipe that connects the supply side of the alarm check valve to the retard chamber.

32. ☐ T ☐ F A gravity tank will **NOT** make a reliable primary water supply for sprinkler systems.

33. ☐ T ☐ F Inspectors should **NEVER** operate, adjust, physically manipulate, or alter any sprinkler system components except in emergencies or supervised training sessions.

34. Determine if a) through f) are true or false when you inspect sprinkler systems.

☐ T ☐ F a) The alarm line shutoff cock valve is open.

☐ T ☐ F b) The pressure gauge valves are open.

☐ T ☐ F c) The static pressure above the clapper is equal to or greater than the static pressure below the clapper. (Systems without check valves may have only one pressure gauge on the riser.)

☐ T ☐ F d) The main drain, auxiliary drain(s), and the inspector's test valve are closed.

☐ T ☐ F e) The ball drip valve in the fire department connection moves freely and allows trapped water to drain.

☐ T ☐ F f) The velocity drip valve will move freely and allow trapped water to drain into the retard chamber.

35. ☐ T ☐ F When changes in occupancies occur, it is not as important that inspectors examine the *type* of sprinklers installed as it is they are sure the sprinklers are working properly.

36. ☐ T ☐ F Flushing underground mains and lead-in connections should be continued until the pressure reaches 250 psi (1 724 kPa).

37. ☐ T ☐ F A pre-action sprinkler system is used when it is especially important that water damage be prevented.

38. ☐ T ☐ F When the deluge valve operates, water flows from **ALL** the sprinklers simultaneously.

39. ☐ T ☐ F Most residential sprinkler systems are wet-pipe systems.

40. ☐ T ☐ F Most residential sprinklers use pendant or sidewall heads.

41. ☐ T ☐ F On a wet-pipe system with an alarm check valve, the alarm bypass valve should be closed so that the alarm can be tested without unseating the valve.

42. ☐ T ☐ F Dry-pipe valves are designed so that a large amount of air pressure in the sprinkler system piping will hold back small amounts of water pressure.

43. ☐ T ☐ F All residential sprinkler systems should store extra sprinklers and a sprinkler wrench near the riser.

44. ☐ T ☐ F Inspecting a residential sprinkler system is the responsibility of the fire department.

45. ☐ T ☐ F Foams are not suitable for water-reactive or three-dimensional fires.

7

46. ☐ T ☐ F There are two types of discharge devices used on foam extinguishing systems protecting indoor hazards: those producing foam in a spray or dispersed pattern, and those producing foam in compact, low velocity streams.

47. ☐ T ☐ F Carbon dioxide is a nonconductor of electricity.

48. ☐ T ☐ F There are two kinds of carbon dioxide storage (supply) systems: low pressure and high pressure.

49. ☐ T ☐ F Low-pressure systems use refrigerated pressure vessels with a capacity of at least 125 tons (127 000 kg).

50. ☐ T ☐ F Refrigerated pressure vessels are designed to maintain a normal pressure of 300 psi (2 069 kPa) corresponding to a temperature of approximately 0°F (-18°C).

51. ☐ T ☐ F High-pressure storage systems have rechargeable cylinders.

52. ☐ T ☐ F A 10% concentration of halogenated agent may be used in areas normally occupied by people.

53. ☐ T ☐ F Halogenated agents are used only for total flooding and never for local application systems.

54. ☐ T ☐ F NFPA 12A and 12B require predischarge alarms for total-flooding Halon 1211 systems.

55. ☐ T ☐ F Wet chemical extinguishing systems are especially effective on fires involving cooking hazards.

56. ☐ T ☐ F The installation of fire detection and alarm systems should conform to its respective NFPA Standard, and applicable provisions of NFPA 70, *National Electrical Code.*

57. ☐ T ☐ F A local alarm system is a combination of alarm components designed to detect a fire and/or transmit an alarm on the immediate premises and to any agencies away from the premises.

58. ☐ T ☐ F A noncoded alarm system is the most complicated type of system.

59. ☐ T ☐ F In a zone noncoded system each circuit serves an area of the building.

60. ☐ T ☐ F When one of the alarm initiating devices operates, the current flow increases and lights the lamp and trips a relay, which activates the signal device.

61. ☐ T ☐ F Master coded systems are employed in occupancies that use the audible signal devices for other purposes.

62. ☐ T ☐ F A presignal alarm is used in occupancies where the potential for panic is high.

63. ☐ T ☐ F Zone coded systems all have a signal device that sounds in a specific and unique pattern for each zone.

64. ☐ T ☐ F A central station alarm system ties several different jurisdictions on a central location.

65. ☐ T ☐ F When a high degree of reliability is required, alarm circuits may be electronically supervised.

66. ☐ T ☐ F A permanent record of all detector tests should be maintained for a minimum of five years.

67. ☐ T ☐ F A fire hydrant that receives water from one side (a dead-end hydrant) has less available water than a fire hydrant supplied from two or more directions.

68. ☐ T ☐ F Hydrant outlets are considered standard if there is at least one $2\frac{1}{2}$-inch (65 mm) outlet and two $1\frac{1}{2}$-inch (32 mm) outlets.

69. ☐ T ☐ F The main function of water main valves is to control water flow as circumstances dictate.

5/94

70. ☐ T ☐ F An indicating valve shows whether the gate valve seat is open, closed, or partially closed.

71. ☐ T ☐ F Nonindicating valves in water distribution systems are usually buried or installed in manholes.

72. ☐ T ☐ F Sediment deposits are caused by tubercular corrosion or rust, biological or organism growth, or biodegradation of pipe materials.

73. ☐ T ☐ F Generally, each fire department repairs and maintains the fire hydrants in their jurisdiction because the fire departments depend on hydrants in top operating condition during a fire.

74. ☐ T ☐ F Inspectors should notify the water utility company when hydrant inspections will be made (at least twice a year).

75. ☐ T ☐ F Fire flow tests are used to determine the direction and expected flame spread rate within specific types of construction.

76. ☐ T ☐ F Before conducting a water flow test, a responsible water department official should be notified.

77. ☐ T ☐ F When testing available water supply, the number of hydrants to be opened will depend upon an estimate of the flow available in the area; furthermore, enough hydrants should be opened to drop the *static* pressure by at least 10 psi (69 kPa).

78. ☐ T ☐ F In general, when flow testing a single hydrant, the flow hydrant should be downstream from the test hydrant.

7

MULTIPLE CHOICE

Circle the letter corresponding to the most appropriate response.

79. Portable fire extinguishers are used, installed, and maintained in accordance with _______.

A. NFPA 10, *Portable Fire Extinguishers*
B. NFPA 20, *Portable Fire Extinguishers*
C. NFPA 15, *Portable Fire Extinguishers*
D. NFPA 25, *Portable Fire Extinguishers*

80. The only type of portable fire extinguisher that is suitable for use on all fires is a(an) _______.

A. A-B type
B. A-B-C type
C. A-B-C-D type
D. none of the above

81. A water-type extinguisher rated 1-A requires _______ of water.

A. 1¼ gallons (4.73 L)
B. 1½ gallons (5.68 L)
C. 2 gallons (7.57 L)
D. 2¼ gallons (8.52 L)

82. Extinguishers for use on Class B fires are classified with numerical ratings from _______.

A. 1-B through 140-B
B. 1-B through 160-B
C. 1-B through 320-B
D. 1-B through 640-B

83. Water extinguishers are suitable for _______.

A. Class A fires
B. Class A-B fires
C. Class A-B-C fires
D. Water-based extinguishers are now obsolete

84. Foam extinguishers are rated and designed for _______.

A. Class A
B. Class B
C. Class A-B
D. Class A-B-C

85. The primary type of foam extinguisher available today is aqueous film forming foam (AFFF) extinguisher. This extinguisher contains a premixed solution of foam concentrate and water and is pressurized in a manner similar to a loaded stream water extinguisher. What creates the bubbles?

A. A special nozzle aerates the foam to produce bubbles.
B. The chemical reaction of the foam concentrate and water produce the bubbles.
C. The high pressure within the cylinder produces the bubbles upon expulsion.
D. A highly concentrated soaplike solution is added to the foam concentrate to produce the bubbles.

86. Carbon dioxide extinguishers are used for ______ fires.

    A. Class B
    B. Class B and C
    C. Class D
    D. Class C and D

87. When Halon 1004 (carbon tetrachloride) comes in contact with flames or very hot metal surfaces, it ______.

    A. evaporates at an excessive rate
    B. solidifies and becomes hard to use
    C. releases a highly toxic gas
    D. vaporizes and becomes ineffective

88. Which of the following elements should **NOT** be considered during extinguisher selection? (One or more answers *may* be possible.)

    A. The chemical and physical characteristics of the combustibles.
    B. The potential severity of any resulting fire.
    C. Environmental conditions that may affect the use of the extinguisher (temperature, winds, presence of toxic gases or fumes).
    D. The type, design, and installation of the automatic sprinkler system.
    E. Any anticipated adverse chemical reactions between the extinguishing agent and the burning material.
    F. Any health and occupational safety concerns, such as exposure of the extinguisher operator to heat and products of combustion during fire fighting efforts.
    G. The inspection and maintenance required to maintain the extinguishers.
    H. Opportunities to actually use the fire extinguisher in a simulated fire condition before it is put into active service.

89. Placement of Class D fire extinguishers from the Class D fire hazard should be no more than ______.

    A. 50 feet (15 m)
    B. 60 feet (18 m)
    C. 75 feet (23 m)
    D. 85 feet (26 m)

90. The height of extinguisher placement affects its accessibility. Extinguishers weighing less than 40 pounds (18.1 kg) should be installed with the *top* not more than ______ from the floor.

    A. 3 feet (1.0 m)
    B. 4 feet (1.2 m)
    C. 5 feet (1.5 m)
    D. 6 feet (1.8 m)

7

91. The clearance between the floor and the bottom of the extinguisher must be at least ______.

A. 4 inches (102 mm)
B. 6 inches (152 mm)
C. 8 inches (203 mm)
D. 9 inches (228 mm)

92. All maintenance procedures should include a thorough examination of the three basic parts of an extinguisher: 1) mechanical parts, 2) extinguishing agents, and 3) ______.

A. accessibility
B. means of expelling
C. inspection tag
D. mounting brackets

93. Stored-pressure extinguishers that require a 12-year hydrostatic test must be emptied every ______ for complete maintenance.

A. 3 years
B. 4 years
C. 6 years
D. 12 years

94. Standpipe systems are generally limited to ______ in height.

A. 275 feet (84 m)
B. 300 feet (91 m)
C. 350 feet (107 m)
D. 400 feet (122 m)

95. The hose connections to the FDC must be of the ______ type.

A. male
B. female
C. sexless or female
D. sexless or male

96. The sprinkler used for a specific application should be based on the maximum temperature expected at the level of the sprinkler under normal conditions. Another important consideration is ______.

A. the ph and mineral content of the water used throughout the system
B. the anticipated rate of heat release produced by a fire in the particular area
C. the number of inhabitants specified in the *Life Safety Code*®
D. the location of portable fire extinguishers

97. Outside screw and yoke (OS&Y) valves should be inspected to ensure that they are fully open, the valve stem is clean, and the operating wheel is backed off approximately ______ turn.

A. one-quarter
B. one-half
C. three-quarters
D. one full

98. Of all sprinkler systems, wet-pipe sprinkler systems are ______.

A. the most trouble
B. the hardest to design
C. the most reliable
D. the most expensive

99. During acceptance tests, when should underground mains and lead-in connections be flushed?

A. BEFORE connection is made to the sprinkler piping
B. AFTER connection is made to the sprinkler piping
C. BEFORE or AFTER (it does not matter) connection is made to the sprinkler piping
D. BEFORE and AFTER connection is made to the sprinkler piping

100. All piping is required to be hydrostatically tested at not less than ______.

A. 100 psi (690 kPa)
B. 150 psi (1 034 kPa)
C. 200 psi (1 379 kPa)
D. 250 psi (1 724 kPa)

101. Foam extinguishing systems are most frequently used to protect ______.

A. electrical hazards
B. combustible metals
C. flammable liquid hazards
D. none of the above

102. Most foams used today are mechanical foams. They are made by mixing ______.

A. reactive solutions in the cylinders with internal mechanisms designed for aeration
B. highly reactive sodium oxides
C. air with a solution of water and foam concentrate
D. inhibitors with vaporization film

103. Which one of the following is **NOT** a synthetic foam.

A. Aqueous Film Forming Foam (AFFF)
B. High-Expansion Foam Concentrate
C. Hydrocarbon active agents (“wetting agents”)
D. Protein Foam Concentrate

104. Carbon dioxide systems must be equipped with an indicator to show that the system has operated and needs ______.

A. inspecting
B. replacing
C. recharging
D. conditioning

7

105. Carbon dioxide extinguishing systems should be thoroughly inspected and tested for operation at least ______.

A. monthly
B. quarterly
C. semiannually
D. annually

106. All high-pressure cylinders should be weighed at least semiannually. The container should be refilled or replaced if it shows a loss in net content of more than ______ percent.

A. 10
B. 12
C. 18
D. 20

107. Low-pressure containers have liquid level gauges which should be inspected on a weekly basis. The container should be refilled if the gauge shows a loss of more than ______ percent.

A. 10
B. 20
C. 25
D. 30

108. The two most common forms of halogenated hydrocarbons are ______.

A. Halon 1211 (bromochlorodifluoromethane)
   Halon 1301 (bromotrifluoromethane)
B. Halon 1121 (bromochlorodifluoromethane)
   Halon 1310 (bromotrifluoromethane)
C. Halon 1201 (bromochlorodifluoromethane)
   Halon 3130 (bromotrifluoromethane)
D. Halon 1221 (bromochlorodifluoromethane)
   Halon 1301 (bromotrifluoromethane)

109. Dry chemicals can be stored under a wide range of temperature conditions. Which NFPA Standard provides detailed information concerning these systems and should be consulted prior to any inspections?

A. NFPA 15, *Dry Chemical Extinguishing Systems*
B. NFPA 17, *Dry Chemical Extinguishing Systems*
C. NFPA 18, *Dry Chemical Extinguishing Systems*
D. NFPA 19, *Dry Chemical Extinguishing Systems*

110. Chemical extinguishing system inspections should be made at least ______.

A. monthly
B. quarterly
C. semiannually
D. annually

111. Chemical extinguishing systems should be refilled or replaced if a container shows a loss in net weight of more than 5% or a loss in pressure (adjusted for temperature) of more than ______ percent.

A. 10
B. 15
C. 20
D. 25

112. An automatic telephone dialer connects a building fire detection or alarm system to ______.

A. the sprinkler system
B. a leased telephone line
C. a standard residential or business telephone
D. special fire/telephone lines

113. When water is converted from liquid to vapor (steam), its volume increases about ______ times.

A. 1,000
B. 1,200
C. 1,700
D. 2,000

114. The network of water mains that make up a water distribution system are sometimes called ______.

A. distributors
B. channels
C. grids
D. loops

115. The threads on *all* hydrant outlets must conform to those determined by ______.

A. the local fire department
B. the NFPA
C. the local water department
D. the American Water Works Association

116. Hydrant location is usually determined by the type, size, occupancy location, and type of occupancy; however, there should be at least ______ between hydrants. In closely built areas, ______ is a more acceptable standard.

A. 600 feet (180 m), 300 feet (90 m)
B. 700 feet (210 m), 400 feet (120 m)
C. 800 feet (245 m), 500 feet (150 m)
D. 900 feet (270 m), 600 feet (180 m)

117. The maximum lengths for water main valve spacing should be ______ in high-value districts and ______ in other areas.

A. 300 feet (90 m), 600 feet (180 m)
B. 400 feet (120 m), 700 feet (210 m)
C. 500 feet (150 m), 800 feet (245 m)
D. 600 feet (180 m), 900 feet (270 m)

7

118. A progressive growth of rust deposits on the iron pipes or the accumulation of various salts due to oxidation is called ______.

A. sedimentation
B. deforestation
C. gestation
D. incrustation

119. The easiest way to determine how much water is flowing from the hydrant outlet(s) is to ______.

A. refer to prepared tables for nozzle discharge
B. use a hydrometer
C. use a pitot tube and gauge
D. use the formula for frictionless discharge

120. Generally, 2½-inch (65 mm) outlets should be used to conduct hydrant flow tests because ______.

A. a pitot tube cannot be held in a 4-inch (100 mm) stream
B. the stream from large hydrant outlets contains voids
C. the pressure from a 4-inch (100 mm) stream is not the same as from a 2½-inch (65 mm) stream
D. the pressure differential can create cavitation

121. When computing the available water for area flow test results, fire protection engineers have established the minimum required residual pressure is ______.

A. 10 psi (69 kPa)
B. 15 psi (103 kPa)
C. 20 psi (138 kPa)
D. 25 psi (172 kPa)

MATCHING

Match the term with the correct description.

122. Standpipe systems must provide a minimum supply of water. Identify the correct rate to the three Classes of standpipes.

___ Class I
___ Class II
___ Class III

A. 100 gpm (378 L/min) for at least 30 minutes
B. 150 gpm (568 L/min) for at least 30 minutes
C. 200 gpm (757 L/min) for at least 30 minutes
D. 250 gpm (946 L/min) for at least 30 minutes
E. 400 gpm (1 514 L/min) for at least 30 minutes
F. 500 gpm (1 890 L/min) for at least 30 minutes
G. 600 gpm (2 271 L/min) for at least 30 minutes
H. 700 gpm (2 650 L/min) for at least 30 minutes

Match the terms with the correct description(s) and place the correct letter(s) that apply to the following fixed extinguishing systems. More than one answer may apply to some systems.

123. ___ Foam fixed systems
124. ___ Dry-chemical fixed systems
125. ___ Carbon dioxide systems
126. ___ Halogenated-agent fixed systems
127. ___ Wet-chemical systems

A. Can be used to extinguish or control fires both in flammable gases or liquids and in electrical equipment.
B. It will leave no residue. Thus, cleanup will be unnecessary and equipment is not damaged by the use of the agent.
C. Used primarily on flammable liquid fires and electrical equipment.
D. NOT RECOMMENDED for delicate electrical equipment where flammable liquids are contained in electrical equipment such as an oil filled transformer.
E. Used primarily in restaurant hood and duct systems.
F. Used mainly for flammable liquids storage.
G. Leave no residue and are sometimes referred to as a "clean extinguishing agent."
H. Highly recommended for areas containing high-value materials that are easily damaged such as computer rooms, fur vaults, and archives.

Match the test with the correct frequency.

128. ___ deluge and pre-action systems
129. ___ residential sprinkler systems
130. ___ alarm test
131. ___ 2-inch (50 mm) main drain test
132. ___ trip test

A. At least monthly; although the inspector does not take an active role in the testing.
B. At least annually; however, a quarterly test is recommended.
C. At least monthly, although a weekly test is recommended.
D. At least annually. (A visual inspection of the system and 2-inch (65 mm) main drain test can be performed along with the trip test.)
E. At least monthly, although a weekly inspection is recommended. They should also determine if a main drain test is being performed at least annually, although a quarterly test is recommended.

7

Match the type of each Products-of-Combustion detector with the correct description.

133. ___ Visible products-of-combustion
134. ___ IR detectors
135. ___ UV detectors
136. ___ Rate-of-rise
137. ___ Fixed-Temperature
138. ___ Invisible products-of-combustion

A. Initiated at a predetermined temperature.
B. Responds to quick changes in temperature.
C. Uses photoelectric cell and a specific light source.
D. Detects electron imbalance.
E. Can give false alarms if in contact with sunlight.
F. Alarm initiates upon flickering action of a flame.
G. Detects motion such as ascending ash.

SHORT ANSWER

Briefly answer each question in your own words.

139. There are five major types of extinguishing equipment and fire protection systems. Name them and briefly describe their function.

A. ______________________________

B. ______________________________

C. ______________________________

D. ______________________________

E. ______________________________

140. There are basically four common ways of expelling extinguishing agents from portable fire extinguishers. Name and briefly describe how each type works.

A. ______________________________

B. ______________________________

C. ______________________________

D. ______________________________

141. Portable fire extinguishers are in four separate Classes. Briefly describe what kind of fire each Class is capable of extinguishing.

Class A: ______________________________

Class B: ______________________________

Class C: ______________________________

Class D: ______________________________

142. There are six major basic extinguishing agents. Name them.

A. ______________________________
B. ______________________________
C. ______________________________
D. ______________________________
E. ______________________________
F. ______________________________

143. To operate a portable fire extinguisher, follow the letters P-P-P-S. Briefly describe P-P-P-S.

Step 1: P ______________________________

Step 2: P ______________________________

Step 3: P ______________________________

Step 4: S ______________________________

144. In order to determine the number of each type of fire extinguisher needed to adequately protect a property, fire inspectors must take into consideration a number of factors. What are the three primary considerations?

A. ______________________________

B. ______________________________

C. ______________________________

145. According to NFPA 10, *Portable Fire Extinguishers,* define the following:

A. Light Hazard Occupancy

B. Ordinary Hazard Occupancy

C. Extra Hazard Occupancy

146. During a routine inspection, fire inspectors should remember that there are three important factors that determine the value of a fire extinguisher. Name them.

A.

B.

C.

147. List seven things that should be checked during every fire extinguisher inspection.

A.

B.

C.

D.

E.

F.

G.

148. Stored-pressure extinguishers containing a loaded stream agent should be disassembled for complete maintenance. Prior to disassembly, what should be done?

7

149. Identify the designed intentions of the following Classes of standpipes.

A. Class I

B. Class II

C. Class III

150. There are four basic types of standpipe systems. Name them.

A.

B.

C.

D.

151. What is the primed system, and what is its major advantage?

152. New standpipe installations should be inspected to ensure all devices (valves, racks, cabinets, and so on) are listed and labeled by a nationally recognized testing laboratory. What else?

____

____

____

____

____

____

153. Wet standpipe systems should be inspected at regular intervals (usually every six months). Listed below are things inspectors should check. One very important item has been omitted. What is it?

A. Ensure the proper water level is maintained in water supply tanks. Precautions against freezing must be taken when necessary.
B. Fire pumps start and operate.
C. Fire hose cabinets and closets are used for the storage of fire fighting equipment only.
D. Water control valves are open and supervised.
E. Individual discharge valves operate properly, gaskets are in good condition, and there is no corrosion or evidence of leaks.
F. The fire department connection is inspected for accessibility and protective caps.
G. Drains are free of dirt and/or sediment.
H. ______________________________

____

____

154. In addition to all the inspection procedures for the previous question, listed below are procedures for Class II and Class III systems. One very important item has been omitted. What is it?

A. The swingout rack should be checked for ease of operation.
B. Threads on the combination nozzles and hose couplings are not damaged and the gaskets are in good condition.
C. The nozzle is not obstructed and the shutoff valve, if there is one, is working properly.
D. Dry standpipe systems should be hydrostatically tested every five years.
E. ______________________________

____

____

155. Name two very important features of automatic sprinkler systems.

A. ______________________________
B. ______________________________

7

156. Fixed fire extinguishing systems are designed to respond rapidly to fire. Name three more advantages of installing fixed fire extinguishing systems.

____

____

____

157. Sprinklers are kept closed by a number of devices. Name two commonly used mechanisms.

____

____

158. There are four basic types of sprinkler systems. Name and briefly describe each one.

A. ______________________________

B. ______________________________

C. ______________________________

D. ______________________________

159. The minimum water flow required is determined by three major considerations. Name them.

A. ______________________________

B. ______________________________

C. ______________________________

160. What four observations are important when inspecting control valves?

A. ______________________________

B. ______________________________

C. ______________________________

____

D. ______________________________

____

161. What should you determine when inspecting all sprinkler piping and hangers?

____

____

____

____

162. When does cold flow occur, and how can this problem be eliminated?

____

____

____

163. Why do inspectors witness instead of perform sprinkler system acceptance tests?

____

____

____

____

164. If a significant pressure drop occurs during a main drain test, what is the probable cause?

____

____

____

165. As with wet-pipe sprinkler systems, acceptance tests for dry-pipe systems are conducted by a representative of the installation firm. Identify the missing test to be performed.

A. Flush the Underground Connections

B. ______________________________

C. Air Test

166. The above question identifies an Air Test. Explain how this procedure is conducted.

____

____

____

____

____

7

167. When conducting a dry-pipe valve trip test, the 2-inch (50 mm) main valve is opened slightly while the water supply control valve is closed and re-opened. Then the 2-inch (50 mm) main drain valve is closed. What happens if the water supply control valve is never opened then re-closed?

____

____

____

____

____

____

168. When conducting a dry-pipe valve trip test, what is the function of the person assigned to open the inspector's test valve?

____

____

____

____

____

169. Trip tests for *small* deluge systems require a variation of dry-pipe testing procedure? What is this procedure?

____

____

____

170. Trip tests for *large* deluge systems require a variation of dry-pipe testing procedure? What is this procedure?

____

____

____

____

____

171. What is the title of NFPA 13D?

____

____

172. The foam concentrates used to make foam solutions are divided into three categories. Identify them.

A. ____

B. ____

C. ____

173. What are ATC foams?

____

____

____

____

174. Periodic inspections must also be made of air-foam concentrates and their tanks or storage containers. Why?

____

____

____

____

175. Identify and label the typical sprinkler system layout.

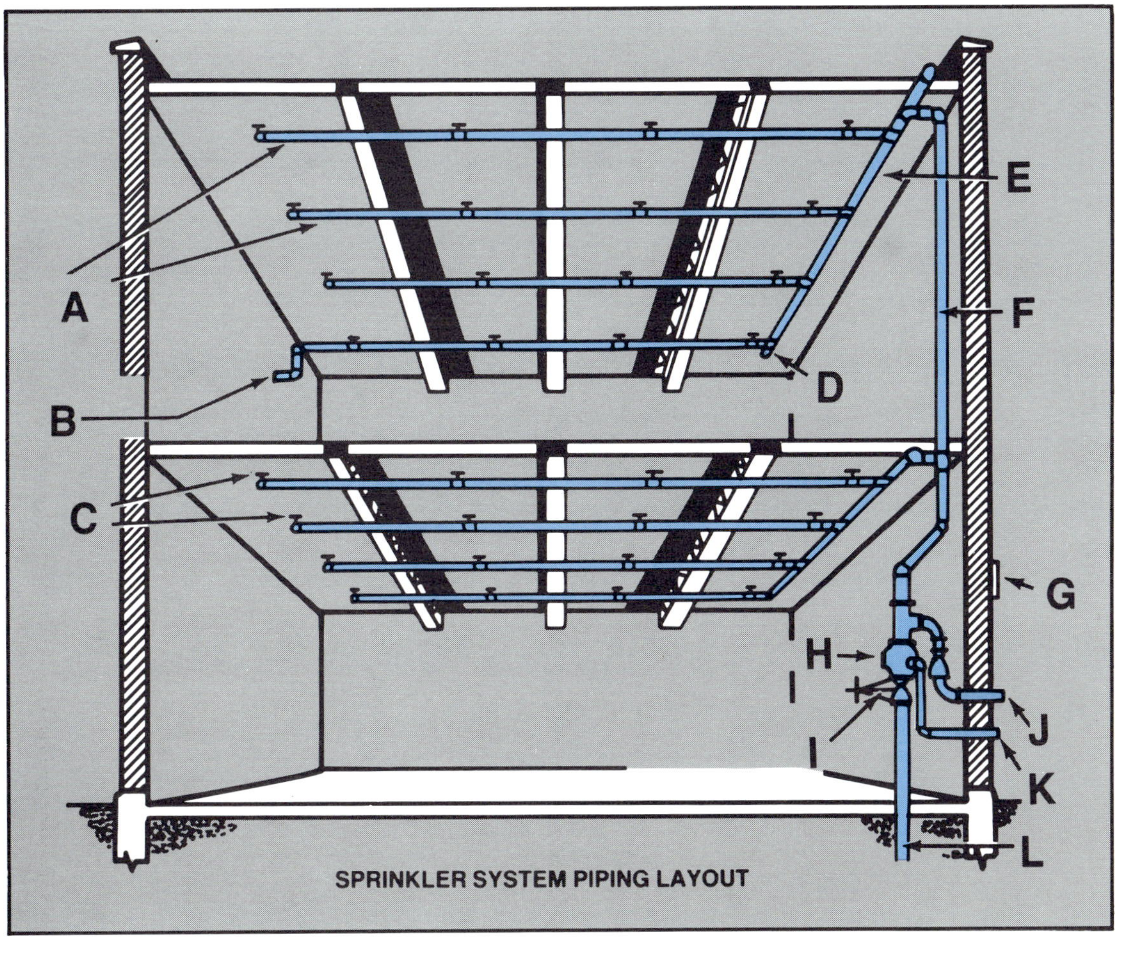

A. ____________________ E. ____________________ I. ____________________

B. ____________________ F. ____________________ J. ____________________

C. ____________________ G. ____________________ K. ____________________

D. ____________________ H. ____________________ L. ____________________

7

176. There are four types of fixed carbon dioxide systems. Name and briefly describe each one.

A.

B.

C.

D.

177. What documentation does NFPA 12 require the manufacturer to provide for the owner?

178. Why are halogenated agents effective in extinguishing surface fires in flammable liquids, most solid combustible fires, and electrical fires? How do they work, and on what fires are they ineffective?

179. Why are dry chemical extinguishers not recommended for use on electronic and computer equipment?

____

____

____

180. Identify the basic components of an alarm system.

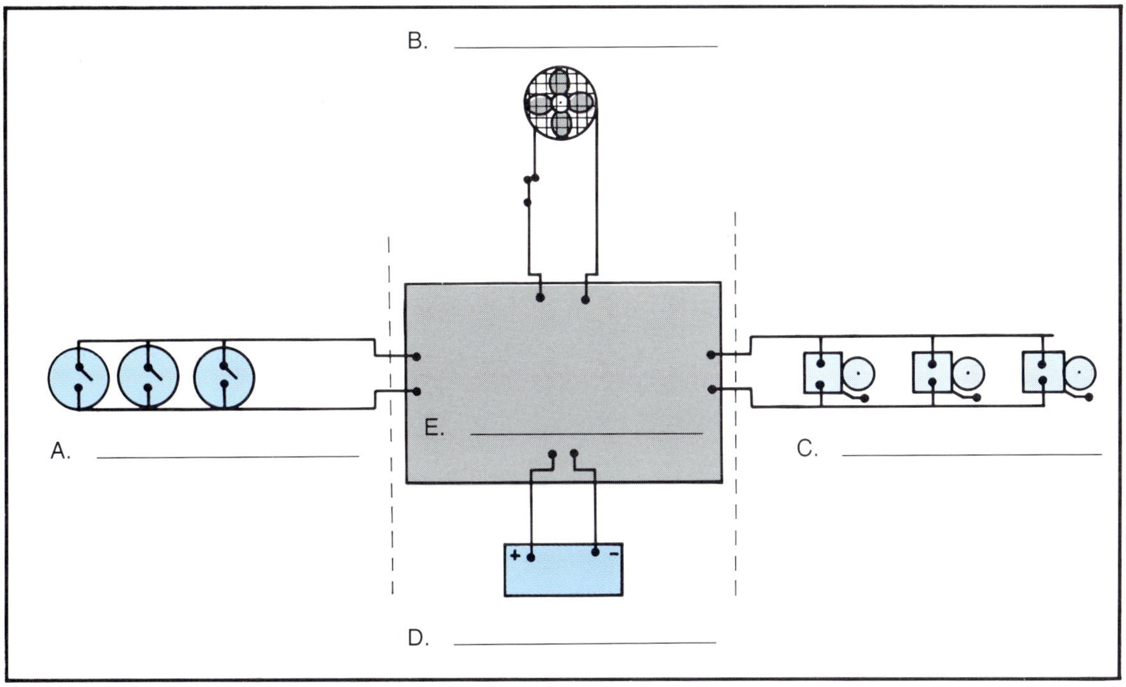

181. Identify the basic types of initiating devices.

A. ____

B. ____

C. ____

D. ____

E. ____

182. What is the main advantage of a proprietary alarm system with a central alarm receiving point?

____

____

____

183. What is the main difference between a central station system and a proprietary alarm system?

____

____

____

7

184. Municipal alarm systems are classified as either Type A or Type B. Briefly identify the main difference of each type.

Type A ______________________________

____

____

Type B ______________________________

____

____

185. What is the chief advantage of signal multiplexing alarm systems?

____

____

____

____

____

____

186. Identify and briefly describe the three types of alarm initiating devices.

A. ______________________________

____

____

B. ______________________________

____

____

C. ______________________________

____

____

187. Many building and fire codes require a voice communication and firefighter telephone system in high-rise buildings. These systems serve two functions. Name them.

A. ______________________________

____

____

____

B. ______________________________

____

____

____

188. Name four general visual observations that must be made when testing detectors.

A. ______________________________

B. ______________________________

C. ______________________________

D. ______________________________

189. What is the procedure for testing the following types of detectors?

A. NONRESTORABLE FIXED TEMPERATURE DETECTORS:

____

B. RESTORABLE DETECTORS:

____

C. FUSIBLE LINK DETECTORS:

____

D. PNEUMATIC-TYPE DETECTORS:

____

E. SMOKE DETECTORS:

F. FLAME DETECTORS:

190. There are four components of an effective water distribution system. Name them.

A.

B.

C.

D.

191. There are three types of distribution systems, name and briefly describe each system.

A.

B.

C.

192. The distribution system consists of three main feeders. Name and describe them.

A.

B. ______________________________

____

____

____

C. ______________________________

____

____

____

193. Identify the minimum pipe dimensions recommended for good water supply distribution in the following:

RESIDENTIAL DISTRICTS:

____

____

____

SHOPPING CENTERS AND INDUSTRIAL AREAS:

____

____

____

MULTIPLE HOUSING DEVELOPMENTS:

____

____

____

194. What main factor determines whether dry- or wet-barrel hydrants are used?

____

____

____

____

____

195. Name three important maintenance areas to check for leaks in hydrants.

A. ______________________________

B. ______________________________

C. ______________________________

196. Name four possible causes for obstruction of water mains.

A. ______________________________

B. ______________________________

C. ______________________________

D. ______________________________

7

197. Name 10 items needed during a fire hydrant inspection.

A. ____________________

B. ____________________

C. ____________________

D. ____________________

E. ____________________

F. ____________________

G. ____________________

H. ____________________

I. ____________________

J. ____________________

198. Name five observations made during hydrant inspections.

A. ____________________

B. ____________________

C. ____________________

D. ____________________

E. ____________________

199. When should water flow tests occur?

____

200. Briefly explain the four-step procedure for using a pitot tube and gauge.

Step 1: ______

Step 2: ______

Step 3: ______

Step 4: ______

201. What is the formula used to compute hydrant flow?

GPM = ______

L/min = ______

Where: C = ______

d = ______

P = ______

202. During a flow test, what is the difference between the test hydrant and the flow hydrant?

______

203. Briefly explain the seven-step procedure for conducting an available water test.

Step 1: ______

7

Step 2: ______

Step 3: ______

Step 4: ______

Step 5: ______

Step 6: ______

Step 7: ______

204. Name three flow test precautions, and determine the solution to each precaution named.

205. There are three ways to compute fire flow test results: graphical analysis, mathematical formula, and nomograph method. Explain how to use each one.

GRAPHICAL ANALYSIS:

Step 1: ______________________________

____

Step 2: ______________________________

____

Step 3: ______________________________

____

Step 4: ______________________________

____

Step 5: ______________________________

____

Step 6: ______________________________

____

Step 7: ______________________________

____

MATHEMATICAL FORMULA:

$Q_r =$

Where Q_r = ______________________________

____

Q_f = ______________________________

h_r = ______________________________

____

____

h_f = ______________________________

____

____

NOMOGRAPH METHOD:

Step 1: ______________________________

____

____

____

Step 2: ______________________________

____

____

____

7

Step 3: ______________________________

206. Determining available water flow answers three questions about the water supply. What are they?

A. ______________________________

B. ______________________________

C. ______________________________

207. Each type of available water flow determination method has its advantages. What is the advantage of each method?

GRAPHICAL ANALYSIS:

____

THE NOMOGRAPH:

____

MATHEMATICAL DETERMINATION:

____

8

Plans Review

This chapter provides information that addresses performance objectives described in NFPA 1031, *Standard for Professional Qualifications for Fire Inspector* (1987), particularly those referenced in the following sections:

Fire Inspector II

4-9.2 Plans and Specifications.

4-9.2.1

4-9.2.2

Plans Review 8

TRUE/FALSE

Mark each statement true or false.

1. ☐ T ☐ F The obvious advantage of establishing a plans review process is that it enables fire service reviewers the opportunity to design the automatic sprinkler system for the occupancy.

2. ☐ T ☐ F Plans for large construction projects are usually divided into four or more basic areas such as architectural, structural, mechanical, and electrical.

3. ☐ T ☐ F One aspect of fire protection to be examined during the architectural drawing review is building compartmentation.

4. ☐ T ☐ F The reviewer should verify the fire-resistance rating of the construction assembly separating vertical openings.

5. ☐ T ☐ F The building inspector verifies that automatic extinguishing systems, if required, are located and installed according to the appropriate standards.

6. ☐ T ☐ F Inspectors should be familiar with different types of sprinkler systems, their operation, and the specifications for each type of system.

7. ☐ T ☐ F The size of each sprinkler system is based on the total square feet (square meters) of floor area controlled by a single riser and control valve.

8. ☐ T ☐ F Fire inspectors should be aware of specified maximum travel distances to pull boxes and code requirements concerning pull box placement for accessibility to the handicapped.

9. ☐ T ☐ F Fire inspectors should be familiar with all types of fire alarm detectors specified and the code requirements for their use.

10. ☐ T ☐ F It is the responsibility of building inspectors to *require* inspection of the alarm system during construction and to observe the final acceptance test to ensure compliance.

11. ☐ T ☐ F Once the inspector has finished reviewing all of the plans, the plans should be returned, and the inspector is finished until after construction is complete.

8

MULTIPLE CHOICE

Circle the letter corresponding to the most appropriate response.

12. The north direction symbol usually points towards the ______.

    A. front view
    B. elevation view
    C. top of the sheet
    D. plan view

13. Structural drawings indicate how the building will be built, what materials will be used, and ______.

    A. how the building will be used
    B. who will use the building
    C. when the building will be used
    D. where the building will be used

14. When reviewing structural drawings, reviewing the overall size of the building in terms of height and area should be the ______ step.

    A. first
    B. second
    C. third
    D. fourth

15. When determining the height of a building, fire inspectors must understand how the jurisdictional code addresses what three factors?

    A. Lowest point, highest point, and automatic sprinkler protection
    B. Lowest point, highest point, and widest point
    C. Highest point, widest point, and automatic sprinkler protection
    D. Highest point, narrowest point, and automatic sprinkler protection

16. After verifying that the project can be built, inspectors should ______.

    A. suggest the type of automatic sprinkler head
    B. specify locations of emergency fire alarms
    C. determine the occupant load
    D. evaluate for life safety

17. After fire inspectors have determined the occupant load, they should ______.

    A. evaluate the means of egress
    B. specify a wet- or dry-pipe sprinkler system
    C. determine standpipe classes
    D. determine portable fire extinguisher number and type

18. Once the means of egress has been identified and the acceptability of each component has been verified, the reviewer should ______.

    A. determine standpipe location
    B. evaluate the capacity of the means of egress
    C. specify gpm (L/min) required for automatic sprinkler system
    D. specify size and location of portable fire extinguishers

19. Fire inspectors should locate and check fire and smoke barriers for continuity, fire-resistance rating, and opening protection. Who should supply this detailed information?

    A. The building inspector
    B. The fire protection engineer
    C. The architect
    D. The contractor

20. Fire inspectors must verify the types of detection devices to be used and their ______.

    A. locations
    B. power requirements
    C. warning frequencies
    D. inspection intervals

21. Inspectors should send copies of the review letter to ______.

    A. the contractor only
    B. the architect only
    C. only the architect and contractor
    D. all parties interested in or affected by the comments

22. The plans review letter should note that the plans review is a/an ______.

    A. initial compliance inspection
    B. official document
    C. pre-inspection process
    D. courtesy to promote fire safety

IDENTIFY

Identify the proper sequence of events inspectors should follow when developing a plans review system.

23. ___ Develop a written policy stating which agency has the authority to enforce code regulations during the plans review stage.

    ___ Establish good record keeping procedures. Both formal and informal communications should be documented because fire inspectors may need these records for a performance evaluation, legal action, or future references.

    ___ Formulate and write goals and objectives of the plans review system.

    ___ After fire inspectors establish a system, they should initiate a public information program targeted at those who are most affected — architects, engineers, contractors, and developers.

    ___ Establish a procedure that specifies the minimum requirements for submitting plans for review; if possible, the requirements should be in booklet form and distributed to all architects, engineers, contractors in the area, and any other contractors who are named to area building projects.

    ___ While planning the record keeping system, fire inspectors should develop the format for a plans review letter.

    ___ Develop methods for coordinating the efforts of the plans review system.

    ___ Identify typical problems that could be prevented if a plans review system were in place.

8

Identify the proper sequence of events for sprinkler review.

24. ___ The inspectors should examine the specifications to verify the temperature rating, type, orifice size, area of coverage, use in special areas, spacing, and location of sprinklers.
___ The inspector should determine whether the system has been designed according to the pipe schedule or has been hydraulically calculated.
___ The inspector should use flow tests to measure the pressure and flow available at the city main.
___ The inspector should check the total capacity of the water supply.
___ The inspector should determine which standard applies and what the basic requirements are.
___ The inspector should check to ensure water supplies for sprinklers are of sufficient capacity and pressure to satisfy the tabular requirements for pipe schedule systems or the calculated requirements for hydraulically designed systems.
___ The inspector should check several system design factors, such as the extent of coverage, type of system, size of system, information about sprinklers and piping, water supply connections and valves, and the fire department connections.

SHORT ANSWER

Briefly answer each question in your own words.

25. There are four main views of working drawings. Name them.

A. ______________________________

B. ______________________________

C. ______________________________

D. ______________________________

26. Briefly describe what each of the following views contain.

A. The Plan View ______________________________

____

The Plan View commonly has three specific areas. Briefly describe each one.

- The Site Plan ______________________________

____

____

____

____

- The Basement Plan ______________________________

____

____

____

____

- The Floor Plan

B. The Elevation View

C. The Sectional View

D. The Detailed View

27. There are three types of cross-sectional views. Briefly describe each one.

A. Horizontal

B. Typical

C. Detail

8

28. When reviewing site plans, inspectors should pay close attention to accessibility, water supply, and general building parameters. Specifically, explain what is meant by each one of these terms.

A. ACCESSIBILITY

B. WATER SUPPLY

C. GENERAL BUILDING PARAMETERS

29. When evaluating hazardous areas, fire inspectors should verify that adequate separation or automatic sprinkler protection has been provided. What are some additional aspects that fire inspectors must consider are special hazards?

30. During the review of the mechanical HVAC system, what observations should the inspector verify?

31. When should smoke control systems be used?

8

32. What is the purpose and intent of stairwell pressurization?

33. During the review of the electrical system, what observations should the inspector verify?

34. Detailed information about fire alarm plans and communications systems is not usually provided on the general construction plans. Generally, separate plans must be submitted and approved before these systems can be installed. What should plans for alarm systems contain?

35. Special extinguishing systems are often required in areas where special hazards exist or where the use of water is undesirable. What type of agents are often used, and what detailed information should be included in the specifications.

36. When reviewing alarm and detection systems, inspectors need certain information. List what is needed.

37. What should inspectors check in the plans regarding portable fire protection equipment?

8

38. What information should the plans review letter contain?

39. What is considered the "final sign-off" for the certificate of occupancy?

9

Hazardous Materials

This chapter provides information that addresses performance objectives described in NFPA 1031, *Standard for Professional Qualifications for Fire Inspector* (1987), particularly those referenced in the following sections:

Fire Inspector I

3-12.1 Properties of Flammable and Combustible Liquids.

3-12.1.1

3-12.1.2

3-12.1.3

3-12.1.4

3-12.1.6

3-12.8 Flammable and Combustible Liquids Fire Extinguishment.

3-12.8.1

3-12.8.2

3-12.8.3

3-12.9 Flammable and Combustible Liquids Labeling.

3-12.9.1

3-13.1 Properties of Compressed and Liquefied Gases.

3-13.1.1

3-13.1.2

3-13.1.3

3-13.1.4

3-13.7 Fire Extinguishment of Compressed and Liquefied Gases.

3-13.7.1

3-14.1 Properties of Explosives.

3-14.2

3-15.1 General.

3-15.1.1

3-15.1.3

3-15.2 Specific Hazardous Materials.

3-15.2.1

3-15.2.2

3-15.2.3

3-15.2.4

3-15.2.5

3-15.2.6

3-15.2.7

3-15.2.8

3-15.3 Combustible Metals.

3-15.3.1

3-15.4 Combustible Dusts.

3-15.4.1

3-15.4.2

Fire Inspector II

4-3 Compressed and Liquefied Gases.

4-3.1

4-4 Explosives, Including Fireworks.

(See NFPA 495, *Code for the Manufacturing, Transportation, Storage and Use of Explosive Materials,* **and NFPA 1124,** *Code for the Manufacture, Transportation, and Storage of Fireworks.***)**

4-4.4

4-5.1 Natural and Synthetic Fibers.

4-5.1.2

Hazardous Materials 9

TRUE/FALSE

Mark each statement true or false.

1. ☐ T ☐ F Disease-causing agents are not considered a hazardous material for fire inspectors.

2. ☐ T ☐ F Flammable liquids are any liquids having a flash point above 100°F (38°C) and having a vapor pressure exceeding 40 psi (256 kPa).

3. ☐ T ☐ F Combustible liquids have flash points below 100°F (38°C).

4. ☐ T ☐ F One acceptable method of extinguishing flammable or combustible liquids is cooling the liquid to stop the flammable vapors from being produced.

5. ☐ T ☐ F Gases are often classified by their principal use.

6. ☐ T ☐ F There are several types of cryogenic containers: spherical tanks, cylindrical tanks, and dewars.

7. ☐ T ☐ F The primary goal in controlling fire emergencies involving flammable gases is to smother the fire.

8. ☐ T ☐ F The principal hazard associated with inorganic acids involves the possibility of leakage.

9. ☐ T ☐ F The reactivity of a flammable or combustible liquid or solid refers to the material's ability to release energy as a result of a chemical reaction.

10. ☐ T ☐ F Reactivity refers to the reaction of two or more chemicals and the ease with which the reaction takes place.

11. ☐ T ☐ F Self-reactivity refers to the external activity of a material and the ease with which a reaction may be initiated.

12. ☐ T ☐ F Reactive materials are categorized by degrees based on their ability to undergo a chemical reaction with another substance and to release some type of energy during this process.

13. ☐ T ☐ F Materials classified as poisons include those substances that are capable of producing serious illness or death once they enter the bloodstream.

14. ☐ T ☐ F Irritants produce some type of local inflammation or irritate the skin, respiratory membranes, or eyes.

9

15. ☐ T ☐ F Anesthetics reduce the muscular powers of vital bodily functions and result in loss of consciousness, suppressed breathing, or even death.

16. ☐ T ☐ F It is imperative that fire inspectors be aware of the possible toxic effects of a material and make sure that sufficient personal protective equipment is available.

17. ☐ T ☐ F The toxicity of a flammable or combustible liquid refers to the ability of that substance to flashover.

18. ☐ T ☐ F Fire inspectors should determine the maximum allowable concentration of toxicity to which an individual may repeatedly be exposed without harmful effects.

19. ☐ T ☐ F When in contact with materials such as oils, greases, hydrocarbons, and various cleaning agents, oxidizers react chemically to ignite the material.

20. ☐ T ☐ F Radioactive materials that may be commonly found in the workplace include radium, plutonium, cobalt, uranium, cesium, and indium.

21. ☐ T ☐ F A thermoluminescent dosimeter (TLD) measures radiation.

22. ☐ T ☐ F Burning plastics sometimes generate large amounts of sooty, dense, black smoke.

23. ☐ T ☐ F Fire inspectors must exercise caution if catalysts, particularly peroxygen compounds, are located near plastics.

24. ☐ T ☐ F When considering explosive materials, the only effective way for fire inspectors to prevent disaster is to ensure the area is protected by an automatic sprinkler system.

25. ☐ T ☐ F Common extinguishing agents used for ordinary combustible and flammable liquids may cause a violent reaction when applied to burning metals.

26. ☐ T ☐ F Combustible dusts include **ALL** of the following: cocoa, grain, flour, starch, graphite, charcoal, coal, plastic, aluminum, rubber, and magnesium.

27. ☐ T ☐ F The ignitability of any dust-air mixture is based on several factors, particularly the humidity.

28. ☐ T ☐ F Explosion vents or release devices actually do very little to reduce the damage sustained by a structure during such an explosion.

29. ☐ T ☐ F Combustible dusts should be blown away from ignition sources.

30. ☐ T ☐ F Protein fibers, such as wool and silk, are derived from animals. These fibers are generally more difficult to ignite than plant fibers; but, when burning do not emit toxic gases.

31. ☐ T ☐ F The main hazard of storing baled cotton and other fibers is that the surface of the bales is covered with minute fibers.

MULTIPLE CHOICE

Circle the letter corresponding to the most appropriate response.

32. The labeling and placarding of hazardous materials may fall under several systems of marking: bulk, nonbulk, and ______.

    A. international
    B. granular
    C. compressed
    D. biological

33. Identification systems of hazardous materials have been developed by the U.S. Department of Transportation, the National Fire Protection Association, and the ______.

    A. National Chemical Society
    B. United Nations
    C. International Hazardous Material Conference
    D. Hazardous Materials Fellowship

34. For bulk shipments, each material that is considered hazardous can be specifically identified by an assigned ______ number.

    A. alpha/numeric code
    B. three-digit
    C. four-digit
    D. numeric/alpha code

35. In the United States, the transportation of hazardous materials is regulated by the ______.

    A. Department of Transportation (DOT)
    B. National Fire Protection Association (NFPA)
    C. Interstate Trucking Association (ITA)
    D. Interstate Commerce Commission (ICC)

36. An extinguishing agent **NOT** suitable for a flammable or combustible liquid fire is ______.

    A. dry chemical
    B. carbon dioxide
    C. water
    D. halogenated compounds

37. Cryogenic gases are produced and stored at ______ and colder.

    A. -100°F (-73°C)
    B. -130°F (-90°C)
    C. -180°F (-118°C)
    D. -273°F (-169°C)

9

38. Because of the temperature and vapor ratio, cryogenic liquids must be stored in special containers. Which material is **NOT** used in its construction?

A. Perlite
B. Aluminized Mylar Film
C. Carbon Steel
D. Copper Alloys

39. Chemicals that provide oxygen for combustion, either as a result of exposure to heat or through natural decomposition are called ______.

A. combustibles
B. anesthetics
C. self-reactive
D. oxidizers

40. Alpha, beta, and gamma rays are measured in ______.

A. remikens
B. ricktors
C. roentgens
D. recenders

41. Plastics, with the exception of cellulose nitrates, are classified as ______ materials.

A. Class A
B. Class B
C. Class C
D. Class D

42. Generally, the best way to reduce dust explosions is ______.

A. collect dust weekly
B. employ good housekeeping practices
C. blow dust away from ignition sources
D. collect dust in 2x2x2 cubes

43. Natural fibers include those materials composed of ______ or more cellulose material.

A. 60%
B. 70%
C. 80%
D. 90%

SHORT ANSWER

Briefly answer each question in your own words.

44. Identify two examples of each of the following:

Fuel Gases:

A. ______________________________

B. ______________________________

Industrial Gases:

A. ______________________________

B. ______________________________

Medical Gases:

A. ______________________________

B. ______________________________

45. Toxic chemicals are classified into three basic categories. Name these categories.

A. ______________________________

B. ______________________________

C. ______________________________

46. Fire inspectors come in contact with many oxidizers. Name ten.

____

____

____

____

____

____

____

____

____

____

47. Information concerning regulations, code requirements, and emergency actions for hazardous materials may be obtained from various agencies. Name six.

____

____

____

____

____

____

48. Hazardous materials are divided into nine numbered classes. Name them.

Class 1 — ______________________________

Class 2 — ______________________________

Class 3 — ______________________________

Class 4 — ______________________________

Class 5 — ______________________________

Division 5.1 — ______________________________

Division 5.2 — ______________________________

9

Class 6 – ____________________

Class 7 – ____________________

Class 8 – ____________________

Class 9 – ____________________

49. What are placards?

50. Name the U.S. Department of Transportation publication for hazardous materials and explain its function.

51. The National Fire Protection Association has developed a nationally recognized labeling system for fixed facilities. Name the standard and explain the labeling system.

52. **Flammable** liquids are divided into Class IA, IB, and IC liquids. Name the **general properties** of each class.

Class IA – ____________________

Class IB – ____________________

Class IC – ____________________

53. **Combustible** liquids are further divided into Class II, IIIA, and IIIB liquids. Name the general properties of each class.

Class II – ____________________

Class IIIA – ____________________

Class IIIB – ____________________

54. For liquids, explain the difference between flash point and fire point.

____

55. Explain boiling point for a liquid and why bubbles appear.

____

9

56. Explain specific gravity of a flammable or combustible liquid.

57. Define the flammable and explosive limits of flammable or combustible liquids.

58. Based on your answer in the previous question, explain LEL and UEL.

59. Explain how a BLEVE occurs.

60. Explain the difference between compressed gases and liquefied gases.

61. Explain vapor density.

62. Define Charles' Law and write the formula.

63. Define Boyle's Law and write the formula.

9

64. Basically, the hazards of cryogenic liquids can be reduced to three categories. What are they?

A. ______________________________

B. ______________________________

C. ______________________________

65. What common three pressure release devices are used to control pressure in cryogenic containers?

A. ______________________________

B. ______________________________

C. ______________________________

66. Define corrosives, and provide five examples of materials considered to be corrosive.

____

Examples: ______________________________

67. Why are reactive materials a particular concern to fire inspectors?

____

68. Define unstable materials, and provide five materials that are considered unstable.

Examples:

69. What four ways can toxic materials enter the body?

A.

B.

C.

D.

70. What are TLV's, and why are they important to fire inspectors?

71. Name two organizations that publish TLV's.

A.

B.

9

72. What are acute toxicity and chronic toxicity, and in what type of occupancies is each usually found?

Acute toxicity: ______________________________

Chronic toxicity: ______________________________

73. Explain acute toxicity in terms of LC_{50}.

74. Explain acute toxicity in terms of LD_{50}.

75. There are three types of radioactive particles. Name them and briefly describe each one's effective penetrability.

A. ______________________________

B. ______________________________

C. ______________________________

76. Plastic materials are characterized as either thermoplastic or thermoset materials. Briefly explain the difference.

77. Define explosive material.

78. There are three groups of explosives: primary or initiating high explosives, secondary high explosives, and low explosives. Explain the differences between each type.

A. Primary or initiating high explosives:

B. Secondary high explosives:

C. Low explosives:

79. Name four sources fire inspectors can contact for technical data on explosives.

9

80. Define combustible metals and name three that are commonly encountered.

Examples:

81. Name four hazards that are potential ignition sources for combustible dusts.

82. Electrical equipment used in a combustible dust area should conform to the requirements set forth by what code?

83. There are a variety of factors that affect the way in which a textile will burn. Name three factors.

10

Storage, Handling, and Use of Hazardous Materials

This chapter provides information that addresses performance objectives described in NFPA 1031, *Standard for Professional Qualifications for Fire Inspector* (1987), particularly those referenced in the following sections:

Fire Inspector I

3-12.2 Storage, Handling, and Use of Flammable and Combustible Liquids.

3-12.2.1

3-12.2.2

3-12.2.3

3-12.2.4

3-12.2.5

3-12.2.6

3-12.2.7

3-12.3 Underground Storage Tanks for Flammable and Combustible Liquids.

3-12.3.1

3-12.3.2

3-12.3.3

3-12.4 Aboveground Storage Tanks for Flammable and Combustible Liquids.

3-12.4.1

3-12.4.2

3-12.4.3

3-12.4.4

3-12.5 Inside Storage Tanks for Flammable and Combustible Liquids.

3-12.5.1

3-12.5.2

3-12.5.3

3-12.5.4

3-12.6 Outside Container Storage for Flammable and Combustible Liquids.

3-12.6.1

3-12.6.2

3-12.6.3

3-12.6.4

3-12.7 Inside Container Storage for Flammable and Combustible Liquids.

3-12.7.1

3-12.7.2

3-12.7.3

3-12.7.4

3-12.10 Transportation of Flammable and Combustible Liquids.

3-12.10.1

3-12.10.2

3-12.10.3

3-13.2 Storage, Handling, and Use of Compressed and Liquefied Gases.

3-13.2.1

3-13.2.2

3-13.2.3

3-13.3 Compressed and Liquefied Gas Containers.

3-13.4 Compressed and Liquefied Gas Transfer Operations.

3-13.5 Compressed and Liquefied Gas Leaks.

3-13.6 Transportation of Compressed and Liquefied Gases.

3-13.6.1

3-13.6.2

3-13.6.3

3-14.1 Properties of Explosives.

3-14.3

3-14.5 Labeling of Explosives, Including Fireworks.

3-14.6

3-14.7 Storage of Explosives, Including Fireworks.

3-14.7.1

3-14.7.2

3-15 Other Hazardous Materials.

3-15.1.2

3-15.2 Specific Hazardous Materials.

3-15.3 Combustible Metals

3-15.3.2

3-15.4 Combustible Dusts

3-15.4.3

Fire Inspector II

4-2 Flammable and Combustible Liquids.

4-3 Compressed and Liquefied Gases.

4-3.2

4-3.3

4-3.4

4-3.5

4-3.7

4-4 Explosives, Including Fireworks.

(See NFPA 495, *Code for the Manufacture, Transportation, Storage, and Use of Explosive Materials,* **and NFPA 1124,** *Code for the Manufacture, Transportation, and Storage of Fireworks.***)**

4-4.1

4-4.2

4-4.5

4-5.2 Combustible Dusts.

4-5.2.1

Storage, Handling, and Use of Hazardous Materials

10

TRUE/FALSE

Mark each statement true or false.

1. ☐ T ☐ F Flammable vapors, released by flammable liquids, are responsible for flame propagation and explosions.

2. ☐ T ☐ F When flammable vapor-air mixtures do explode, they usually do so in a confined space such as a building, room, or container.

3. ☐ T ☐ F When evaluating storage practices of flammable and combustible liquids, fire inspectors must remember that the size of the tank is extremely important.

4. ☐ T ☐ F Flammable and combustible storage receptacles referred to as *portable tanks that have a storage capacity greater than 660 gallons (2 498 L)* should be treated according to the same standards as fixed storage tanks.

5. ☐ T ☐ F There are four basic classifications of storage tanks: aboveground, underground, tanks located inside buildings, and special conditions.

6. ☐ T ☐ F Vent discharges must be arranged to prevent flame impingement on any part of the tank or nearby tanks in case the vapors exiting the vent ignite.

7. ☐ T ☐ F All aboveground storage tanks, except Class IIIB exceeding 12,000 gallons (45 429 L) in a diked area with, or in the path of, Class I or Class II liquids, must have some device or inherent design that will relieve any excess pressure caused by *nearby* fires.

8. ☐ T ☐ F Underground tank storage is perhaps the safest form of storage for flammable and combustible liquids.

9. ☐ T ☐ F Vent pipings should be protected from physical damage.

10. ☐ T ☐ F Under normal circumstances, underground tanks that are installed correctly may be expected to last approximately 50 years.

11. ☐ T ☐ F Inside storage tanks containing Class I, Class II, or Class IIIA liquids must have overflow prevention devices such as float valves, fill-line meters, low heat pumps, or liquidtight overflow pipes that are at least one pipe size smaller than the fill pipe.

12. ☐ T ☐ F The most common form of flammable and combustible liquid storage vessels encountered are containers and portable tanks.

10

13. ☐ T ☐ F Portable tanks must conform to *Chapter 1, Title 49* of the *Code of Federal Regulations* (DOT Regulations) or NFPA 386, *Portable Shipping Tanks for Flammable and Combustible Liquids.*

14. ☐ T ☐ F The liquids *must be* dispensed through approved pumps or self-closing faucets.

15. ☐ T ☐ F Class I and Class II liquids should be kept in covered containers when not actually in use.

16. ☐ T ☐ F Only Class I liquids may be used in the presence of any possible ignition source, such as open flames, electrical arcs, or heating elements.

17. ☐ T ☐ F Operations that use spray booths should have an exhaust duct leading to the outside by the most direct route, even if these ducts pass through floors.

18. ☐ T ☐ F All dip tank operations must be located on the ground floor of noncombustible buildings.

19. ☐ T ☐ F If a static discharge is present at the same time that a flammable mixture is near, a fire or explosion can result.

20. ☐ T ☐ F To protect against static discharge, tanks must be bonded together with a metal chain or strap.

21. ☐ T ☐ F Transfer systems should be designed so liquids will flow by gravity or by siphoning.

22. ☐ T ☐ F The basic difference in the two vapor recovery systems for gasoline service stations currently in operation is the way in which the closed loop is accomplished.

23. ☐ T ☐ F During any inspection of a VRS, special emphasis should be placed on connections, piping, and nozzles and equipment.

24. ☐ T ☐ F Cylinders for flammable gases must be built according to specifications and regulations set forth by NFPA 30B, *Construction Specifications for Flammable Gas Cylinders and Portable Containers.*

25. ☐ T ☐ F Tanks used to store relatively small quantities of gas at moderate pressures are designed and developed by the American Society of Mechanical Engineers (ASME).

26. ☐ T ☐ F Tanks designed to hold large quantities of low pressure gas are built according to standards set forth by the American Petroleum Institute (API).

27. ☐ T ☐ F All cylinders should be stored in a safe, dry, well-ventilated area specifically designed for storing compressed liquefied gases.

28. ☐ T ☐ F Empty cylinders should be stored to the immediate left of its specific type of gas to ensure the same type of gas is refilled in that container.

29. ☐ T ☐ F Cylinders stored outside should be protected from adverse weather conditions.

30. ☐ T ☐ F Static electricity is **NOT** a potential ignition source where gases are transferred.

31. ☐ T ☐ F All cylinders on loading stations must be clearly labeled with the name of the gas being used in order to reduce the possibility that someone will connect the wrong containers.

32. ☐ T ☐ F Fire extinguisher requirements for compressed and liquefied gases fall into the category of Class D hazards.

33. ☐ T ☐ F Electrical equipment used in dust-laden atmospheres must be of the explosion-proof type as specified by NFPA 70, *National Electrical Code.*

34. ☐ T ☐ F To prevent the possibility of a dust explosion, the dust should be blown away from surfaces where it could accumulate.

35. ☐ T ☐ F When fire inspectors consider storage provided for explosives, they must ensure that the explosives are protected from external sources of energy and that employees are protected in case of explosion.

36. ☐ T ☐ F A major consideration in the storage of explosives involves the separation distances between storage facilities and other structures.

MULTIPLE CHOICE

Circle the letter corresponding to the most appropriate response.

37. Flammable and combustible storage receptacles referred to as *containers* have a storage capacity of ______ or less.

    A. 40 gallons (151 L)
    B. 50 gallons (189 L)
    C. 60 gallons (227 L)
    D. 70 gallons (265 L)

38. Flammable and combustible storage receptacles referred to as *portable tanks* are larger than ______ and are not intended for a fixed installation.

    A. 40 gallons (151 L)
    B. 50 gallons (189 L)
    C. 60 gallons (227 L)
    D. 70 gallons (265 L)

10

39. Flammable and combustible storage receptacles referred to as a *storage tank* refers to a vessel greater than ______ and in a fixed location.

A. 25 gallons (95 L)
B. 30 gallons (114 L)
C. 55 gallons (208 L)
D. 60 gallons (227 L)

40. When fire inspectors check aboveground tanks, they should ensure the tanks are placed on sturdy foundations with adequate supports, and exposed supports under the tanks must be protected by fire-resistant materials with ratings of at least ______.

A. 1 hour
B. 2 hours
C. 3 hours
D. 4 hours

41. Fire inspectors must also consider carefully the spacing between aboveground tanks. The spacing between two tanks should be at least ______.

A. 3 feet (1 m)
B. 4 feet (1.2 m)
C. 6 feet (1.8 m)
D. 7 feet (2.1 m)

42. In aboveground tanks containing liquids classified as Class I, Class II, or Class III, the distances between the tanks must be at least ______ the sum of their diameters.

A. 1/6
B. 1/4
C. 1/2
D. 3/4

43. For those tanks containing unstable flammable or combustible liquids, the distance must be at least ______ the sum of their diameters.

A. 1/6
B. 1/4
C. 1/2
D. 3/4

44. When liquefied petroleum gas containers are located in the same area as flammable or combustible liquid aboveground storage tanks, the gas containers and storage tanks must be at least ______ apart.

A. 20 feet (6 m)
B. 30 feet (9.1 m)
C. 40 feet (12.2 m)
D. 50 feet (15.2 m)

45. Fire inspectors should also make sure that there are measures taken to prevent the flammable or combustible liquids from accumulating under the gas containers. If the liquid storage tanks are enclosed by dikes, any nearby liquefied petroleum gas containers must be on the outside of the dike and at least ______ from the wall of the dike.

    A. 10 feet (3 m)
    B. 12 feet (4 m)
    C. 15 feet (5 m)
    D. 25 feet (8 m)

46. The inside nominal diameter of the vents must be at least ______.

    A. 1 inch (25 mm)
    B. 1¼ inches (32 mm)
    C. 1½ inches (38 mm)
    D. 2 inches (51 mm)

47. Vents located near buildings or public places must be arranged so that vapors are released outside in a safe area and at least ______ from the ground.

    A. 10 feet (3 m)
    B. 12 feet (3.6 m)
    C. 15 feet (4.6 m)
    D. 18 feet (5.5 m)

48. Underground tanks **NOT** subject to vehicular traffic over them must be covered with at least 2 feet (0.6 m) of earth, or at least 1 foot (0.3 m) of earth on top of which is a reinforced concrete slab at least ______ thick.

    A. 3 inches (77 mm)
    B. 2 inches (51 mm)
    C. 4 inches (102 mm)
    D. 6 inches (152 mm)

49. Underground tanks *likely* to have vehicles passing over them must be protected against damage by at least 3 feet (1 m) of earth, or 1½ feet (0.46 m) of well-tamped earth plus ______.

    A. 6 inches (152 mm) of concrete or 8 inches (203 mm) of reinforced asphaltic concrete
    B. 8 inches (203 mm) of reinforced concrete or 6 inches (152 mm) of asphaltic concrete
    C. 4 inches (102 mm) of reinforced concrete or 6 inches (152 mm) of asphaltic concrete
    D. 8 inches (203 mm) of concrete or 8 inches (203 mm) of reinforced asphaltic concrete

50. The vents used in underground storage should have at least a ______ nominal inside diameter.

A. 1¼-inch (32 mm)
B. 1½-inch (38 mm)
C. 2¼-inch (42 mm)
D. 2½-inch (65 mm)

51. Vents for Class I liquids must discharge outside buildings, must be higher than the fill pipe opening, and must be at least ______ above the adjacent ground level.

A. 12 feet (4 m)
B. 15 feet (5 m)
C. 18 feet (5.5 m)
D. 20 feet (6 m)

52. The most common types of tanks found inside buildings are those used to store fuel oil. Tanks of less than 660 gallons (2 500 L) require ______.

A. a fire-resistant room
B. a 3-hour fire resistant rated enclosure
C. a self-closing door
D. no special fire protection features

53. Each portable tank must be installed with an emergency venting device to limit internal pressures to ______ of the bursting pressure of the tank, whichever is greater.

A. 5 psig (34.5 kPa), or 25 percent
B. 10 psig (69 kPa), or 30 percent
C. 15 psig (104 kPa), or 35 percent
D. 20 psig (138 kPa), or 40 percent

54. Storage rooms for flammable or combustible liquids should be specially constructed of fire-resistive materials, a 4-inch (102 mm) sill that is liquidtight and composed of noncombustible materials, and ______.

A. a deluge sprinkler system
B. a 3-hour fire rated enclosure
C. a self-closing door
D. no other special fire protection features are required

55. Storage rooms for flammable or combustible liquids must have ______ ventilation.

A. gravity
B. mechanical
C. either gravity or mechanical
D. both gravity and mechanical

56. The area designated for outside storage of flammable and combustible liquids must be protected by a fence or ______.

A. a 3-foot (0.9 m) deep trench around the perimeter
B. an approved emergency self-containment system
C. a security guard
D. an approved emergency alarm/lighting system

57. Loading and unloading stations for Class I liquids should be located no closer than ______ from storage tanks, property lines, or adjacent buildings.

    A. 20 feet (6 m)
    B. 25 feet (8 m)
    C. 30 feet (9 m)
    D. 35 feet (11 m)

58. Loading and unloading stations for Class II and Class III liquids should be located no closer than ______ from these same objects.

    A. 15 feet (5 m)
    B. 20 feet (6 m)
    C. 25 feet (8 m)
    D. 30 feet (9 m)

59. Fire inspectors are expected to know the basic techniques for extinguishing fires involving flammable and combustible liquids. To extinguish these fires, personnel should use a ______ extinguishing agent.

    A. Class A
    B. Class B
    C. Class C
    D. Class D

60. The Department of Transportation requirements apply only to those cylinders and tanks involved in ______ travel.

    A. intrastate
    B. interstate
    C. interborder
    D. all

61. When inspecting storage of compressed and liquefied gases, fire inspectors should ensure that six basic safety precautions are observed. Which one is **NOT** a basic safety precaution?

    A. *Absolutely No Smoking* in the area of the cylinders.
    B. Adequate ventilation installed to prevent accumulation of flammable gas vapors.
    C. Electric lights are in a fixed position, enclosed in glass, and the switch to the light is located outside the storage room.
    D. All activity within the inspection area ceases until the inspection is complete.

62. The primary hazard associated with the storage of compressed and liquefied gases is the ______.

    A. high pressure caused by the storage itself
    B. low flashpoint of the individual gas
    C. awkward handling associated with cylinders
    D. refill operations

63. Older stock of explosives should be used or shipped first; furthermore, packages must be opened or repacked at least ______ from the magazine.

    A. 30 feet (9 m)
    B. 40 feet (12 m)
    C. 50 feet (15 m)
    D. 60 feet (19 m)

64. Vehicles used to transport explosives should have a closed body or the load should be covered with a flame retardant and moistureproof tarpaulin; further, they should carry at least ______ fire extinguishers with a combined rating of ______.

    A. three, 5-A-20-B-C
    B. two, 2-A-10-B-C
    C. two, 6-A-20-B-C
    D. four, 5-A-10-B-C

65. At no time should vehicles transporting explosives be left unattended, nor should they be driven within ______ of each other.

    A. 200 feet (60 m)
    B. 300 feet (91 m)
    C. 400 feet (122 m)
    D. 500 feet (150 m)

SHORT ANSWER

Briefly answer each question in your own words.

66. Fire prevention measures are based on one or more techniques or principles. Name these five techniques or principles.

    A. ______
    B. ______
    C. ______
    D. ______
    E. ______

67. Aboveground storage tanks for flammable and combustible liquids are classified in three categories, depending upon the pressures for which they are designed. Name those three categories.

    A. ______
    ______
    ______

    B. ______
    ______
    ______

    C. ______
    ______
    ______

68. Certain aboveground tanks should have additional spacing so that inside tanks are accessible for fire fighting operations. When should this hold true?

____

69. In large aboveground storage applications, one of the most important considerations is the properly designed storage vessel. In addition to normal venting, what is required for most aboveground tanks to prevent a BLEVE?

____

70. All commercial venting devices should be stamped with three distinct pieces of information. Name them.

A. ______________________________

B. ______________________________

C. ______________________________

71. All Class I, II, or IIIA storage tank areas must have dikes or some form of drainage to prevent any leaks or accidental discharges. Briefly explain:

A. Why dikes are needed

____

B. The volume requirements

____

C. Construction methods/techniques

____

72. What method is perhaps the simplest and most economical method of detecting leaks in underground storage tanks?

73. Abandoned underground tanks can be safeguarded in either of two ways. Name them and explain the procedure.

A.

B.

74. The amount of flammable and combustible liquids that can be stored in an occupancy depends upon the occupancy classification. Briefly explain the proper storage of the following occupancies.

DWELLING OCCUPANCIES/BUILDINGS CONTAINING THREE OR FEWER DWELLING UNITS:

ASSEMBLY OCCUPANCIES/BUILDINGS CONTAINING MORE THAN THREE UNITS:

OFFICE, EDUCATIONAL, AND HEALTH CARE OCCUPANCIES:

MERCANTILE OCCUPANCIES AND RETAIL STORES:

WAREHOUSES AND BUILDINGS USED STRICTLY FOR STORING FLAMMABLE LIQUIDS AND LOCATED NO MORE THAN 50 FEET (15 m) FROM ANOTHER BUILDING OR PROPERTY LINE:

75. Small quantities of flammable or combustible liquids in normal operating areas should be stored in approved metal storage cabinets. Generally, what is the maximum capacity of Class I, Class II, and Class IIIA liquids (Gallons [L]) permitted to be stored in one cabinet?

10

76. There are two types of VRS for gasoline service stations in operation. Name and briefly describe each system.

A. ______________________________

B. ______________________________

77. What agency regulates transportation of flammable and combustible liquids at the following levels?

A. Interstate Level: ______________________________

B. Intrastate Level: ______________________________

C. Within your jurisdiction: ______________________________

78. If a hazard has been declared due to an unconfined leak, who usually assumes jurisdiction and why?

____

79. When flammable and combustible liquid leaks are suspected from an underground source, the liquid or its vapors are normally reported in the following areas. Provide two examples from each of the following categories.

A. Inhabited subsurface structures:

____

____

____

B. Uninhabited substructures:

____

____

____

C. Groundwater:

____

____

____

80. If the leak or suspected leak is in an inhabited area, the condition should be considered a potential hazard to human life. What is the fire inspector's immediate action?

____

____

____

____

____

____

____

81. Name five local agencies that can offer assistance within the local jursidiction during an incident and identify what type of support they can provide.

____

____

____

____

____

____

____

____

____

____

82. Name five state government agencies that can offer assistance within the local jurisdiction during an incident and identify what type of support they can provide.

83. After all precautions have been taken to protect life and property during a flammable or combustible liquid leak, what is the next step in controlling the incident?

84. Name five common possible sources of contamination for flammable or combustible liquid leaks.

85. A leak usually occurs in one of two ways: (1) a liquid spills during transfer and escapes into porous soil or a sewer; (2) a leak develops during storage, transportation, or handling. Equipment and storage devices are prime candidates for being the sources of the leak. When inspecting equipment, name six observations that are helpful in determining causes for an unconfined material.

86. Identify the four basic causes of container failure that lead to uncontrolled release of energy.

A. ______________________________

B. ______________________________

C. ______________________________

D. ______________________________

87. Give four examples of possible ignition sources fire inspectors must analyze to prevent fires and explosions in areas common to compressed and liquefied gas use or storage.

____

88. Name eight general rules that will help control hazards when accepting and handling compressed gas cylinders.

A. ______________________________

B. ______________________________

C. ______________________________

D. ______________________________

10

E. ______

F. ______

G. ______

H. ______

89. The National Safety Council Research and Development Agency has developed a fact sheet that lists poor handling and storage practices involving gases. This list includes 20 items. List as many as you can. If necessary, refer to the manual to complete this list.

A. ______

B. ______

C. ______

D. ______

E. ______

F. ______

G. ______

H. ______________________________

____

____

I. ______________________________

____

____

J. ______________________________

____

____

K. ______________________________

____

____

L. ______________________________

____

____

M. ______________________________

____

____

N. ______________________________

____

____

O. ______________________________

____

____

P. ______________________________

____

____

Q. ______________________________

____

____

R. ______________________________

____

____

S. ______________________________

____

____

T. ______________________________

____

90. What publication lists the strict federal regulation of the transportation of compressed and liquefied gases?

91. If investigation has determined that a concentration of gas is inside a building, identify the six steps (in correct order) to eliminate the hazard inside the building.

Step 1:

Step 2:

Step 3:

Step 4:

Step 5:

Step 6:

92. What is the first objective in controlling flammable gas leaks?

93. What is the basic technique for extinguishing fire involving compressed and liquefied gases?

94. Briefly explain the requirements (in general) for storing combustible metals.

95. Using and storing combustible dusts presents a unique hazard.

A. Why are they hazardous?

B. How can they be removed safely?

96. What government agency issues regulations concerning the manufacture, distribution, and storage of explosives?

97. The BATF regulations contain the requirements for the five types of storage facilities, or magazines. Briefly explain these requirements for each of the following magazines.

A. Magazine Type 1:

B. Magazine Type 2:

C. Magazine Type 3:

D. Magazine Type 4:

E. Magazine Type 5:

98. When hazardous materials incidents occur, local government agencies, especially fire and police departments, are usually the first to arrive at the scene of an incident. What are the initial responsibilities of these individuals?

99. Name five local agencies that can offer assistance within the local jurisdiction during a hazardous materials incident and identify what type of support they can provide.

100. Name five state agencies that can offer assistance within the local jurisdiction during a hazardous materials incident and identify what type of support they can provide.

10

101. Name five federal agencies that can offer assistance within the local jurisdiction during a hazardous materials incident and identify what type of support they can provide.

Case Studies

Chapter 1 Case Study

1.1 You suspect improper use and storage of hazardous materials in an industrial plant. You call the plant manager Monday morning and request permission to inspect the premises. He politely thanks you for the concern, assures you they are within acceptable limits, and then hangs up the telephone. What are your options and actions?

1.2 You inspected a nightclub within a hotel Thursday afternoon and found a current Certificate of Occupancy allowing a maximum of 175 people in the nightclub at a time. As you conduct the inspection, you notice there are 20 tables with 10 chairs each (seating for 200). You did not issue a cease to operate order that afternoon, but you did file your standard inspection form noting there was more seating than allowed. You gave the owner two weeks to correct this problem. You return to the nightclub (off-duty) that evening at 11:45 p.m. and find a full house; every chair is taken; furthermore, patrons standing. What authority do you have, what actions can be taken?

1.3 The nightclub you inspected Thursday afternoon had a three-alarm fire that Friday morning at 1:00 a.m. The club was full when you left at midnight. Ten people died, twenty-three were hospitalized, and a firefighter broke her arm because of the number of people trying to vacate the burning building. What is your liability, and who could, if any, take action against you? Why or why not?

Chapter 2 Case Study

2

2.1 You have decided to inspect the local fairgrounds exposition building before the boat show next month. A crowd of 20,000 people is expected. What preparations are necessary before the inspection?

2.2 You have just finished inspecting a restaurant. On the inspection form you noted the grill area is a fire hazard, tables block emergency exits, and miscellaneous decor is a fire hazard. The owner tells you that to comply with what you suggest is cost prohibitive. What are her options, if any, and what is your reply?

2.3 You are asked by the District Attorney to testify against a local chemical manufacturing plant you inspected four months ago. The charges include refusing to comply with your recommendations. What should you include in your documentation for the court case? When on the stand to testify, what should be your demeanor?

2

2.4 You are called by a local resident to witness, critique, and make recommendations for their family fire drill at their home. What materials are available to you to promote home fire safety and efficient fire drills, also what procedure would you use during the drills?

____

____

____

____

____

____

Chapter 3
Case Study

3.1 You have accepted an invitation to speak to a 12th grade chemistry class on the theory and phases of fire. Assemble a 15-minute presentation on this subject.

3.2 You are preparing to inspect a local new car dealership. Since the last inspection, they have added a paint and body shop (5, 000 square feet [465 m^2]) to their service department, and a new waiting room with a fast food snack bar. You have a good working relationship with the building department and have obtained the new construction blueprints and permits for review. Which sections of the new construction could be special fire hazards and which sections are common hazards?

Chapter 4
Case Study

4

4.1 Fire inspectors are sometimes called upon to stand by at major public events where large crowds will be present. You have been assigned the responsibility of fire protection and safety for the state fair in your area. The fair will begin in three months. The planning committee has asked you to identify

- possible problem areas
- locations for
  —automobile, boat, and motorcycle exhibits
  —midway rides, games, and amusements
  —restaurant booths
  —animal exhibits
  —vendor exhibits
- a base of operations

Develop plans using your local fairgrounds as the location for the fair to present to the planning committee, and identify and list your duties to protect the public.

Chapter 5
Case Study

5.1 You have accepted an invitation to speak at the State Builders Convention. Attendance is expected to exceed 300 veteran builders. Your topic is "Fire Safety in Building Construction," and you are expected to include visuals (slides, overheads, etc.) in your 30-minute program. Design this program by writing a formal outline to identify the content, timing, major topics, subtopics, and integration of visuals.

5

5.2 A group of architects has requested a presentation explaining the significance of fire-resistance ratings and the classification of interior finishing materials. These issues are confusing to them and, in particular, they do not understand where and how the ratings are established. What can you use to thoroughly explain how and where ratings originate, and what would you develop to clarify fire-resistance ratings?

Chapter 6
Case Study

6

6.1 See Figure 6.1. This floor plan is a structure originally built eight years ago as a warehouse. The building has been leased and remodeled. The name of the new occupancy is the "#3 Lift." It features a 2,500 watt sound system and a 18,000 watt light show. Its main business is cocktails and dancing to Top 40 music. A DJ provides the entertainment. The target audience is 21-40.

It has the atmosphere of a ski resort. Outside the building rough cedar and wood shingles provide the appearance of a Swiss Alps Chalet. The inside decor includes: rough cedar rafters and trim; cork trim; pine trees; four free-standing metal gas fireplaces; mirrored walls; spinning mirrored balls; four smoke machines (carbon dioxide) for the dance floor area; hanging plastic and fabric strips; flashing and spinning lights in the floors, the walls, and hanging from the 20-foot (6 m) black ceiling.

The decor is plush and features thick carpet throughout seating areas, oak tables with oak/fabric armchairs, and fuel-cylinder decorator candles on every table. During normal business hours, the club is dim to accent the special effects. The interior is protected by an adequate sprinkler system; but, it has inadequate emergency lighting and the exit signs become lost within the special effects lighting. Emergency exit #4 and the "maze" entrance/exit are new additions to the occupancy.

The manager has ordered more seating to accommodate her increasing business. She added emergency exit #4 and requests you to raise the allowable occupancy from 625 to 1,200. You are called to review the occupancy for life and fire safety.

A. Determine the occupancy type and class.

____

____

____

____

____

____

B. Compute the occupancy number using the "Floor Area Method" and the "Unit of Width Method."

____

____

____

____

____

____

6

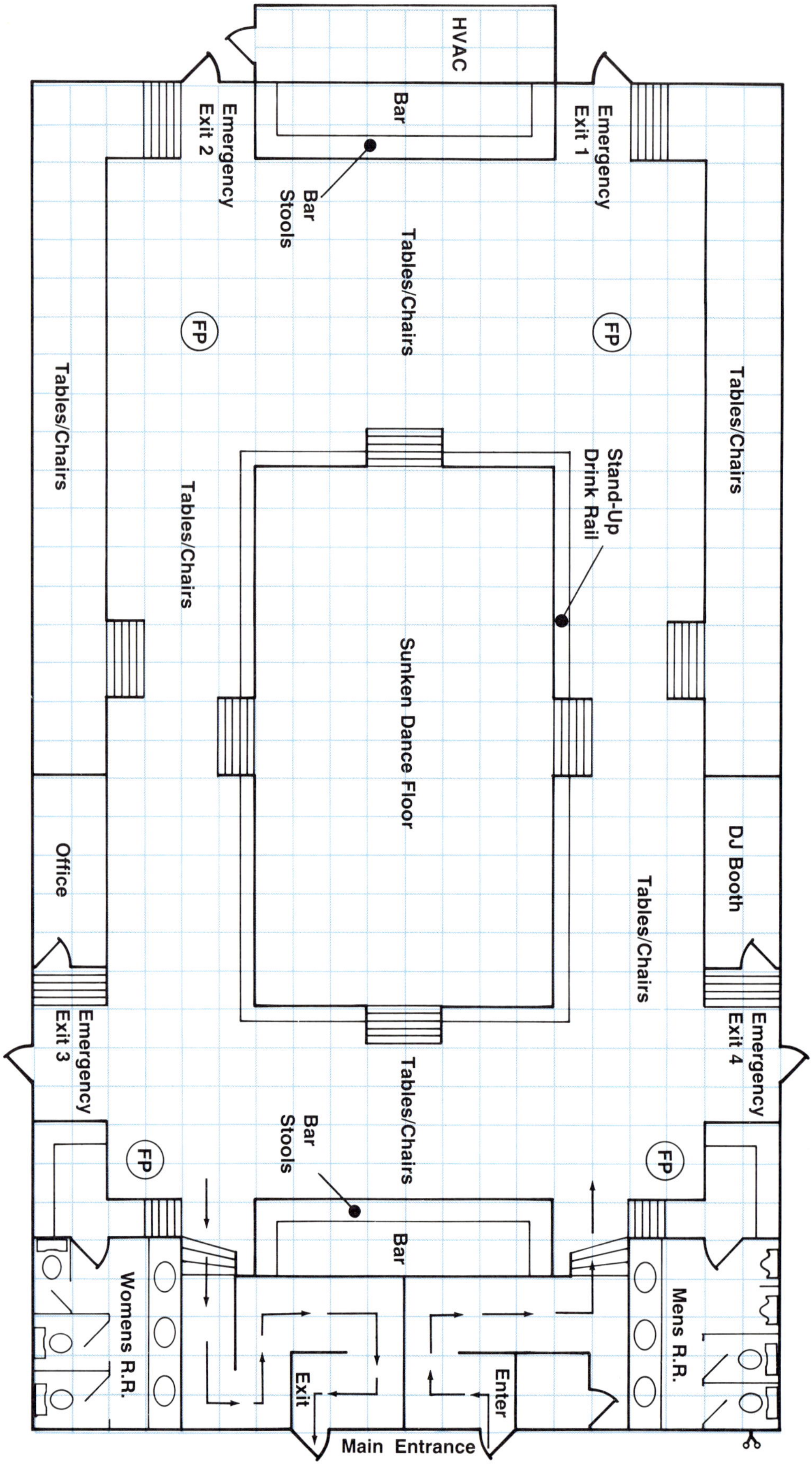
HVAC
Bar
Emergency Exit 1
Emergency Exit 2
Bar Stools
Tables/Chairs
FP
FP
Tables/Chairs
Tables/Chairs
Tables/Chairs
Stand-Up Drink Rail
Sunken Dance Floor
Office
DJ Booth
Tables/Chairs
Emergency Exit 3
Emergency Exit 4
Tables/Chairs
Bar Stools
FP
FP
Bar
Womens R.R.
Mens R.R.
Exit
Enter
Main Entrance

Figure 6.1

C. What is the maximum number of patrons you will allow in the club?

____

D. What are your recommendations for emergency lighting and exit signs?

____

____

____

____

____

____

E. Does the "maze" entrance/exit comply with the codes in your jurisdiction?

____

____

____

____

____

____

F. Do the four freestanding fireplaces pose a problem? Why or why not?

____

____

____

____

____

____

G. All the steps leading to and from the different levels are 8 feet (2 m) wide. Where, if any, are handrails required?

____

____

____

____

____

____

H. What other specific areas of this occupancy are you going to check thoroughly to ensure compliance?

____

____

____

____

____

6

I. List good qualities, and problems and their solutions for this occupancy. Also note what the manager is going to have to do to comply with the codes in your jurisdiction.

Chapter 7
Case Study

7.1 You are asked to inspect Flash Industries Inc., a local manufacturing company that recently designed their plant to accommodate the exclusive manufacture of the following small-engine, gas-powered products: portable generators, chain saws, and ventilation fans used by firefighters. The plant manager has called your office to ask for your assistance. The building is 112,000 square feet (10 405 m^2). See Figure 7.1 on page 187.

Evaluate and use Figure 7.1 to determine the following:

A. The type of occupancy.

____

____

____

B. The best-suited portable fire extinguisher type for *each* area.

Specific individual descriptions of each AREA are as follows:

Area A—Loading Docks—5 Employees

Seven unloading/loading bays are controlled by a center office located behind dock 4. Docks 1 through 3 are used for incoming freight; whereas, docks 5 through 7 are used for shipping. Dock 4 is used as necessary for both functions. LPG-powered forklifts are used to move pallets and materials in and out of the plant.

Area B—High Rack Storage for Incoming Freight, Vendor Parts, Raw Materials, Manufacturing Supplies

Each of the four metal high storage racks are 20 x 20 x 30 feet with 10 square feet (6 m x 6 m x 10 m with 1 m^2) of vacant space around the perimeter for loading/unloading. This is a holding area for the incoming inventory that is dispersed as needed to each department within the plant. Area B inventory includes items such as raw materials (steel, aluminum, plastic), spools of insulated wire, styrofoam and cardboard boxes used for packaging, miscellaneous tools, and office supplies. These racks have in-rack sprinklers.

Area C—High Rack Storage for Raw materials—1 Employee

This area is a feed storage for Areas D (Steel), E (Aluminum), and F (Plastic). Raw materials are kept in this area and moved to the furnace areas as needed. The high rack storage units are 20 x 20 x 30 feet with 10 square feet (6 m x 6 m x 10 m with 1 m^2) of vacant space between each unit. Area B feeds Area C to maintain a constant level of raw materials. A forklift truck operator moves materials as required.

Area D—Aluminum Furnace/Casting—10 Employees

This area contains a natural gas furnace that melts bulk aluminum to liquid. The liquid aluminum is then poured into molds, cooled, and removed from the molds. The raw casting is then placed in 4 x 4 x 4 feet (1.2 m x 1.2 m x 1.2 m) containers for storage in Area G, Raw Casting High-Rack Storage.

Area E—Steel Furnace/Casting—9 Employees

This area contains a natural gas furnace that melts bulk steel to liquid. The liquid steel is then poured into molds, cooled, and removed from the molds. The raw casting is then placed in 4 x 4 x 4 foot (1.2 m x 1.2 m x 1.2 m) containers for storage in Area G, Raw Casting High-Rack Storage.

Area F—Plastic Furnace/Casting/Finishing—12 Employees

This area contains a natural gas furnace that melts bulk plastic to liquid. The semifluid plastic is injected into molds, cooled, and removed from the molds. The raw casting is then placed in 4 x 4 x 4 foot (1.2 m x 1.2 m x 1.2 m) metal containers for storage in Area G, Raw Casting High-Rack Storage. This area also contains drill presses, hole saws, and band saws. The plastic parts leaving this area are finished parts; they are then moved to Area N for storage. Proper plastic dust collecting systems are provided for this area.

Area G—High Rack Storage for Raw Castings—2 Employees

This area is storage space for the raw castings from Area H (Steel) and Area I (Aluminum). The high rack storage units are 20 x 20 x 20 feet with 10 square feet (6 m x 6 m x 6 m with $1m^2$) of vacant space between each unit. The steel and aluminum raw castings are moved respectively to Areas H and I as needed for machining.

H—Steel Machining—9 Employees

This area has milling machines, drill presses, and tapping machines used to make finished parts (herein known as "parts"). All machines use electric motors to power the various machines and are all grounded, bonded, and use proper dust/waste removal techniques.

Area I—Aluminum Machining—10 Employees

This area has milling machines, drill presses, and tapping machines used to make finished parts (herein known as "parts"). All machines use electric motors to power the various machines and are all grounded, bonded, and use proper dust/waste removal techniques.

Area J—Part Washing/Drying—4 Employees

This area consists of two vapor-degreasers. One for steel parts and one for aluminum parts.

> **NOTE:** Vapor-degreasers are used to clean the metal filings, dust, and oil residue left on the parts from the machining process. The basic principle of a vapor-degreaser is a two-step process. First, a tank of liquid cleaner (inhibited triclorethylene) is heated. The parts are dipped into the hot bath for the initial cleaning. In the second phase of

the cleaning process, the same chemical is vaporized and the parts are sprayed with pressurized vapors. It is an extremely efficient method of cleaning metal parts, but highly flammable.

Between the steel vapor-degreaser and the aluminum vapor-degreaser is a one-hour fire wall with parapets. The aluminum vapor-degreaser uses triclorethylene diluted 1:2. Proper exhaust units are installed to remove hazardous vapor by-products.

Area K—Dip Painting with Hot Air Dryer—5 Employees

This area is used to prime and dip paint some of the steel and aluminum parts. The area contains a natural gas hot air dryer to ensure complete drying. It is safety interlocked for emergency shut down.

Area L—Paint Storage and Painting Supplies—1 Employee

This area is used to store and mix all primers, paints, cleaning solvents (including for the vapor-degreaser), and painting tools. All supplies are stored on metal storage racks and cabinets as required.

Area M—Spray Painting with Hot Air Dryer—5 Employees

This area is used to spray paint any steel and aluminum parts that are not dip painted. Parts received to this area are primed (in Area K) and are ready for spray painting. The area contains a natural gas hot air dryer to ensure complete drying. The painted parts are then moved to Area N for storage.

Area N—High-Rack Storage (finished parts)—2 Employees

This area contains high-rack storage of finished plastic, aluminum, and steel parts ready for the assembly lines. The racks are 20 x 20 x 30 feet (6 m x 6 m x 10 m).

Area O—General Offices—22 Employees

This area contains the accounting, engineering, and customer service general offices. The fire load includes desks, chairs, computers, copiers, paper storage, and other general office supplies and equipment.

Area P—Computer Room—1 Employee

This area contains a mainframe computer that communicates with the terminals in the general office and in/out of the plant.

Area Q—Toolroom/Vender Parts—1 Employee

This area contains all miscellaneous hand tools, vendor supplies (screws, nuts, bolts, etc), and machining tools such as drill bits, fixtures, and taps for the entire plant.

Area R—Product Testing Laboratory—2 Employees

This area contains testing facilities for products manufactured and for engineering applications. Since the products are gas powered, a 5-gallon (19 L) gasoline can is stored for use in the room. This room is compartmentalized. It is soundproof and surrounded by a 2-hour fire wall and protected by an approved 2-hour fire door, 2-hour frame, and automatic door closer.

7

Area S—Breakrooms (one on each side of the plant)

These areas contain breakrooms for employees. Each contain vending machines, restrooms, microwave ovens, and tables and chairs. The function of the room is to give employees an area out of the plant for lunch and breaks.

Area T—Assembly Line 1—18 Employees

This area is for assembly of portable generators. The parts of the generators are placed throughout various stations and the employees assemble the generator. Pneumatic and hand tools are used during the assembly process.

Area U—Assembly Line 2—15 Employees

This area is for assembly of portable ventilation fans. The parts of the ventilation fans are placed throughout various stations and the employees assemble the product. Pneumatic and hand tools are used during the assembly process.

Area V—Assembly Line 3—10 Employees

This area is for assembly of portable chain saws. The parts of the portable chain saws are placed throughout various stations and the employees assemble the product. Pneumatic and hand tools are used during the assembly process.

Area W—Packaging—9 Employees

This area contains the packaging and boxing machines. All finished products are placed in premolded styrofoam and packed in corrugated cardboard. The boxed products are then placed on pallets, wrapped in plastic tubes, and moved to Area X.

Area X—Product Storage—2 Employees

This area contains products ready for shipping. One employee operates an LPG forklift to move products from Area W, and one employee moves products from storage to Area A for shipping. Employees in Area A fill orders and prepare products for shipping.

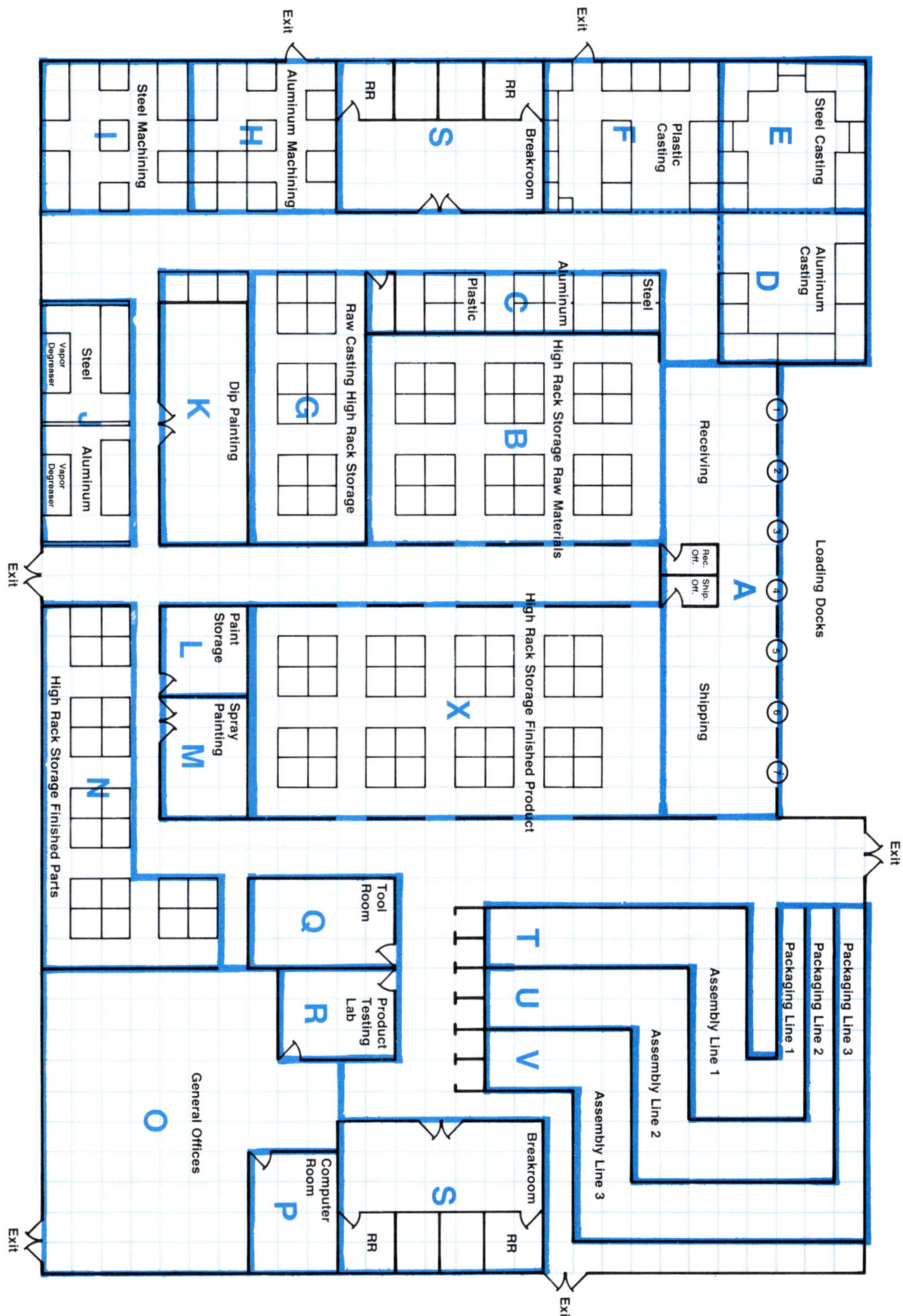

Figure 7.1 Place the number, type, and location of portable fire extinguishers on this drawing.

Chapter 8
Case Study

8

8.1. You have been asked to review the site plan (see Figure 8.1 on page 191) of Flash Manufacturing (Figure 7.1 is the floor plan) for apparatus accessibility and pre-incident planning.

A. Determine available flow at hydrant #3. What is the available flow at hydrant #4. Use the Universal Water Flow Summary Sheet on page 190 to determine available flow. Use Scale A. Are they different? Briefly justify your answer.

B. Are fire department access roadways wide enough, and do they have an adequate road base to permit apparatus to operate and to pass?

8

Fire Protection Publications
Oklahoma State University
Stillwater, OK 74078

Universal Water Flow Test Summary Sheet

Conducted by ____________ Location ____________ Date ________

Hydrant coefficient ______ Elevation ______ Static ______ Residual ______ @ Flow ______

PRESSURE

(Bars = kPa ÷ 100)

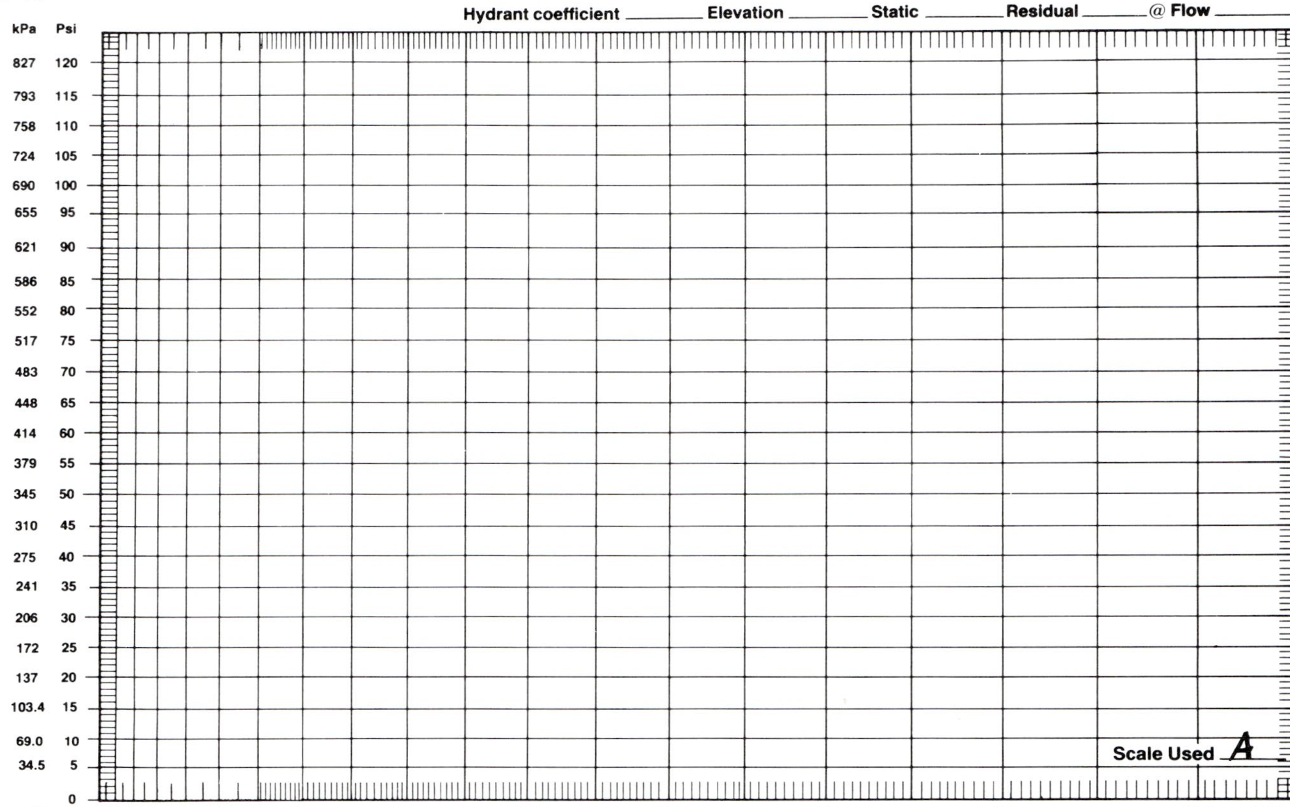

GPM	100	200	300	400	500	600	700	800	900	1000	Scale A
Imp. Gal.	83	167	250	333	416	500	583	666	749	833	
Liters	380	759	1139	1519	1899	2278	2658	3038	3418	3797	
	200	400	600	800	1000	1200	1400	1600	1800	2000	Scale B
	167	333	500	666	833	999	1166	1332	1499	1665	
	759	1519	2278	3038	3797	4557	5316	6075	6835	7594	
	400	800	1200	1600	2000	2400	2800	3200	3600	4000	Scale C
	333	666	999	1332	1665	1998	2332	2665	2998	3331	
	1519	3038	4557	6075	7594	9113	10,632	12,151	13,670	15,188	

FLOW

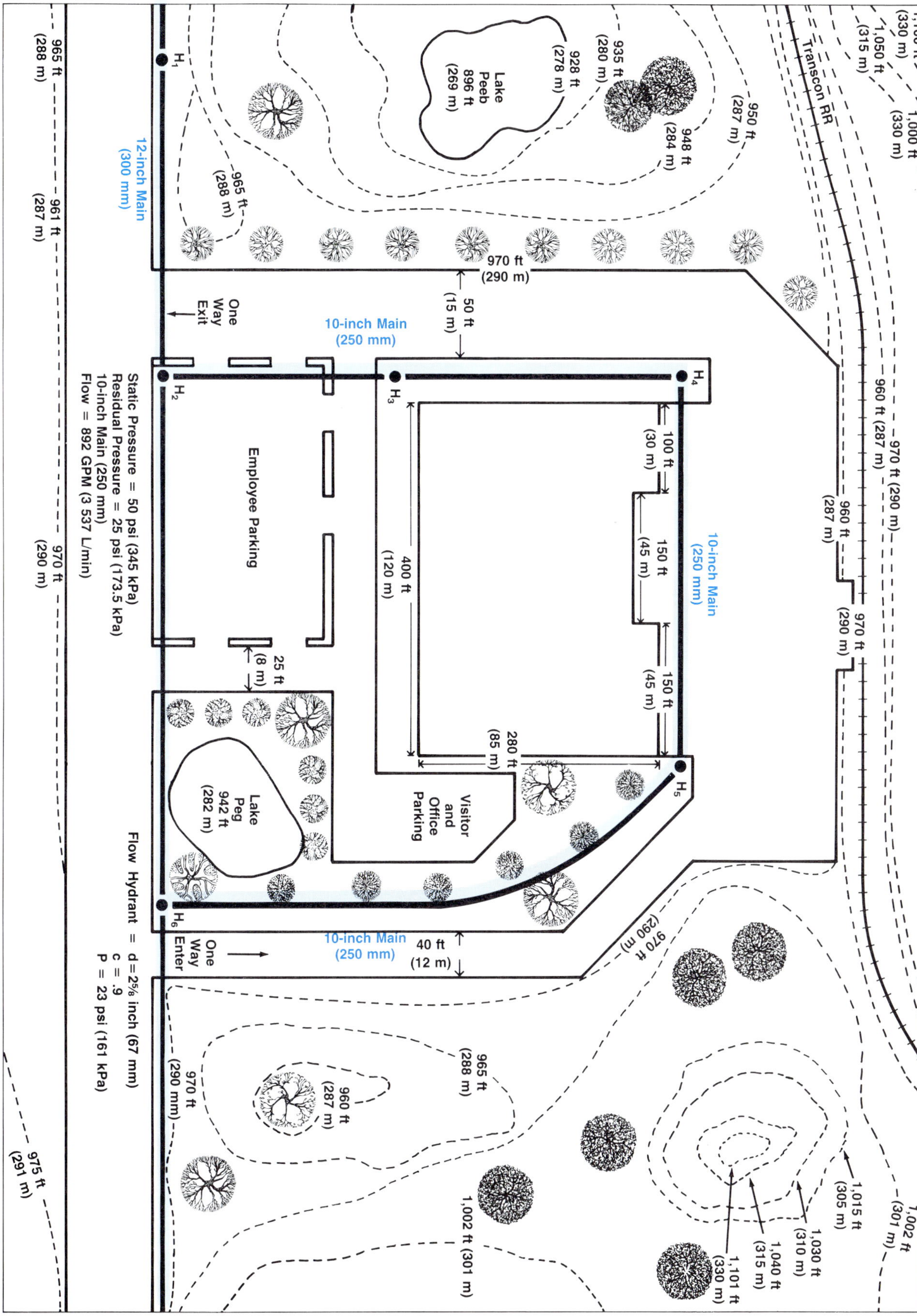

Lake Peeb
896 ft
(269 m)
Transcon RR
12-inch Main
(300 mm)
10-inch Main
(250 mm)
One Way Exit
One Way Enter
Employee Parking
Visitor and Office Parking
Lake Peg
942 ft
(282 m)
Static Pressure = 50 psi (345 kPa)
Residual Pressure = 25 psi (173.5 kPa)
10-inch Main (250 mm)
Flow = 892 GPM (3 537 L/min)
Flow Hydrant = d = 2⅝ inch (67 mm)
c = .9
P = 23 psi (161 kPa)
Vacant Field
50 ft
(15 m)
25 ft
(8 m)
40 ft
(12 m)
100 ft
(30 m)
150 ft
(45 m)
400 ft
(120 m)
280 ft
(85 m)
970 ft
(290 m)
1,002 ft (301 m)

Figure 8.1

9

Chapter 9
Case Study

9.1 At 1040 hours you receive an anonymous telephone call from an employee of REHAZMAT Inc. The caller complains that the owner of the company hires unskilled laborers at a low hourly wage instead of qualified chemists or chemical technicians to perform the repackaging. The sole purpose of this hiring practice is to increase profits. He contends the employees are asked to perform tasks beyond the scope of their education and understanding, and he thinks the operation is not safe and a possible fire hazard. There was a Class A fire in the plant two days ago. The fire department extinguished the fire with portable extinguishers. He did not want to lose his job, so he asked to remain anonymous.

REHAZMAT Inc. is a two-story occupancy conducting business as a chemical wholesale and distribution warehouse that specializes in buying chemicals in bulk quantities and repackages them into smaller quantities under their own label.

The warehouse area is divided into two sections: Side A stores incoming bulk product and Side B stores repackaged smaller quantities. The rest of the building contains mixing and repackaging laboratories and general offices. (See Figure 9.1 on pages 196 and 197.) The entire building has an impressive fusible link, wet pipe automatic sprinkler system except rooms 104 and 109. These two rooms are protected by Halon 1301 systems.

A fire wall with a parapet separates the storage areas from the laboratory/office section of the structure. Near the center of the building is an atrium surrounding the staircase. At the top of the atrium is a skylight. The building interior is extremely clean; but, it has definite odors from the chemicals in the building.

PART ONE

What Is Your Authority

A. What is your authority for this type of operation?

9

B. Do you have the power to require the owner to hire chemists or chemical technicians? Why?

C. When can you make the inspection and what procedures should you follow? Since the caller wants to be anonymous, does this have any impact on your method of action?

PART TWO

Evaluation of the Chemicals

Evaluate the following chemicals in chart 9.1, and rate each for Health, Flammability, Reactivity, and identify any extra hazard associated with each of the chemicals listed below. Keep in mind the fire, explosion, and life hazards associated with each chemical. Use NFPA 704 as your reference guide.

CHART 9.1 — Chemicals used in REHAZMAT Inc.

Chemical	Health	Flam	React	Extra	State	Rm #	St#
Ammonia	___	___	___	___	Liq	111	14
Acetic Acid	___	___	___	___	Liq	116	12
Amyl Nitrate	___	___	___	___	Liq	105	11
Bromopropyne	___	___	___	___	Liq	205	13
Hydrogen Peroxide ›52%	___	___	___	___	Liq	214	14
Isopropyl Alcohol	___	___	___	___	Liq	204	24
Hydrochloric Acid	___	___	___	___	Liq	112	23
Sulfuric Acid	___	___	___	___	Liq	109	10
Turpentine	___	___	___	___	Liq	204	15
Chloroform	___	___	___	___	Liq	204	22
Diethyl Ether	___	___	___	___	Liq	108	25
Perchloric Acid	___	___	___	___	Liq	112	26
Nitric Acid	___	___	___	___	Liq	116	27
Phosphorus	___	___	___	___	Sol	216	29
Picric Acid	___	___	___	___	Sol	116	30
Sodium Nitrate	___	___	___	___	Sol	218	31
Aluminum Chloride	___	___	___	___	Sol	218	32
Aluminum	___	___	___	___	Sol	103	9
Lithium	___	___	___	___	Sol	109	8
Zinc	___	___	___	___	Sol	102	7
Zirconium	___	___	___	___	Sol	102	17
Sodium	___	___	___	___	Sol	104	18
Magnesium	___	___	___	___	Sol	104	20
Potassium	___	___	___	___	Sol	104	19
Chlorine	___	___	___	___	Gas	202	1
Butane	___	___	___	___	Gas	111	2
Acetylene	___	___	___	___	Gas	110	3
Formaldehyde	___	___	___	___	Gas	110	4
Cyanogen	___	___	___	___	Gas	205	5
Ethene	___	___	___	___	Gas	203	6

9

PART THREE

Hazard Marking

Use the information compiled in chart 9.1 and assign diamonds to each of the rooms in Figure 9.1. Consult NFPA 704, *Standard for the Identification of Fire Hazards of Materials,* if necessary.

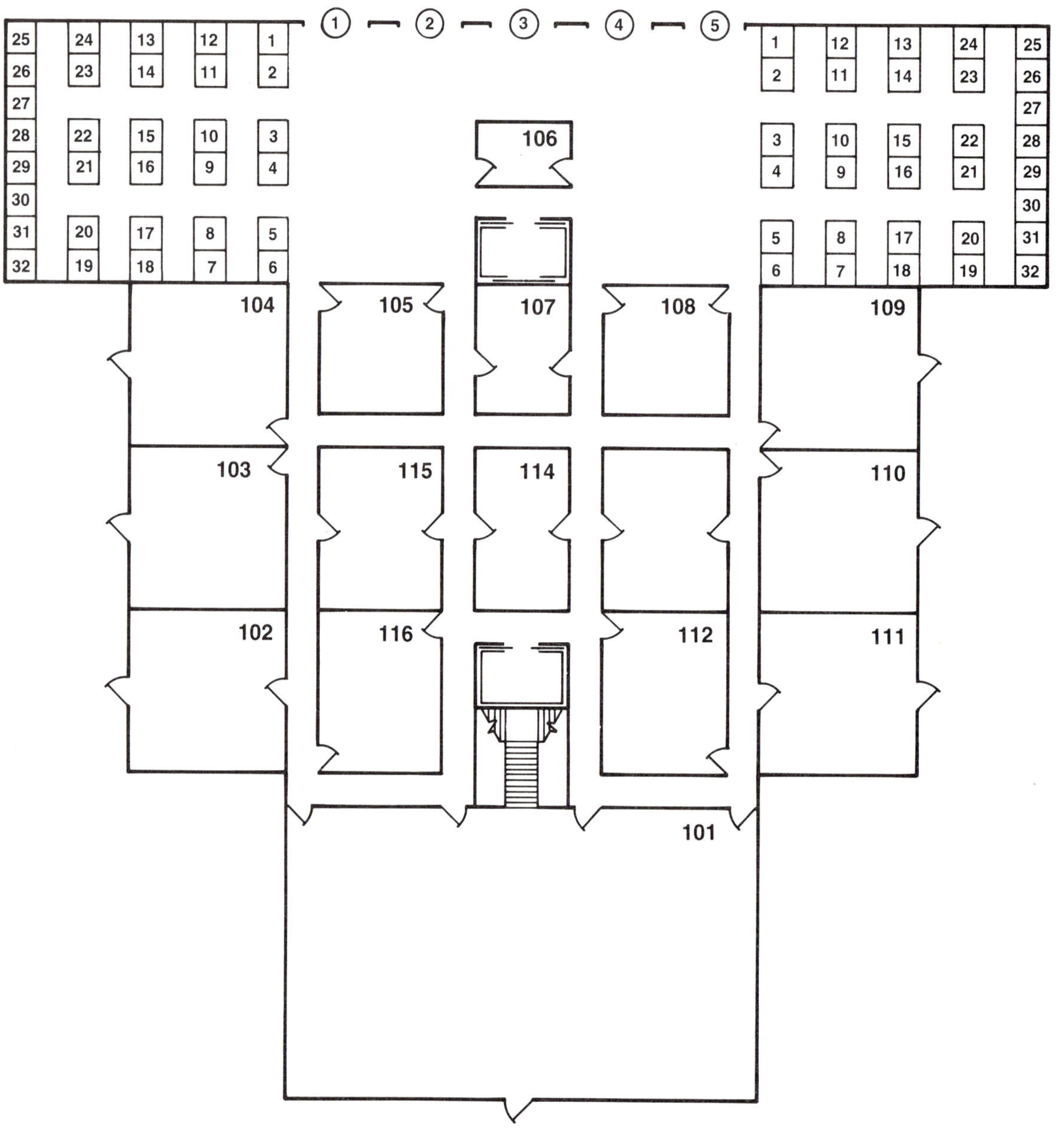

Figure 9.1 Ground Floor.

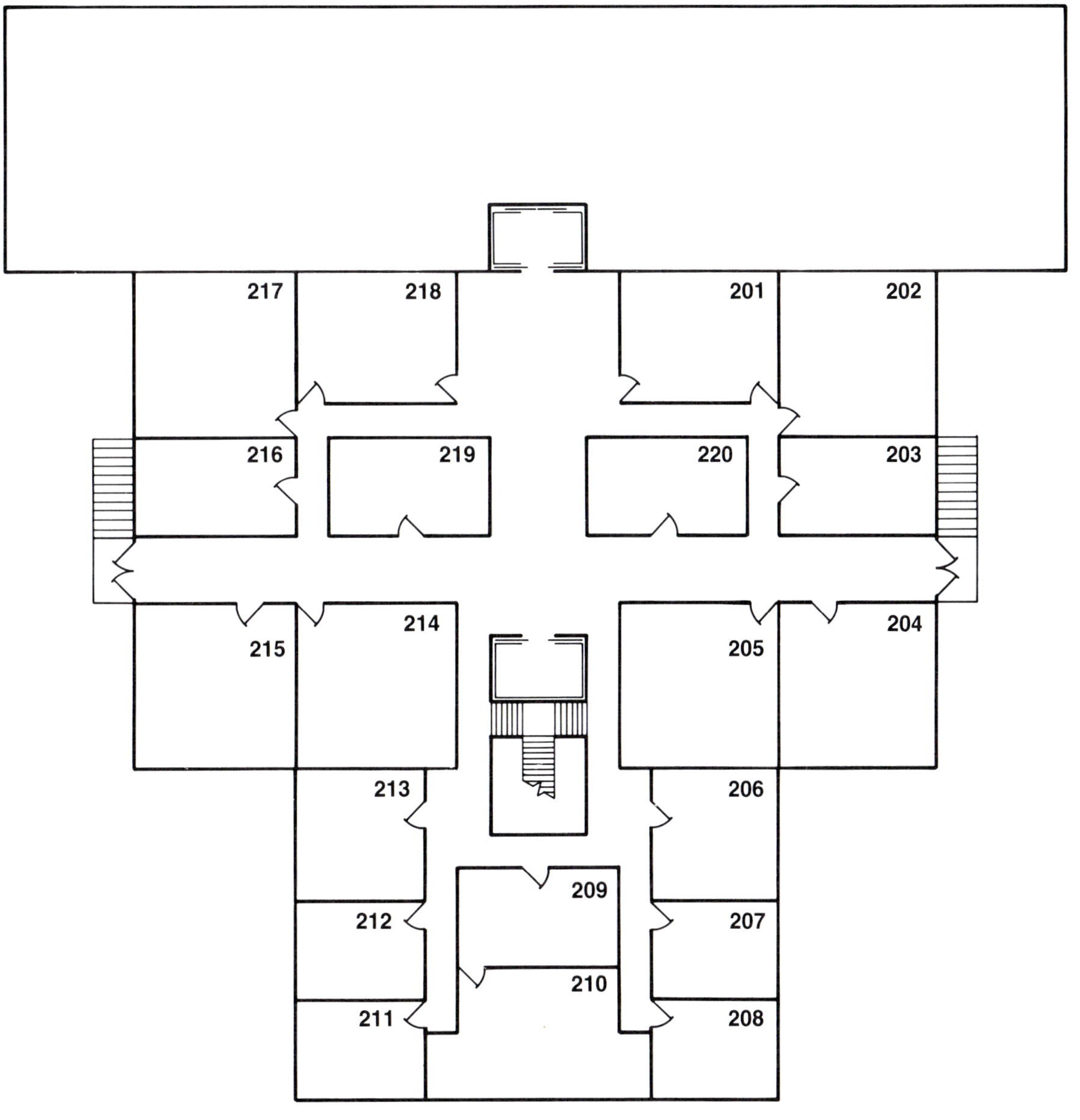

Figure 9.1 Second Floor.

Chapter 10
Case Study

10

10.1 Use a separate sheet of paper to answer the following:

PART ONE—Determine the usual type of shipping container(s) used to contain each material listed in Figure 10.1 on pages 200 and 201. If necessary consult NFPA 49.

PART TWO—Evaluate Figure 10.1 on pages 200 and 201. Note the location of each chemical within the building, the building design, its contents, its systems, and methods of operations for fire and life safety. Identify hazardous situations, violations, or any potential problems that might exist.

PART THREE—Write a formal report (addressed to your chief or any other agency you deem appropriate). Use either the guidelines established in your jurisdiction or the **Inspection and Code Enforcement Manual** for your report.

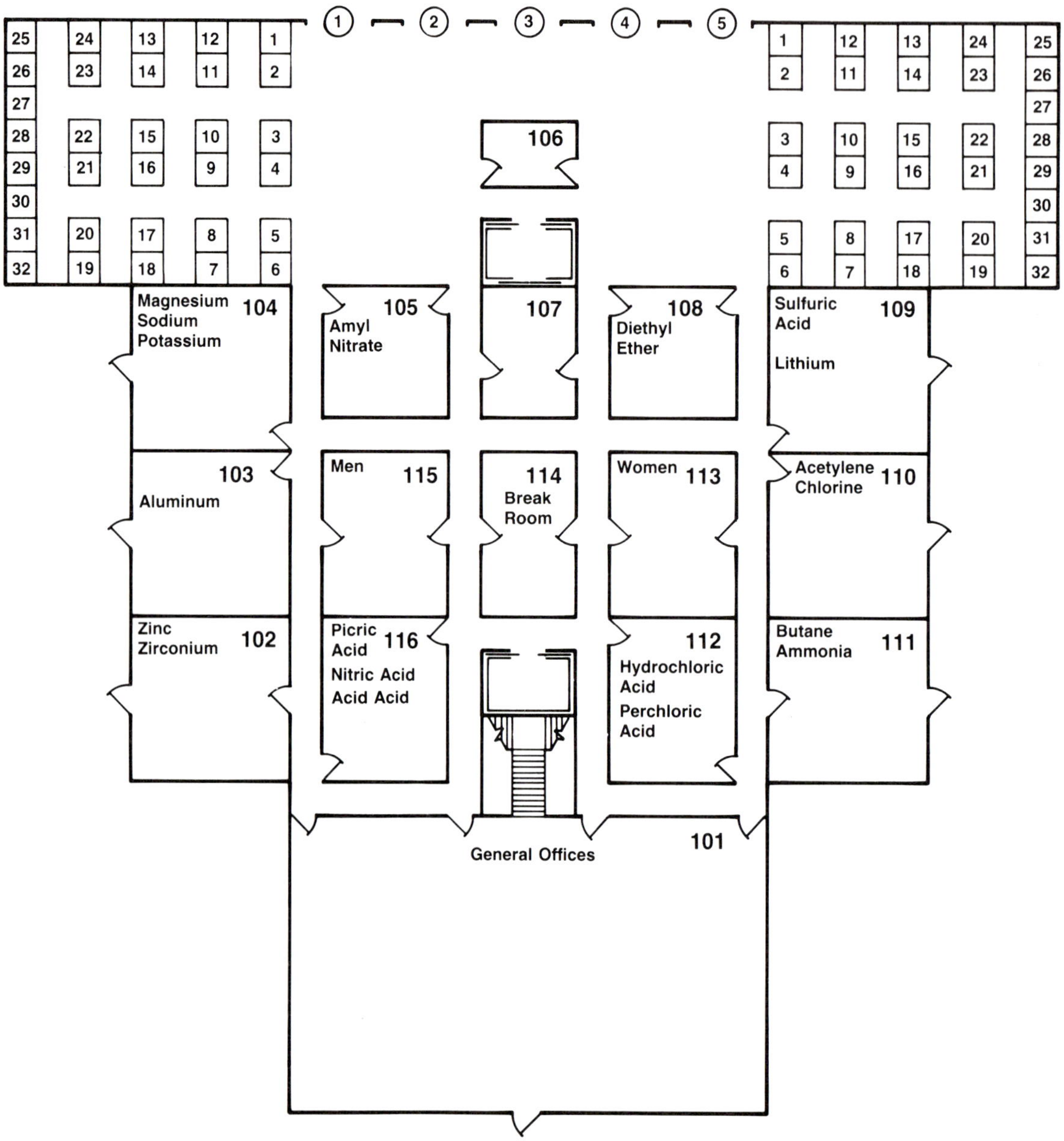

Figure 10.1 Ground Floor.

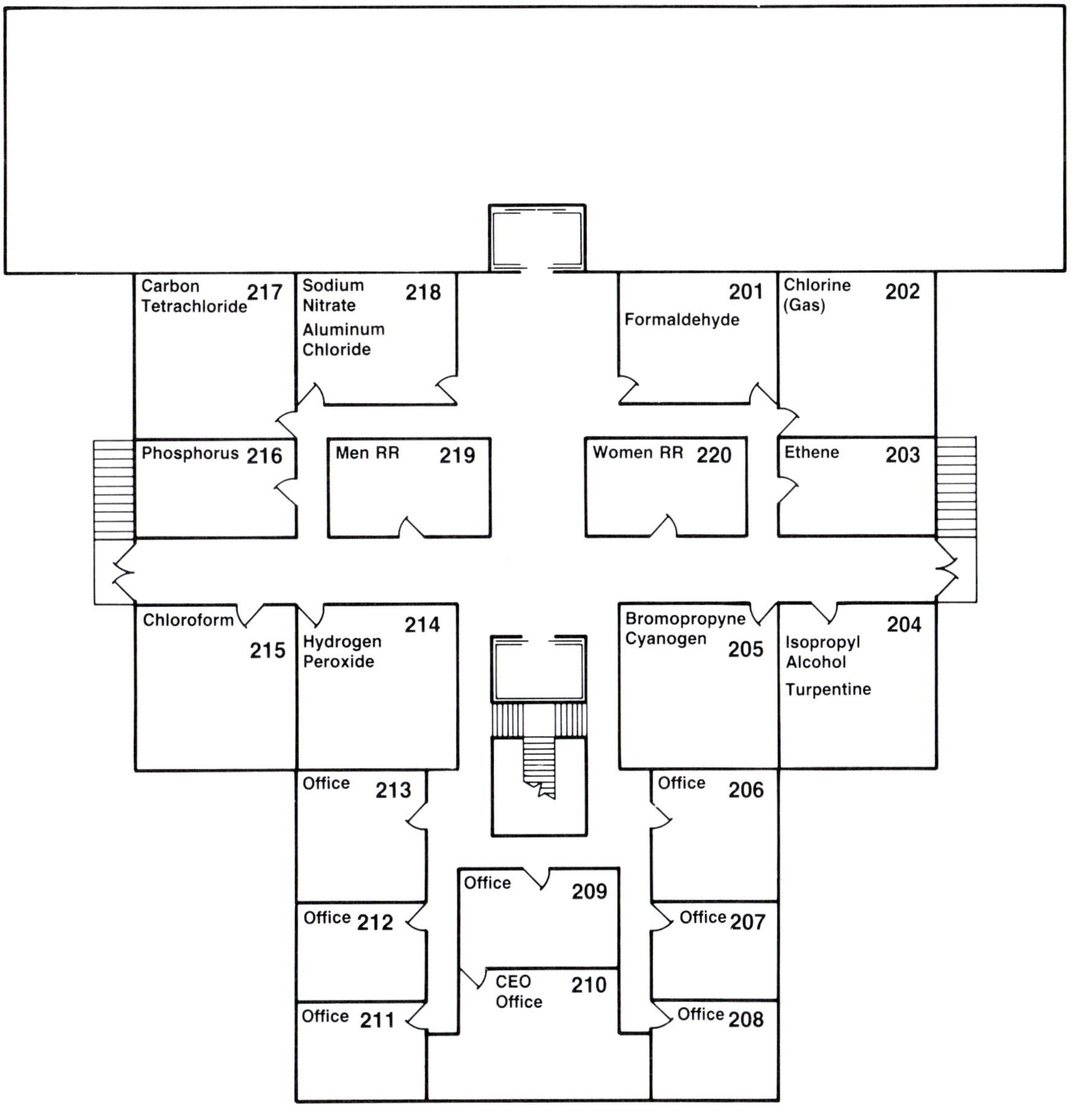

Figure 10.1 Second Floor.

Answers

Chapter 1 Answers

1

TRUE/FALSE

1. False (5)
2. True (5)
3. True (5)
4. False (6)
5. True (7)
6. True (7)
7. False (7)
8. True (7)
9. True (7)
10. True (9)
11. True (9)
12. True (9)
13. True (10)
14. False (11)
15. True (11)
16. True (12)
17. False (12)
18. True (12)
19. True (12)
20. True (13)
21. False (13)
22. False (14)
23. True (14)
24. True (14)

MULTIPLE CHOICE

25. D (5)
26. B (5)
27. D (6)
28. A (7)
29. B (11)
30. C (11)
31. D (11)
32. B (15)
33. D (11)

SHORT ANSWER

34. A. Employees as public officers
    B. Limits and scope as fire inspectors (5)
35. A. criminal or civil
    B. compliance
    C. inducements
    D. penalties (10)
36. Adequate reason to believe that the property contains fire hazards and has obtained a warrant to allow entry. (9)
37. A. The Fourth Amendment
    B. The Fourteenth Amendment (10)
38. A. Issue a final notice.
    B. Involve the jurisdiction's attorney.
    C. Assistance from the police (issue a citation). (11)
39. A. The local department or division.
    B. The other related, outside agencies. (12)
40. The following are correct: employee safety, transportation of hazardous materials, patient safety in health care facilities, and minimum housing standards. (13)
41. A. Building and Safety Codes. Those that govern the construction and occupancy of a building when it is being planned and constructed.
    B. Fire Codes. Those that regulate activities that are conducted within a building once it has been constructed. (15)

2

Chapter 2 Answers

TRUE/FALSE

1. False (21)
2. True (22)
3. True (22)
4. False (23)
5. True (23)
6. True (23)
7. False (23)
8. False (24)
9. False (25)
10. True (26)
11. True (27)
12. False (27)
13. False (27)
14. True (29)
15. False (29)
16. False (29)
17. True (29)
18. True (32)
19. True (32)
20. True (32)
21. False (32)
22. True (33)
23. True (33)
24. True (33)
25. False (33)
26. True (33)
27. True (33)
28. False (34)
29. False (34)
30. True (34)
31. True (35)
32. True (35)

MULTIPLE CHOICE

33. C (21)
34. A (21)
35. B (22)
36. B (23)
37. C (25)
38. D (26)
39. A (27)
40. C (27)
41. C (29)
42. D (32)
43. B (33)
44. B (33)
45. C (34)
46. B (34)

MATCHING

47. C (288)
48. H (288)
49. K (288)
50. B (288)
51. I (288)
52. G (288)
53. L (288)
54. A (288)
55. D (288)
56. M (288)
57. J (288)
58. E (288)
59. N (288)
60. F (288)
61. E (288)
62. D (288)
63. A (288)
64. C (288)
65. B (288)

SHORT ANSWER

66. A. Preplanning
    B. Developing standard operating procedures
    C. Maintaining equipment readiness (21)

67. A. A hard hat
    B. Safety shoes (22)
68. The following are correct: information about the building dimensions, construction materials, exposures, water sources, hydrants, valves, and the surrounding area. The location of doors, windows and fire escapes can be also noted at this time. (23)
69. The following are correct: information about floor plans, building dimensions, fire hydrants, streets, exposure distances, and permanent objects of importance. (24)
70. Be polite but firm. Do not return any of the hostility toward the owner/manager. In every instance, inspectors should use the closing interview to express thanks for any courtesies extended. (26)
71. The following are correct: citations, fines, court summons, or stop work orders. (29)
72. A. Photographs.
    B. Documentation. (Notes taken during the inspection, formal reports, inspection forms, illustrations.)
    C. Exhibits used for demonstration purposes. (32)
73. *Code Administration Resource Directory* (32)
74. Yes, the management should evacuate the building. The smoke is an indication fire exists and evacuation should be implemented immediately. (33)
75. A. Phase I — Evacuate a single room.
    B. Phase II — Evacuate an entire zone.
    C. Phase III — Evacuate a floor and zones above.
    D. Phase IV — Evacuate the building. (34)
76. Maintain Security. (34)
77. Note: Depending on the type of inspection the equipment may slightly vary between jurisdictions.

X	coveralls
X	clipboard
	telephone book
X	paper and pencil
	matches or lighter
	small caliber handgun
X	safety hat and shoes
	goggles
X	50-foot measuring tape
X	flashlight
	turnout gear
X	camera with strobe
X	pitot tube and gauges
	1/4-inch socket set
X	reference books
	atmospheric detection equipment (22)

Chapter 3 Answers

TRUE/FALSE

1. True (39)
2. False (39)
3. True (39)
4. False (39)
5. True (39)
6. True (39)
7. False (39)
8. True (40)
9. True (40)
10. False (40)
11. True (40)
12. True (40)
13. False (41)
14. True (42)
15. False (42) 5/94
16. False (42)
17. True (43)
18. False (45)
19. True (47)
20. False (48)
21. False (48)
22. True (48)
23. False (49)

MULTIPLE CHOICE

24. A (39)
25. C (39)
26. D (39)
27. A (39)
28. C (40)
29. A (40)
30. D (40)
31. B (40)
32. B (41)
33. A (41)
34. D (47)
35. C (49)

MATCHING

36. A (40)
37. B (40)
38. E (42)
39. F (42)
40. G (43)
41. H (43)
42. I (43)
43. N (42)
44. D (40)
45. J (43)

SHORT ANSWER

46. A. Oxygen
    B. Fuel
    C. Heat (39)
47. A. Chemical heat energy
    B. Electrical heat energy
    C. Mechanical heat energy
    D. Nuclear heat energy (39)
48. A. Solid
    B. Liquid
    C. Gas (39)
49. A. Oxygen
    B. Fuel
    C. Heat (40)

50. The chemical chain reaction when materials burn. (40)
51. Heat is a form of energy and temperature is the measurement of the intensity of the heating of a material. (40)
52. A. During the incipient phase, the oxygen has not been significantly reduced, and heat is being generated and will increase as the fire progresses.
    B. During the free-burning phase, the fire consumes the free oxygen until there is insufficient oxygen to react with the fuel.
    C. During the hot smoldering phase, flame may cease to exist if the area of confinement is sufficiently airtight. (41)
53. In terms of the relative ease with which the fuel may be ignited. (43)
54. A. Flammable gases are measured by their flammable or explosive limits.
    B. Flammable liquids are measured in terms of flash points.
    C. Solids are measured relative to their ease of ignition and rate of flame spread. (44)
55. Hazards can vary from jurisdiction to jurisdiction; however, examples of common fire hazards include: heating and cooking equipment, smoking and matches, environmental control housekeeping practices, environmental control systems, cleaning agents, and storage incompatibilities. (45)

    Special hazards include: painting, welding, chemicals, acids, flammable liquids, explosives, combustible dusts, and flammable gases. (46)
56. A. Low Hazard — Contents of low combustibility in which no self-propagating fire is likely to occur.
    B. Ordinary Hazard — Contents that would burn moderately fast or that produce a considerable amount of smoke.
    C. High Hazard — Contents that would burn extremely fast or that would result in poisonous fumes explosions during a fire. (47)
57. The following are correct: point of origin; cause of fire; (fuel ignited, form of heat of ignition, source of heat of ignition, and human involvement); how the fire spread; flame spread characteristics; who or what was responsible for the fire; need for further investigation; and corrective action needed. (48)
58. A. Pick up broken glass carefully, with two fingers at the edges. Pick up bottles by inserting a finger into the neck or by gripping the upper extremity of the neck. (49)
    B. Ash and most fire debris should be placed into a can, glass container, or a special evidence bay.
    C. Flammable liquid containers should be carefully sealed in metal or plastic containers.
    D. Flammable liquid samples should be put into cans, glass vials, or special plastic evidence bags. Hydrocarbons will usually destroy or vaporize through ordinary plastic. (50)
    E. Charred documents can be protected by placing them between sheets of tissue in a box or between two panes of glass.
    F. Tire tracks or footprints have two methods of being saved: 1) photograph using sidelighting and placing a ruler on the impression to provide scale, and 2) cover the tracks with boxes to prevent dust accumulation until molds can be made.

4

Chapter 4 Answers

TRUE/FALSE

1. True (53)
2. True (53)
3. False (53)
4. False (53)
5. True (54)
6. False (54)
7. True (55)
8. False (55)
9. True (57)
10. True (57)
11. False (57)
12. True (58)
13. True (58)
14. False (58)
15. False (58)
16. True (58)
17. True (58)
18. True (58)
19. True (59)
20. False (59)
21. False (60)
22. False (60)
23. True (60)
24. True (60)
25. True (61)

MULTIPLE CHOICE

26. C (53)
27. B (55)
28. C (55)
29. A (57)
30. B (57)
31. D (57)
32. C (57)
33. A (57)
34. B (57)
35. B (58)
36. B (58)
37. A (58)
38. C (58)
39. A (58)
40. A (58)
41. C (59)
42. C (59)
43. D (60)

SHORT ANSWER

44. The following are correct: smoking materials, oily rags, any highly combustible materials, and any highly reactive materials. (53)
45. The containers must have self-closing, tightly fitting lids and should be supported by legs so that the bottom is several inches (millimeters) off the floor. (53)
46. The basic structural components include walls, floors, ceilings, and drains. Inspectors should be looking to be sure that hazardous chemicals, flammable liquids, fuel by-products, or dusts have not accumulated or impregnated these components. (54)
47. These metal cans should be constructed of sturdy metal with 3- or 4-inch (76 mm or 102 mm) legs and have self-closing lids and carrying handles. (55)
48. Ashtrays should be made of noncombustible materials and contain grooves or snuffers that hold cigarettes securely. The sides should be steep enough that users must place smoking materials entirely within the ashtray. They should also be small enough that people cannot use them for trash containers. (55)
49. To make sure it is sufficiently remote from buildings and outside storage so there is little or no danger from flames, sparks, or flying brands. (57)

50. The test material or a sample of the material should be removed for testing at a safe location. To perform a flame test, apply a small flame from a ¾-inch (19 mm) paraffin candle to the material for 1 minute. The material should not flash, support combustion, or continue to flame for more than 2 seconds. The material should not glow for more than 30 seconds following removal of the test flame. (57)

51. Static electricity is the presence of a nonflowing electrical charge (usually caused by friction) that may develop on almost any surface. (58)

52.

Measurement	*Water*	*Electricity*
Quantity	gpm (L/min)	amperage
Pressure	psi (kPa)	voltage
Resistance	friction loss	ohms (58)

53. A. The amount of current that passes through the body.
    B. The type of current (alternating or direct).
    C. The path the electricity takes through the body.
    D. The length of time of contact. (58)

54. The proper grounding of electrical equipment is important because the appliance user develops a false sense of security and has a greater chance of getting shocked. (59)

55. Incorrectly wired grounds literally energize the shell of the appliance, thus providing a means for the user to be shocked. (59)

56. A. The possibility of a person receiving acid burns during connection and refill operations.
    B. Hydrogen gas is produced during battery recharging, which can ignite and explode. (59)

57. The following are correct: nonconductive fluids flowing through pipes; liquids breaking into drops and the drops then hitting liquid or solid surfaces; air, gas, or steam flowing from an opening in a hose or pipe; pulverized materials traveling through chutes or pneumatic transfer devices; belts in motion; moving vehicles; moving air masses (weather); and clothing. (60)

58. A. Is there a source that generates a dangerous amount of static electricity?
    B. Is there a conductor that will accumulate the charges generated and maintain a suitable difference of electrical potential between the materials involved?
    C. Will there be a spark discharge of sufficient energy to create a hazardous situation?
    D. Is there a fuel present that may ignite? (60)

59. Telephone:
    — 911 or Appropriate Number
    — Fire Department Direct
    — "0"perator
      Report Type of Incident
      Address
      Cross Street
      Your Name and Location

    Fire Alarm Box:
    — Send Signal
    — Stay at Location
    Fire Alarm Station:
    — Send Signal
    — Notify Fire Department (63)

5

Chapter 5 Answers

TRUE/FALSE

1. True (69)
2. False (69)
3. False (71)
4. True (69)
5. True (71)
6. True (71)
7. True (71)
8. False (72)
9. True (72)
10. False (72)
11. True (72)
12. False (72)
13. True (73)
14. True (73)
15. True (74)
16. False (73)
17. True (76)
18. True (76)
19. False (76)
20. False (76)
21. False (77)
22. False (77)
23. False (77)
24. True (77)
25. True (78)
26. True (78)
27. False (79)
28. True (80)
29. True (80)
30. True (80)
31. False (80)
32. True (80)
33. True (80)
34. True (80)
35. False (81)
36. True (83)
37. False (85)
38. False (85)
39. True (85)
40. True (81)
41. True (89)
42. True (86)

MULTIPLE CHOICE

43. A (71)
44. C (71)
45. A (72)
46. A (72)
47. A (72)
48. B (72)
49. B (72)
50. D (72)
51. A (72)
52. B (72)
53. A (73)
54. D (74)
55. B (75)
56. B (75)
57. C (77)
58. B (79)
59. A (80)
60. C (80)
61. A (81)
62. B (82)
63. C (82)
64. C (86)
65. B (86)
66. D (89)

MATCHING

67. B (85)
68. B (85)
69. A (85)
70. B (85)
71. A (85)
72. B (85)
73. B (85)
74. A (85)
75. B (85)
76. D (85)
77. C (85)
78. D (85)
79. E (85)
80. B (85)
81. B (85)
82. B (85)
83. B (85)
84. B (85)
85. A (75)
86. C (75)
87. B (75)
88. B (75)
89. A (75)

SHORT ANSWER

90. A. The first digit refers to the fire-resistive rating (in hours) of the exterior bearing walls.
    B. The second digit refers to the fire-resistive rating (in hours) of structural frames or columns and girders that support loads of more than one floor.
    C. The third digit indicates the fire-resistive rating (in hours) of the floor construction. (69)

91. A. 19,800 square feet
    B. 4,800 square feet
    C. 8,400 square feet
    D. No limit
    E. No limit
    F. 4,800 square feet
    G. Two stories
    H. Four stories
    I. Not permitted (Reference *Basic Building Code*)

92. In order to test roof coverings, several test decks of each type of roof are constructed. The intermittent flame exposure test, the spread of flame test, the burning brand test, the flying brand test, and the rain test are conducted on each type of test roof. The tests involving flame require a gas burner for the flame source, a wind tunnel, and an air blower. (71)

93. A. Type I construction has structural members, including walls, columns, beams, floors, and roofs of noncombustible or limited combustible materials having the degree of fire resistance shown in Table 5.1. (70)
    B. Type II construction is similar to Type I construction except that the degree of fire resistance is lower. Note that in subtype 000, noncombustible materials with no fire-resistance rating are used. (70)
    C. Type III construction has exterior walls and structural members that are of approved noncombustible or limited-combustible materials. Interior structural members, including walls, columns, beams, floors, and roofs, are entirely or partly constructed of wood. The wood used in these members is of smaller dimensions than required for heavy timber construction. In addition, structural members must have fire-resistance ratings not less than those set forth in Table 5.1 (70)
    D. Type IV construction has exterior walls, interior walls, and structural members that are portions of these walls of approved noncombustible or limited-combustible materials. Other interior structural members, including columns, beams, arches, floors, and roofs are of solid or laminated wood without concealed spaces. The wood used in these interior structural members must be of the dimensions required for heavy timber construction. The specific requirements for these members can be found in NFPA 220, Chapter 3. (71)
    E. Type V construction has exterior walls, bearing walls, floors, roofs, and supports made entirely or partly of wood or other approved materials of smaller dimensions than those required for Type IV construction. In addition, structural members have fire-resistance ratings that are not less than those set

in Table 5.1. **NOTE:** For an explanation of the way fire-resistive ratings are determined, fire inspectors should refer to NFPA 251, *Standard Methods of Fire Tests of Building Construction and Materials.* (71)

94. Class A materials possess the best fire retardant properties, Class C the least. (72)

95. A. Failure to support the load.
    B. Passage of flame through the occupancy.
    C. Excessive increase in temperature on the unexposed side of an assembly. (73)

96. The following are correct: Underwriters Laboratories, Inc., National Bureau of Standards, Factory Mutual System, Forest Products Laboratory, Portland Cement Association, and Southwest Research Institute. (73)

97. A. NFPA 251, *Fire Tests of Building Construction and Materials.*
    B. NFPA 255, *Test of Surface Burning Characteristics of Building Materials.* (73)

98. NFPA 252, *Fire Tests of Door Assemblies.* This standard determines relative fire integrity. The test consists of a fire endurance test and a hose stream test. Acceptable criteria require that the door remain in the opening throughout both the fire endurance test and hose stream test. (73)

99. NFPA 257, *Fire Tests of Window Assemblies.* These tests are made to determine the ability of a window or light-transmitting assembly to remain in an opening during a specified level of fire exposure for 45 minutes. Like the tests for door assemblies, tests for window assemblies involve both fire endurance and hose stream tests. (73)

100. A. It affects the rate of fire buildup to a flashover condition.
     B. It may contribute to fire extension through flame spread over its surface.
     C. It may add to the intensity of a fire by contributing additional fuel.
     D. It may produce smoke and toxic gases that can contribute to life hazard and property damage. (74)

101. The Steiner Tunnel is a horizontal furnace 25 feet (7.6 m) long. The interior of the furnace is 17½-inches (445 mm) wide and 12 inches (305 mm) high. The top of the tunnel furnace is removable. The specimen to be tested is attached to the underside of the furnace top and the assembly is lowered into place. A gas burner located at one end of the tunnel produces a gas flame that is projected against the test material. The flame is adjusted to produce approximately 5,000 Btus (5 270 kJ) per minute. The extent of flame travel along the material is observed through view ports along the side of the tunnel. (74)

102.

Class of Material	Flame Spread
A	0-25
B	26-75
C	76-200 (75)

103. These ratings are listed in the *Building Materials Directory* published by Underwriters Laboratories, Inc. (75)

104. A fire wall is a wall with a specified degree of fire resistance designed to prevent the spread of fire within a structure or between two structures. (75)

105. The following are correct: The walls must be of the proper fire resistivity. The code being enforced should specify the required rating of fire walls; typical requirements will range from two to four hours. Walls should be checked for a) cracks, b) crumbling bricks, c) rotten mortar joints, and, d) in older structures, wooden lintels that carry masonry walls. Penetrations for utilities should be limited and holes completely resealed. Ducts penetrating fire walls should have proper fire dampers within the ducts. Doors in fire walls must be examined to determine if they are defective, inoperative, or blocked open. The inspector should also evaluate manufacturing or operating processes in the structure to determine if there is a possibility of a flash fire or explosion that could destroy or damage the wall. (76)

106. A. A clear path for closing and should move easily.
B. Fusible links and/or stay rollers must not be painted.
C. All components of the assembly must be listed by Underwriters Laboratories (UL) or approved by Factory Mutual Laboratories (FM) for a specific use.
D. Installations should be installed and maintained in accordance with local building codes and with NFPA 80, *Fire Doors and Windows*. (79)

107. Venting also results in rapid fuel consumption by the fire, in other words, the fire grows faster. (80)

108. The following are correct: stationary shutters, slots, breakable glass, hinged dampers, fusible links, counterweights, and smoke- and heat-actuated solenoids are all considered automatic features of venting systems. Venting systems may include the use of monitors, continuous gravity vents, unit-type vents, sawtooth skylights, exterior wall windows, or power roof ventilators. (80)

109. Wooden fire stops cut off the draft within walls and prevent the spread of fire and smoke within the concealed space. (81)

110. The following are correct: sheet metal, gypsum board, brick, plaster, mineral fiber insulation, cement grout, ceramic fiber boards, silicone elastomer insulation, and, in some cases, sand. (81)

111. A. Central heating appliances
B. Unit heaters
C. Room heaters
D. Portable heaters (82)

112. Warm air furnaces. Because these units contain plenums and duct work that may become hot enough to ignite adjacent unprotected woodwork, they require the use of appropriate clearances and insulation. Automatic controls should also be provided that will shut off the heating elements when the warm air plenum reaches 250°F (418°C). (82)

113. A floor furnace. Most are designed and approved for installation underneath combustible floors. However, they require proper clearances from miscellaneous combustibles and temperature limit controls. (83)

114. The following are correct: air-fuel interlocks, atomizer-fuel interlocks, pressure regulation interlocks, oil temperature interlocks, manual restart mechanisms, remote shutoffs, and safety shutoff valves. (85)

5

115. A gas, such as freon, is compressed in coils into a liquid, then allowed to expand back into a gas. During the expansion process, the freon cools. Air is blown across the coils to cool the surrounding air. (85)

116. A. Class 0
B. Class 1
C. Class 2 (85)

117. Because a lengthy time is needed for evacuation, fire apparatus cannot reach upper floors, and there are strong air flow patterns in vertical shafts (stack effect phenomenon). The system must be capable of maintaining smoke- and heat-free exit routes for occupants. (86)

118. A. NFPA 54, *National Fuel Gas Code*, provides recommendations for the safe installation of gas-fired cooking devices.
B. NFPA 96, *Installation of Equipment for the Removal of Smoke and Grease-Laden Vapors from Commercial Cooking Equipment*, addresses ventilation practices for fixed cooking equipment. (86)

119. A. Location of hazardous contents in the building.
B. Proximity to combustible structural members.
C. Capacity and location of HVAC systems.
D. Maximum temperature required for the particular process.
E. The way in which materials are handled, moved, or stored after heating. (88)

120. The following are correct: sound construction and installation, good housekeeping practices, automatic sprinkler protection, automatic humidity control, good air circulation, and proper ventilation. (88)

121. Flammable and combustible liquids storage rooms should have interior walls, ceilings, and floors that are constructed of materials with a minimum fire-resistive rating of 2 hours. The doorway openings in the walls should have noncombustible, liquidtight, raised sills or ramps at least 4 inches (101 mm) in height to prevent spilled liquids from flowing into adjoining areas. With the exception of drains, all floors should be liquidtight. Further, the room should be liquidtight at the places where the walls join the floor. The storage room should have mechanical or gravity ventilation that removes vapors from the atmosphere. All electrical wiring and equipment used in rooms storing Class 1 flammable liquids should be appropriate for Class I, Division 2 locations, as specified by NFPA 70, *National Electrical Code*. Aisles at least 3 feet (0.9 m) wide should be maintained in the facility, and in places where Class I or II liquids are stored in 30-gallon (132 L) or larger containers, they should be stored no more than one container high. (88)

Chapter 6 Answers

TRUE/FALSE

1. True (93)
2. False (93)
3. False (96)
4. True (96)
5. True (98)
6. True (98)
7. False (98)
8. True (98)
9. False (99)
10. True (99)
11. True (99)
12. True (100)
13. True (100)
14. True (100)
15. True (100)
16. True (101)
17. True (100)
18. False (101)
19. True (102)
20. True (102)
21. True (103)
22. True (103)
23. True (103)
24. True (103)
25. True (104)
26. False (104)
27. False (105)
28. True (105)

MULTIPLE CHOICE

29. C (93)
30. A (98)
31. C (98)
32. A (98)
33. B (98)
34. A (98)
35. B (98)
36. A (99)
37. C (99)
38. A (100)
39. D (100)
40. C (100)
41. B (101)
42. A (103)
43. B (105)
44. A (106)

SHORT ANSWER

45. A. **Places of Assembly** include, but are not limited to, all buildings or portions of buildings used for gathering together 50 or more persons for such purposes as deliberation, worship, entertainment, dining, amusement, or awaiting transportation. Assembly occupancies are further classified according to the number of persons that the structure can accommodate: Class A — Facilities capable of handling 1,000 persons or more. Class B — Facilities capable of handling 300 to 1,000 persons. Class C — Facilities capable of handling 50 to 300 persons. (93)

B. **Educational Occupancies** include all buildings used for educational purposes up through the twelfth grade by six or more persons for 4 hours per day or more than 12 hours per week. Some examples are part-day nursery preschools, kindergartens, and other schools whose purpose is primarily educational even though the children are of preschool age. Other occupancies within educational occupancies are governed by regulations for the specific occupancy. (94)

C. **Health Care Occupancies** are used for medical treatment or care of persons suffering from physical or mental illness, disease, or infirmity; or for the care of

6

infants, convalescents or infirm aged persons. Included are hospitals, nursing homes, residential-custodial care facilities, supervisory care facilities, and ambulatory health care centers. (94)

D. **Detention and Correctional Occupancies** provide sleeping facilities for four or more residents and are occupied by persons who are generally prevented from protecting themselves because of security measures not under their control. Included are jails, detention centers, correctional institutions, reformatories, houses of correction, pre-release centers, and other residential restrained-care facilities where occupants are confined or housed under some degree of restraint or security. (94)

E. **Residential Occupancies** are those in which sleeping accommodations are provided for normal residential purposes and include all buildings designed to provide sleeping accommodations. Included in this classification are hotels, apartments, dormitories, lodging and rooming facilities, and one- and two-family dwellings. (94)

F. **Mercantile Occupancies** include stores, markets, and other rooms, buildings, or structures used to display and sell merchandise. Some examples are supermarkets, department stores, drugstores, auction rooms, and shopping centers. Minor merchandising operations in buildings predominantly of another occupancy are subject to the requirements of the predominant occupancy. (95)

G. **Business Occupancies** are those used for transacting business (other than covered under mercantile), for keeping accounts and records, and for similar purposes. Some examples are doctors' and dentists' offices, outpatient clinics for the ambulatory, general offices, city halls, town halls, courthouses, college and university instructional buildings housing classrooms for less than 50 persons, and instructional laboratories. A minor office occupancy incidental to the operations of another occupancy is considered to be a part of the predominant occupancy. (96)

H. **Industrial Occupancies** include factories making products of all kinds and properties devoted to such operations as processing, assembly, mixing, packing, finishing, decorating, and repairing. These occupancies include laboratories, dry cleaning plants, power plants, pumping operations, smokehouses, laundries, creameries, gas plants, refineries, sawmills, and college and university noninstructional laboratories. (96)

I. **Storage Occupancies** include all buildings or structures used primarily for storing or sheltering goods, merchandise, products, vehicles, or animals. Examples are warehouses, cold storage facilities, freight terminals, truck and marine terminals, bulk oil storage facilities, parking garages, aircraft hangars, grain elevators, barns, and stables. (96)

J. **Unusual structures** include any building or structure that cannot be properly classified in any of the other classifications by reason of some function not encompassed or some unusual combination of functions necessary to the purpose of the building or structure. (96)

46. A. The **exit access** is that portion of a means of egress that leads to an exit. Hallways, corridors, and aisles commonly serve as exit access. (96)

B. The **exit** is that portion of a means of egress that is separated from all other spaces of the building structure by construction or equipment and that provides a protected way of travel to the exit discharge. A door leading directly outside or through a protected passageway to the outside, a horizontal exit, smokeproof tower, and interior and exterior stairs and ramps are examples of exits. (96)

C. The **exit discharge** is that portion of a means of egress that is between the end of an exit and a public way. An alley that joins a street or sidewalk is a typical exit discharge. (96)

47. A. To act as a barrier to fire and smoke.
    B. To serve as components in a means of egress. (98)

48. The stair enclosure may be made smokeproof by the use of natural ventilation, mechanical ventilation, or by pressurizing the stair enclosure. (99)

49. A. Class A ramps must be at least 44 inches wide (1 120 mm), with a maximum slope of 1 to 10. Class A ramps are not limited to a certain height between landings. This type of ramp is especially useful in certain health care occupancies for moving patients in wheelchairs or cots. (100)
    B. Class B ramps must be at least 30 inches wide (760 mm), with a maximum slope of 1 to 8. Several exceptions to these requirements are detailed in Chapters 8-30 of the *Life Safety Code*®. (100)

50. Unreliable exits. Often, they are poorly maintained and may be wet or icy, creating an additional hazard for those who must use them. Fire escape stairs are an unusual means of exiting; as such, individuals often hesitate to use them. Further, persons with a fear of heights may find fire escape stairs extremely difficult to use, slowing the progress of others who are trying to use the stairs. (100)

51. Occupant load is defined by NFPA 101, *Life Safety Code*® as "the total number of persons that may occupy a building or portion thereof at any one time." (101)

52. A. Floor Area Method
    Step 1: Multiply the building's length times its width. (L x W = A)
    Step 2: Consult NFPA 101 and determine the allowed area for occupancy.
    Step 3: Use the following formula to calculate the occupant load: (102)

$$\text{Occupant Load} = \frac{\text{Net Floor Area (ft}^2\text{ or m}^2\text{)}}{\text{Area per Occupant (ft}^2\text{ or m}^2\text{)}}$$

    B. Unit of Width Method
    Step 1: Determine from NFPA 101 a level unit of exit width.
    Step 2: Multiply number of people able to exit by units wide.
    Step 3: Multiply the number of persons per exit by the number of exits. (102)

53. A. If the area/person is not reduced below 5 square feet ($0.46m^2$).
    B. If the authority having jurisdiction approves this deviation. (102)

54. Step 1: Consult NFPA 101, and determine unit of level exit width per person allowed for that occupancy.
    Step 2: Multiply number of people able to exit by units wide.
    Step 3: Multiply the number of persons per exit by the number of exits. (103)

55. Step 1: Consult NFPA 101, note that two remote means of egress are required on each level.
    Step 2: Determine the total exit capacity per floor.
    Step 3: Determine if the stairs and ground egress level will be able to accommodate the largest number of people from any single floor above. (103)

56. Fire load is defined as the *maximum heat* that can be produced if all the combustible materials in a given area burn. Maximum heat release is the product of the weight of each combustible multiplied by its heat of combustion. In a normal building, fire load is calculated for the structural components, interior finish, floor finish, and combustible contents of the building. (106)

57. SLIGHT: TYPICAL FIRE LOAD 5 PSF (Pounds per square foot [24 kg/m^2]). The following are correct: well-arranged office, metal furniture, noncombustible building; welding areas containing few combustibles; noncombustible power house; and noncombustible buildings, small amount of combustibles. (106)
 MODERATE: TYPICAL FIRE LOAD 10 PSF (49 kg/m^2). The following are correct: cotton and waste paper storage (baled) and well-arranged noncombustible building; paper manufacturing, noncombustible building; noncombustible institutional building with combustible occupancy. (106)
 MODERATELY SEVERE: TYPICAL FIRE LOAD 10 TO 15 PSF (49 kg/m^2 to 73 kg/m^2). The following are correct: well-arranged combustible storage, noncombustible building; machine shops with combustible floors. (106)
 SEVERE: TYPICAL FIRE LOAD 15 TO 20 PSF (73 kg/m^2 to 93 kg/m^2). The following are correct: manufacturing areas, combustible products, noncombustible buildings; congested combustible storage areas, and noncombustible building. (106)
 VERY SEVERE: TYPICAL FIRE LOAD GREATER THAN 20 PSF (93 kg/m^2). The following are correct: flammable liquids; woodworking areas; office, combustible furniture, and buildings; paper working, printing, etc; furniture manufacturing and finishing; machine shop with combustible floors. (106)

58. This information can be useful in preparing prefire plans, water requirements for automatic sprinkler and fire flow demands, and fire extinguisher placement. (106)

Chapter 7 Answers

TRUE/FALSE

1. False (111)
2. True (111)
3. True (111)
4. False (111)
5. False (111)
6. True (112)
7. True (114)
8. True (114)
9. False (114)
10. True (115)
11. False (115)
12. True (116)
13. True (116)
14. False (116)
15. True (116)
16. False (116)
17. False (118)
18. True (118)
19. True (119)
20. False (120)
21. True (120)
22. True (120)
23. False (121)
24. False (123)
25. True (122)
26. False (125)
27. True (125)
28. True (128)
29. True (130)
30. False (130)
31. True (130)
32. False (130)
33. True (132)
34. All are True (132-133)
35. False (134)
36. False (134)
37. True (142)
38. True (142)
39. True (144)
40. True (144)
41. False (135)
42. False (136)
43. True (144)
44. False (144)
45. True (144)
46. True (145)
47. True (145)
48. True (146)
49. False (146)
50. True (146)
51. True (146)
52. True (148)
53. False (148)
54. True (148)
55. True (150)
56. True (150)
57. False (150)
58. False (151)
59. True (152)
60. True (152)
61. True (152)
62. True (152)
63. True (152)
64. False (153)
65. True (161)
66. True (163)
67. True (165)
68. False (167-168)
69. True (168)
70. True (168-169)
71. True (170)
72. False (170)
73. False (170)
74. True (172)
75. False (173)
76. True (173)
77. True (176)
78. True (177)

7

MULTIPLE CHOICE

79. A (112)
80. D (113)
81. A (114)
82. D (114)
83. A (116)
84. C (116)
85. A (116)
86. B (116)
87. C (118)
88. D, H (119)
89. C (121)
90. C (121)
91. A (121)
92. B (122)
93. C (122)
94. A (125)
95. C (126)
96. B (129-130)
97. A (132)
98. C (134)
99. A (134)
100. C (135)
101. C (144)
102. C (144)
103. D (145)
104. C (146)
105. D (146-147)
106. A (147)
107. A (147)
108. A (147)
109. B (149)
110. D (150)
111. A (150)
112. C (161)
113. C (163)
114. C (165)
115. A (168)
116. C (168)
117. C (168)
118. D (170)
119. A (174-175)
120. B (175)
121. C (176)

MATCHING

122. F, A, F, (124)
123. F (144)
124. C, D (148-149)
125. A, B (145)
126. G, H (148)
127. E (150)
128. E (143)
129. A (144)
130. C (142)
131. B (142)
132. D (142)
133. C (158)
134. F (160)
135. E (160)
136. B (157)
137. A (155)
138. D (159)

SHORT ANSWER

139. A. Automatic Sprinkler Systems — Fixed-pipe water extinguishing systems that are designed to extinguish or limit the spread of fire until such a time that fire fighting personnel arrive to control the incident.

B. Special-Agent, Fixed-Extinguishing Systems — Special-agent, fixed-extinguishing systems are used in those situations where automatic sprinkler systems, which apply water, are not appropriate. Such systems use carbon dioxide ($C0_2$), dry or wet chemicals, foam, or halogenated agents.

C. Standpipe Systems — Standpipe systems provide a quick and convenient means for deploying fire streams within a building, particularly in large area or multiple-story buildings. Depending upon the type installed, standpipe systems may be used by occupants, firefighters, or both.

D. Portable Fire Extinguishers — The most common type of private fire protection appliance is the portable fire extinguisher. Fire prevention and suppression personnel must thoroughly understand the characteristics and applicability of each type, as well as the classification and distribution requirements.

E. Fire Detection and Alarm Systems — Fire detection and alarm systems, otherwise known as protective signaling systems, provide visual and/or audible signals to alert building occupants and/or organized fire protection units. These systems are also designed to operate fire protection system components. (111-112)

140. A. Stored Pressure — These models contain both the extinguishing agent and expellent gas in a single chamber; both are discharged directly from the control valve. Nearly all of these units have a pressure gauge located on or near the control valve. Stored pressured extinguishers must be recharged by a qualified repair firm. These extinguishers are usually found in low-risk areas such as schools, department stores, and office buildings. (112-113)

B. Cartridge Pressure — These models contain the expellent gas in one cartridge and the extinguishing agent in another cartridge. During operation, the expellent gas must be released into the extinguishing agent cylinder. This type of extinguisher does not use a pressure gauge, but may have an indicator to show that the unit has been charged. Recharging is accomplished by replacing the expellent gas cylinder and refilling the extinguishing agent. This procedure can be an in-house operation since no special equipment is required. These types of extinguishers are commonly found in such industries as oil refineries, solvent manufacturing, and paper manufacturing.

C. Mechanically Pumped — These models feature an internal pump. The operator provides the expelling energy by manually pumping pressure into the cylinder. Recharging is accomplished by refilling the cylinder with water. This type of extinguisher is limited to Class A fires.

D. Hand Propelled — This method of fire extinguishment includes 10- to 12-quart (9.5 L to 11.4 L) covered buckets of water, a 55-gallon (298 L) barrel filled with water with bails hung around or above the barrel, buckets filled with sand, and fire blankets. All of these containers should be clearly stenciled with the word "Fire" across them. Hand-propelled extinguishers are valid when theft or vandalism of standard fire extinguishers is a problem. (113)

141. *Class A*: Fires involving ordinary combustibles such as wood, cloth, or papers.
Class B: Fires involving flammable or combustible liquids, greases, and gases.
Class C: Fires involving energized electrical equipment where the electrical nonconductivity of the extinguishing agent is of first importance. The materials involved are either Class A or B and can be handled as such once the equipment is deenergized. (114)
Class D: Fires involving combustible metals, such as magnesium, titanium, zirconium, and potassium. These fires may require special extinguishing agents or techniques. (114)

142. A. Water
B. Carbon dioxide
C. Halogenated agents
D. Dry chemical
E. Dry powder
F. Foam (116)

143. Step 1: PULL the pin at the top of the extinguisher that keeps the handle from being pressed. Break the plastic or thin wire inspection band.
  Step 2: POINT the nozzle or outlet toward the base of the fire. Some hose assemblies are clipped to the extinguisher body. Release it and point. Stand about 8 to 12 feet (2.4 m to 3.7 m) from the base of the fire.
  Step 3: PRESS the handle above the carrying handle to discharge the agent inside. The handle can be released to stop the discharge at any time.
  Step 4: SWEEP the nozzle back and forth at the base of the flames to disperse the extinguishing agent. After the fire is out, probe for remaining smoldering hot spots or possible reflash of flammable liquids. Make sure the fire is out. (118)

144. A. The type needed to protect the hazard.
  B. The location of the extinguisher.
  C. The personnel to operate the extinguisher. (118)

145. A. *Light Hazard Occupancy*: An occupancy where the amount of combustibles or flammable liquids present is such that a fire of small size may be expected. Some examples are offices, school classrooms, churches, and assembly halls.
  B. *Ordinary Hazard Occupancy*: An occupancy where the amount of combustibles or flammable liquids present is such that fires of moderate size may be expected. Some examples are mercantile storage and display, automobile showrooms, parking garages, light manufacturing, school shop or laboratory areas, and warehouses not classified as extra hazard.
  C. *Extra Hazard Occupancy*: An occupancy where the amount of combustibles or flammable liquids present is such that a fire of large size may be expected. Some examples are manufacturing processes such as painting, dipping, coating, flammable liquids handling, auto repair garages, and aircraft and boat maintenance facilities. (119)

146. A. Serviceability.
  B. Accessibility.
  C. User's ability to operate it. (121)

147. A. Ensure proper location and accessibility.
  B. Ensure discharge nozzle/horn is free of obstructions.
  C. Ensure the operating instructions on the extinguisher nameplate are legible.
  D. Visually inspect the lockpins and tamper seals.
  E. Determine if the extinguisher is full of agent and/or fully pressurized by checking the pressure gauge, weighing the extinguisher, or inspecting the agent level.
  F. Check the inspection tag for the date of the previous inspection, maintenance, or recharging.
  G. Examine the condition of the hose and its associated fittings. (121-122)

148. The extinguisher should be discharged to check the operation of the discharge valve and pressure gauge. (122)

149. A. Class I standpipes are intended for use by fire departments and individuals trained in handling heavy fire streams (2½-inch [65 mm] hose).
  B. Class II standpipes are intended for use primarily by building occupants until the arrival of the fire department. Class II systems feature smaller hose, either 1½-inch or 1-inch (38 mm or 25 mm).

C. Class III standpipe systems combine the features of Class I and II systems. Because Class III systems feature both the smaller 1½-inch (38 mm) hose and the larger 2½-inch (65 mm) outlet, they are intended for use either by fire department personnel and those trained in handling heavy streams or by building occupants. (123)

150. A. Wet standpipe systems that have the water supply valve open and water maintained through the system at all times.
B. Dry standpipe systems that admit water to the system through the operation of a manually activated, approved remote control device located at each hose station.
C. Dry standpipe systems that admit water to the system automatically by the use of a device similar to a dry-pipe valve in an automatic sprinkler system. When a discharge outlet valve is opened, the air pressure in the system is depleted and the dry-pipe valve opens to admit water into the system. This type of system is suitable for use in unheated structures.
D. Dry standpipe systems that have no permanent water supply and must be charged by the fire department pumping into a connection outside the building. (124)

151. A variation of the wet standpipe system is known as a primed system. Water is maintained in the system using a ¾- to 1-inch (20 mm to 25 mm) water line connection. The system cannot be used until the fire department pumps into the connection on the outside of the building. The advantages of a primed system are that it is usable as soon as the fire department starts pumping into it, it does not have to be filled with water, and air does not evacuate from the system through the hoseline. Corrosion of the internal surface of the piping system is also reduced. (124)

152. The following are correct: hose stations are not over 6 feet (1.8 m) from the floor and are within easy reach when standing on the floor; each hose cabinet or closet for Class II or Class III systems is provided with a conspicuous sign that reads "FIRE HOSE" and/or "FIRE HOSE FOR USE BY OCCUPANTS OF BUILDING"; fire department connections have the proper fire department hose threads or connection and are designated with a sign reading "STANDPIPE"; dry standpipes are posted with a sign reading "DRY STANDPIPE FOR FIRE DEPARTMENT USE ONLY"; piping, feed mains, and connections are flushed to remove all debris; system components are tested hydrostatically at not less than 200 psi (1 379 kPa) for two hours. (126)

153. H. Ensure discharge outlet threads are compatible with fire department threads and are not damaged. The standpipe is useless if the local fire department cannot connect to it. (126)

154. E. The hose is in good condition, dry, and properly racked. (127)

155. A. They automatically initiate a fire alarm.
B. They begin to combat the fire while it is in its incipient phase. (127)

156. The following are correct: building and fire code concessions granted during construction that allow for longer allowable exit travel distances, reduced construction costs by using less fire-resistive materials, greater architectural design freedom, reduced insurance premiums, and less water damage during a fire than that caused by firefighters' handlines. (127)

157. The following are correct: fusible links, glass bulbs, and chemical pellets, all of which fuse or open in response to heat. (129)

158. A. *Wet-pipe systems* contain water in the system at all times.
     B. *Dry-pipe systems* maintain air under pressure in the sprinkler piping. When sprinklers fuse, air escapes and water is automatically admitted into the system.
     C. A *pre-action system* is a type of dry system that employs a deluge-type valve, fire detection devices, and closed sprinklers. This system only discharges water into the piping in response to the detection system.
     D. The *deluge system* is another type of dry-pipe system. It is usually equipped with open sprinklers and a deluge valve. Upon fire detection, the deluge valve opens, permitting water to flow out of all the sprinklers at once. (129-130)

159. A. Hazard to be protected.
     B. The occupancy classification.
     C. Fire loading conditions. (130)

160. A. They are fully open and supervised in an approved manner.
     B. The valve is accessible at all times.
     C. The valve and its associated components are not subject to mechanical damage.
     D. If the control valve is enclosed in a room, ensure that the room is kept clean, has adequate lighting, and is sprinklered. (132)

161. Determine if they are in good condition. Check for corrosion and areas that could be subject to physical damage. (133)

162. Cold flow occurs when a sprinkler is repeatedly heated near its operating temperature. Cold flow is evidenced by a creeping or sliding apart of the fused parts (which is known as cold flow) or water leakage around the sprinkler. Cold flow problems can be eliminated by using frangible-bulb sprinklers with the same temperature rating or by using fusible-link sprinklers with a higher temperature rating. (134)

163. In many jurisdictions, fire inspectors witness sprinkler system acceptance tests conducted by a representative of the installation firm. This releases the fire department from liability resulting from damaged equipment due to improper operation or installation. (134)

164. A supply main valve may be partially closed or the supply main may be obstructed. (136)

165. B. Hydrostatic Testing. (137)

166. In this test, the entire system is placed under an air pressure of 40 psi (276 kPa). After 24 hours the air pressure is measured again. If there is a loss of more than 1½ psi (10 kPa), the leaks should be located and corrected. (137)

167. The 2-inch (50 mm) main drain valve is used to prevent accidental tripping. Closing the water supply valve without opening the 2-inch (50 mm) main drain valve can cause water trapped between the water supply control valve and the dry-pipe clapper to push the clapper off its seat. (139-140)

168. This person should record the time that the test valve is opened and the time when water discharges. This discharge should not take longer than 60 seconds. (140)

169. For a small deluge system, open sprinklers are replaced with standard sprinklers, plugs, and caps. (143)

170. For large deluge systems where it is not practical to replace or plug sprinklers, the main water supply valve (OS&Y) is closed to within two turns of being completely shut. The deluge valve is then tripped and the main supply valve (OS&Y) is closed immediately. The system may be activated by using a heating device on a detector or by manual means. (143)

171. NFPA 13D, *Sprinkler Systems in One- and Two-Family Dwellings and Mobile Homes.* (143)

172. A. Protein
     B. Fluoroprotein
     C. Synthetic (144-145)

173. They are special alcohol-type foam concentrates that have an insoluble barrier in the bubble structure that resists breakdown when used to attack polar solvent fires. Manufacturers typically designate these foams as "alcohol-type concentrate" or "ATC." (145)

174. For evidence of excessive sludging or deterioration. (145)

175. A. Branch Lines
     B. Inspector's Test Connection
     C. Automatic Sprinklers
     D. Cap for Flushing
     E. Cross Main
     F. Bulk Main (Riser)
     G. Alarm
     H. Alarm Valve
     I. OS&Y Gate Valve to Control Water Supply to System
     J. Fire Department Connection
     K. Main Drain Connection
     L. Water Supply (129)

176. A. *Total Flooding.* A total flooding system has nozzles arranged to discharge carbon dioxide into an enclosed space or an enclosure around the fire hazard. Piping connects the nozzles to a fixed supply of carbon dioxide.
     B. *Local Application.* A local application system has nozzles arranged to discharge carbon dioxide directly on burning material. Piping connects the nozzles to a fixed supply of carbon dioxide.
     C. *Hand Hoselines.* A hand hoseline system has hoselines located next to hazards. This system is designed for manual local application. Piping connects the hoselines to a fixed supply of carbon dioxide.
     D. *Standpipe with Mobile Supply.* A standpipe with a mobile supply system has fixed nozzles or hoselines, or both, connected to fixed piping. These systems may be used for either total flooding or local applications. A mobile supply of carbon dioxide is maintained where it can be quickly moved into position and manually connected to the fixed piping. (145-146)

177. Testing and maintenance procedure manuals. Inspectors should review this material before conducting an inspection or witnessing any tests. (146)

178. Halogenated agents chemically stop the combustion process by breaking the chemical chain reaction. Halogenated agents are not effective on fires involving fuels that contain their own oxidizing agent, such as potassium or sodium, or on deep-seated fires in Class A materials. (147)

179. Because of problems caused by residue, dry chemicals are usually **NOT** recommended for use on electronic and computer equipment. (149)

180. A. Initiating Devices
     B. Auxiliary Devices
     C. Indicating Signaling Devices
     D. Power Source
     E. Control Panel (151)

181. A. Manual
     B. Thermal sensitive
     C. Products of combustion
     D. Flame detectors
     E. Extinguisher system related (151)

182. The advantage is it provides 24-hour monitoring by trained personnel responsible for taking specific action. (153)

183. The difference is in a central station system a central station receives alarms from different properties not under its ownership. (153)

184. Type A — Manual: The signal transmitted through a Type A system has to be retransmitted to the fire stations.
     Type B — Automatic: The signal transmitted through a Type B system is automatically received from system alarm boxes to the fire stations. (154)

185. The chief advantage of signal multiplexing is that minimum wire is needed to connect alarm-initiating devices to the control panel; yet, alarm devices or zones can be individually identified. (154)

186. A. Manual — Commonly called pull stations. A person must recognize a fire emergency exists and manually pull, or call in an alarm.
     B. Products of Combustion — Detectors that automatically respond to heat, smoke, or flame.
     C. Waterflow Detectors — Detects movement of water within the sprinkler or standpipe system. (155)

187. A. They enable firefighters to give instructions to building occupants.
     B. They enable communication with the incident commander or other suppression personnel within the building. (160)

188. A. Detectors should not show any sign of damage.
     B. Detectors should not have been painted unless the testing laboratory has found them to be unaffected by painting. No attempt should be made to remove paint.
     C. Detectors on systems that are being restored to service after a period of use should be checked by a testing laboratory.
     D. Detectors should not be perceptibly corroded. (162)

189. A. Nonrestorable Fixed Temperature Detectors. These detectors cannot be tested periodically because the application of heat, which is required for testing, will destroy the unit.
B. Restorable Detectors. Restorable detectors can be tested with a portable heat source, such as a hair dryer or heat lamp with a temperature shield.
C. Fusible Link Detectors. Fusible link detectors with REPLACEABLE links should be tested semiannually by having the link removed and observing whether or not the contacts close.
D. Pneumatic-Type Detectors. These may be tested with a heating device or with an approved pressure pump.
E. Smoke Detectors. Smoke detectors should be tested semiannually according to the manufacturer's instructions.
F. Flame Detectors. Instructions from the manufacturer for test procedures, training, and testing equipment, if obtainable, should be required by the bid specifications for the flame detectors. Testing may be included in a service contract. (162-163)

190. A. Water supply source.
B. Processing or treatment facilities.
C. Means or methods of moving the water.
D. Delivery system, including storage. (164)

191. A. Gravity — A true *gravity system* delivers water from the source to the distribution system without pumping equipment.
B. Direct pumping — When elevation pressure cannot provide sufficient pressure for the community, a pump is placed relatively close to the water source to create the pressure within the distribution system.
C. Combination — Uses both gravity and pumping to provide adequate pressure. Water is pumped into the distribution system and into elevated storage tanks (gravitational pressure). (164)

192. A. Primary feeders — Largest pipes (mains) with relatively widespread spacing that convey large quantities of water to various points of the system for local distribution to the smaller mains.
B. Secondary feeders — Intermediate pipes within the primary feeder network that reinforce the grid with a concentrated supply of water.
C. Distributors — Smallest of the mains that serve the individual fire hydrants and blocks of consumers. (165-167)

193. RESIDENTIAL DISTRICTS should use 8-inch (200 mm) pipe unless a 6-inch (150 mm) pipe will complete a good grid and is cross-connected at intervals not exceeding 600 feet (180 m).
SHOPPING CENTERS AND INDUSTRIAL AREAS should use 12-inch (300 mm) pipe, or 8-inch (200 mm) pipe if it will complete a good grid. Larger sized mains may be needed depending upon the size, layout, and occupancy of the structure.
MULTIPLE HOUSING DEVELOPMENTS should use at least 8-inch (200 mm) pipe; in many cases, however, industrial area standards are needed. (167)

194. The weather. Dry-barrel hydrants are used in areas that have freezing temperatures at least part of the year under normal circumstances, and wet-barrel hydrants are used in mild climates where typical weather conditions are above freezing. (168)

195. A. The main valve when it is closed.
 B. The drip valve when the main valve is open but the outlets are capped.
 C. The water mains near the hydrant. (168)

196. A. *Incrustation* — caused by the tubercular corrosion or rust, chemical constituents of water, biological or organism growth, or biodegradation of water agents/pipe materials.
 B. *Sedimentation Deposits* — such as sedimentary decay (mud, clay, leaves), or foreign matter other than sediment.
 C. *Valves* — closed or partially closed.
 D. *Foreign Matter* — stones, tools, wood, or lead. (170)

197. A. Notebook
 B. Gauging device
 C. Can of lubrication oil
 D. Pot with a mixture of light lubrication oil and graphite
 E. Small, flat brush
 F. Gate valve key
 G. Pressure gauge and a tapped hydrant cap
 H. Pitot gauge
 I. 12-quart (11.4 L) pail
 J. Hydrant wrench (170-171)

198. A. Check for any obstructions near the hydrant.
 B. Check for proper outlet(s) direction and clearance between the outlet and the surrounding ground.
 C. Check for mechanical damage to the hydrant such as dented outlets or rounded (stripped) stem nuts.
 D. Check the condition of the paint for rust or corrosion.
 E. Check water flow by having the hydrant fully opened and then checking its ability to drain. (171)

199. Flow tests should occur after any extensive water main improvements, after extensions have been made, or at least every five years if there have been no changes. (173)

200. Step 1: Open the petcock on the pitot tube and make certain the air chamber is drained. Then close the petcock.
 Step 2: Edge the blade into the stream parallel to the outlet, with the small opening or point centered in the stream and held away from the butt or nozzle approximately one-half the diameter of the opening.
 Step 3: Take and record the velocity pressure reading from the gauge. If the needle is fluctuating, read and record the value located in the center between the high and low extremes.
 Step 4: After the test is completed, open the petcock and be certain all water is drained from the assembly before storing. (174)

201. $GPM = (29.83) \times C \times d^2 \times \sqrt{P}$
 $L/min = (0.0667766) \times C \times d^2 \times \sqrt{P}$
 Where: C = The coefficient of discharge
 d = The actual diameter of the hydrant or nozzle orifice in inches (mm)
 P = The pressure in psi (kPa) as read at the orifice (175)

202. The "test" hydrant is the closest hydrant to the location requiring the test results. Static and residual pressure is measured from this hydrant. The "flow" hydrants are those hydrants where pitot readings are taken to find their individual flows. These readings are then added to find the total flow during the test. (177)

203. Step 1: Locate personnel at the test hydrant and at all flow hydrants to be used.
Step 2: Remove a hydrant cap from the test hydrant and attach the pressure gauge cap with the petcock in the open position. After checking the other caps for tightness, slowly open the hydrant several turns. Once the air has escaped and a steady stream of water is flowing, the petcock should be closed and the hydrant opened fully.
Step 3: Read and record the static pressure as seen on the pressure gauge.
Step 4: The individual(s) at the flow hydrant(s) should remove the cap(s) from the outlet(s) to be flowed. Check and record the flow hydrant's coefficient and actual inside diameter of the orifice. **NOTE:** If a nozzle is placed on the outlet, its coefficient and diameter should be measured and recorded.
Step 5: Open flow hydrants and record the pitot reading of the velocity pressures. The individual at the test hydrant should simultaneously record the residual pressure. **NOTE:** The residual pressure should not drop below 20 psi (138 kPa) during the test. If this happens, the number of flow hydrants must be reduced.
Step 6: Slowly close the flow hydrant to prevent water hammer in the mains. Drain the hydrant and secure all hydrant caps. Report any hydrant defects.
Step 7: Check the test hydrant for a return to normal operating pressure, then close the hydrant. The petcock valve should be opened to prevent a vacuum on the pressure gauge. Drain the hydrant, secure the hydrant cap. Report any hydrant defects. (177-178)

204. The following are correct: *Precaution:* Minimize damage to property from the flowing stream. *Solution:* Flow in a direction away from property. Property damage control measures include opening and closing hydrants slowly to avoid water hammer, not flowing hydrants where drainage is inadequate, and always remembering to check downstream to see where the water will flow.

Precaution: Control both pedestrian and automobile traffic during all phases of the testing. *Solution:* Obtain assistance from the local law enforcement agency. Since flowing water across a busy street could cause an accident, take proper measures beforehand to slow or stop traffic.

Precaution: Unnecessary injury from hydrant caps. *Solution:* Safety measures include tightening caps on hydrant outlets not being used, not standing in front of closed caps, and not leaning over the top of the hydrant when operating it.

Precaution: Avoid creating a sheet of ice. *Solution:* Water should not be flowed during freezing weather unless proper drainage minimizes icing problems.

Precaution: A good rule to follow is: WHEN IN DOUBT — DO NOT FLOW! *Solution:* Know the consequences of an action. Thought must be given to any action so the flow test can be completed without disruptions or property destruction. (178)

7

205. GRAPHICAL ANALYSIS:
Step 1: Obtain a Fire Flow Graph and determine which gpm (L/min) scale should be used.
Step 2: Locate and plot the static pressure on the vertical scale at 0 gpm (0 L/min).
Step 3: Locate the total water flow measured during the test on the chart.
Step 4: Locate the residual pressure noted during the test on the chart.
Step 5: Plot the residual pressure above the total water flow measured.
Step 6: Draw a straight line from the static pressure point through the residual pressure point on the waterflow scale.
Step 7: Read the gpm available at 20 psi (138 kPa) and record this figure. This reading represents the total available water that can be relied upon. (180)

MATHEMATICAL FORMULA:
A variation of the Hazen-Williams formula for determining available water is written as follows:

$$Q_r = \frac{Q_f \text{ x } h_r^{0.54}}{h_f^{0.54}}$$

Where Q_r = Flow available at desired residual pressure
Q_f = Flow during test
h_r = Pressure drop to residual pressure (normal operating pressure minus required residual pressure)
h_f = Pressure drop during test (normal operating pressure minus residual pressure during flow test)

The values for h_r or h_f to the 0.54 power are listed in Table 7.6 (185)

NOMOGRAPH METHOD:
The procedure for determining available water by nomographic analysis is as follows:
Step 1: Use a straightedge to connect points h_r and h_f. Use a sharp point pencil or pen and mark the intersection on line S.
Step 2: Rotate the straightedge about the intersection point on S until it is in line with the observed flow on the Q_f scale.
Step 3: Mark the intersection of the line on the Q_r scale. This Q_r point is the available flow at the assumed pressure drop. (186)

206. A. Does the water system meet the needed fire flow for the occupancy or area?
B. Is the available system flow adequate to provide sprinkler system demands in the area?
C. Where will water system improvements be needed? (186)

207. *Graphical analysis* provides a visual graph that indicates system capability at any pressure.
The *nomograph* is often useful for field measurements and provides close approximations.
Mathematical determination provides the most exact answer for any given situation and may be desirable for use in computer applications where large amounts of flow test data must be analyzed. (186)

Chapter 8 Answers

TRUE/FALSE

1. False (191)
2. True (192)
3. True (204)
4. True (204)
5. False (205)
6. True (209)
7. True (209)
8. True (211)
9. True (211)
10. False (212)
11. False (212)

MULTIPLE CHOICE

12. C (194)
13. A (202)
14. A (202)
15. A (203)
16. C (203)
17. A (203)
18. B (203)
19. C (204)
20. A (211)
21. D (212)
22. A (212)

IDENTIFY

23. 1. Identify typical problems that could be prevented if a plans review system were in place.
    2. Formulate and write goals and objectives of the plans review system.
    3. Develop methods for coordinating the efforts of all the agencies that take part in the plans review process.
    4. Develop a written policy stating which agency has the authority to enforce code regulations during the plans review stage.
    5. Establish a procedure that specifies the minimum requirements for submitting plans for review; if possible, the requirements should be in booklet form and distributed to all architects, engineers, contractors in the area; and any other contractors who are named to area building projects.
    6. Establish good record keeping procedures. Both formal and informal communications should be documented because fire inspectors may need these records for a performance evaluation, legal action, or future reference.
    7. While planning the record keeping system, fire inspectors should develop the format for a plans review letter.
    8. After fire inspectors establish a system, they should initiate a public information program targeted at those who are most affected — architects, engineers, contractors, and developers. (198)

24. 1. The inspector should determine which standard applies and what the basic requirements are.
    2. The inspector should determine whether the system has been designed according to the pipe schedule or has been hydraulically calculated.
    3. The inspector should check several system design factors, such as the extent of coverage, type of system, size of system, information about sprinklers and piping, water supply connections and valves, and the fire department connection.

8

4. The inspectors should examine the specifications to verify the temperature rating, type, orifice size, area of coverage, use in special areas, spacing, and location of sprinklers.
5. The inspector should check to ensure water supplies for sprinklers are of sufficient capacity and pressure to satisfy the tabular requirements for pipe schedule systems or the calculated requirements for hydraulically designed systems.
6. The inspector should use flow tests to measure the pressure and flow available at the city main.
7. The inspector should check the total capacity of the water supply. (209)

SHORT ANSWER

25. A. The Plan View
    B. The Elevation View
    C. The Section View
    D. The Detailed View (192)

26. A. The Plan View is a two-dimensional view of the site or the building as seen from directly above the area. A plan view provides information concerning the overall layout of the site or building. The fire inspector will commonly review three basic plan views: the Site Plan, the Basement Plan, and the Floor Plan.
    - The Site Plan (plot plan), usually the first sheet of a set of drawings, identifies conditions currently existing on the site and relates information needed to locate the building. This information includes the north direction, the lot dimensions, utility lines (gas, water, sewer, power, and telephone), grade level, contour lines, structures to be removed, concrete walks and driveways, and areas to be landscaped. (193)
    - The Basement Plan shows the below-ground view of the building. The thickness and external dimensions of the basement walls are given, as are floor joists locations, strip footings, and other attached foundations. Since footings are hidden under the slab or the ground, they are displayed by broken lines.
    - The Floor Plan, like the basement plan, is viewed from the top. The floor plan provides information for constructing external walls, internal partitioning, doors and windows, ceiling and roof joists or trusses, cabinets, closets, shelving, electrical outlets, and fixtures. (194)

    B. The Elevation View is a two-dimensional view of the building as seen from the exterior. There are four exterior elevation views on any rectangular building. Elevation views contain information about the exterior components of the building, such as type of exterior finish or combinations of finishes, and location, sizes, and types of doors and windows. As in the site plan, an elevation view of the grade level is shown as a dark line. (195)

    C. Sectional View is a vertical view of a building as if it were cut into two parts. The purpose of a sectional view is to show the internal construction of each assembly. (198)

    D. The Detailed View is a close-up, detailed section or part of a drawing that relates additional specific construction information.

27. A. Horizontal — Cross section of the complete building from exterior wall to exterior wall and from foundation to roof.
    B. Typical — Cross section of a common construction feature, such as a wall.
    C. Detailed — Cross section of some construction feature to show exact detail. (198)
28. A. Accessibility refers to the ability of fire department apparatus to get close enough to the building during an emergency. Some of the things an inspector should check include: Access roadways should be wide enough to permit apparatus to operate and pass. There are no physical, topographical, or architectural obstructions on site. The intersections are looped to permit traffic flow and they are adequate turning radii. There are enough access roads within minimum building access distance. The surrounding grades are not too steep.
    B. Fire inspectors should determine if water is available in sufficient quantities and pressures to satisfy potential emergency demands. After inspectors have determined the minimum fire flows, they can verify the adequacy of the water supply by examining the type and location of hydrants (both public and private), pump systems, cross-connected water supplies, and the location and size of public water mains. Records of water flow testing performed in the area in question will be invaluable, assuming that they are recent and accurate. It is often necessary to use hydraulic calculations to verify the adequacy of water supplies. (201)
    C. Fire inspectors should review the general building parameters: location, occupancy, fire and land-use zones, property line clearances, and special hazards. It is important to determine the use of the building in order to assign an occupancy classification. The occupancy classification often dictates the total allowable area, maximum height, exposure protection, occupant load, necessity for fixed fire protection, and other factors unique to each building. Most cities have fire and land-use zones; therefore, fire inspectors must check to see that the building is located in the proper zones. During the exterior wall examination, the reviewer should determine if there is adequate property clearance to prevent fire spread. Finally, fire inspectors must identify any special hazards, such as tank installations or high-piled stock, and check for any corrections that are required. (201, 202)
29. Interior finishes, furnishings and decorations, insulation materials, and materials that produce smoke and toxic gases could be considered special hazards. (204)
30. The style and design of the heating, ventilating, and air conditioning (HVAC) system. The refrigerant used in the system should be checked for possible health or fire hazards. Fire inspectors should be familiar with code requirements concerning the automatic shutdown of heating systems to control the spread of fire and smoke. (206)
31. Usually, smoke control systems are used in buildings involving either a large number of people or that have a large quantity of combustibles such as shopping malls and buildings with open atriums. (206)
32. Exit stairwell pressurization is another method of smoke control. The intent of stairwell pressurization is to maintain a smoke-free atmosphere for occupants to exit during a fire. Stairwell pressurization systems must also be engineered and tested to ensure that the applied pressure does not make it difficult, if not impossible, for the average person to open stairwell doors. (206)

8

33. During the review of the electrical systems, the inspector must verify that illumination of exit ways is adequate. Exit illumination must be continuous during the time that the building is occupied. The stairs, aisles, corridors, ramps, escalators, and passageways leading to an exit must be lit. (206)
34. Plans for alarm systems should contain signal initiation, signal notification, supervision of alarm systems, power supply, elevator control, automatic door closers, stair pressurization, smoke control, damper control, initiation of automatic extinguishing equipment, fire pumps, doors that unlock automatically when the alarm activates, and lightning protection. (208)
35. These situations call for the use of halon, foam, carbon dioxide, or dry or wet chemical extinguishing systems. Fire inspectors should be familiar with each type of system and the applicable code requirements. The information should include the definition of the area or equipment to be protected; type of system (local application or total flooding); type of extinguishing agent being used; amount of agent required; concentration of extinguishing agent to be developed; storage container size; type of expellent gas; rate of discharge; duration of flow; location and type of piping included, whether engineered or pre-engineered; location and type of discharge nozzles; method of acutation and auxiliary alarm function such as shutting off ventilation; type of presignaling devices used, if required; and area and volume of the protected space. The architect should also include the calculation sheets or computer data sheets used to design the system. (209)
36. To review the alarm and detection system, fire inspectors need information from the specifications, floor plans, equipment list, and symbol list. The specifications should include the type and gauge of wire, protection provided for the wire (conduit or raceways), wiring methods, and methods of supervision. (212)
37. The inspector should check the plans to make sure all portable fire protection equipment required by the codes will be placed in the building. This includes hand-held fire extinguishers, axes, standpipe hoselines, and any other particular portable equipment that may be required. The inspector should check to see that all maximum travel distances to these pieces of equipment are within the distances set forth by the code and that the equipment to be placed in the building is of the proper type to protect the hazards found in the building. (212)
38. The plans review letter should contain the following:
    - Reviewer's name.
    - Name of the project.
    - Date review is started and completed.
    - Scope of work to be performed.
    - Description of the building and fire protection features to be provided.
    - Applicable codes that must be followed.
    - Comments as a result of the plans review.
    - Specific code references for each comment.

    The plans review letter should be clear and concise. Those who carry out plans review need some equipment and reference materials. These include an architect's scale, a calculator having scientific functions, a well-lit drawing table, the applicable code books, and design manuals. Code books and design manuals can be obtained from the model code organization, trade associations, manufacturers, and independent testing laboratories. (212)

39. The plans review should not be considered as the "final sign-off" for the certificate of occupancy. The final sign-off by the fire inspector can only be given after an official test of the fire protection equipment installed in the finished building is performed.(212)

Chapter 9 Answers

TRUE/FALSE

1. False (217)
2. False (219)
3. False (219)
4. True (221)
5. True (221)
6. True (223)
7. False (223)
8. True (224)
9. True (224)
10. True (224)
11. False (224)
12. True (224)
13. True (225)
14. True (225)
15. True (225)
16. True (225)
17. False (225)
18. True (225)
19. True (225)
20. True (226)
21. True (226)
22. True (227)
23. True (227)
24. False (227)
25. True (229)
26. True (229)
27. False (229)
28. False (230)
29. False (230)
30. False (231)
31. True (231)

MULTIPLE CHOICE

32. A (217)
33. B (217)
34. C (218)
35. A (218)
36. C (221)
37. B (222)
38. C (223)
39. D (225)
40. C (226)
41. A (226)
42. B (230)
43. D (230)

SHORT ANSWER

44. Fuel Gases:
    A. Liquefied Natural Gas
    B. Propane
    Industrial Gases:
    A. MEP gas, or acetylene
    B. Freon, or chlorine
    Medical Gases:
    A. Oxygen, or cyclopropane
    B. Nitrous Oxide (222)

45. A. Poisons
    B. Irritants
    C. Anesthetics (224)

46. The following are correct: sodium nitrate, potassium nitrate, ammonium nitrate, cellulose nitrate, nitric acid, ammonium nitrite, sodium peroxide, potassium peroxide, strontium peroxide, hydrogen peroxide, barium peroxide, benzoyl peroxide, potassium chlorate, potassium perchlorate, sodium chlorite, calcium hypochlorite, ammonium perchlorate, ammonium dischromate, sodium perchlorate, magnesium perchlorate, potassium permanganate, potassium persulfate, and perchloric acid. (225)

47. National Fire Codes — NFPA; U.S. Department of Transportation (DOT); Federal Emergency Management Agency (FEMA); Federal Bureau of Alcohol, Tobacco, and Firearms (BATF); Environmental Protection Agency; Coast Guard; Occupational Safety and Health Administration (OSHA); National Institute of Occupational Safety and Health (NIOSH); CHEMTREC (1-800-424-9300); National Response Center; Institute of Manufacturers of Explosives; Association of American Railroads; State Fire Marshal's Office; State or County Health Department; and Police Agencies. (217)

48. Class 1 — Explosives
Class 2 — Gases (compressed, liquefied or dissolved under pressure)
Class 3 — Flammable liquids
Class 4 — Flammable solids or substances
Class 5 — Oxidizing substances
5.1 Oxidizing substances or agents
5.2 Organic peroxides
Class 6 — Poisons and infectious substances
Class 7 — Radioactive substances
Class 8 — Corrosives
Class 9 — Miscellaneous dangerous substances (217)

49. Placards are diamond-shaped signs that are affixed to each side and to each end of any motor vehicle or rail carrier transporting hazardous materials. The placards must be used according to the DOT regulations for transportation of hazardous materials by motor vehicle or rail carrier. The placard indicates the primary Class of the hazard of the cargo and, in some cases, the specific hazardous material being transported. (218)

50. The Department of Transportation has issued the *DOT Emergency Response Guidebook (ERG)*. Its function is to complete the identification system. The ERG lists hazardous materials by both name and four-digit number. It also gives guidelines for the initial actions fire inspectors can take in handling an incident involving hazardous materials. (218)

51. This system is known as NFPA 704, *System for the Identification of the Fire Hazards of Materials*. The 704 label is diamond-shaped, like a placard, but is divided into four different colored sections, which denote health, flammability, reactivity, and special hazards. Blue is used for the health hazard, red for flammability, and yellow for reactivity. These three sections are further classified with a number from 0 to 4; 4 is the most hazardous and 0 is the least hazardous. The bottom section contains special information such as radiation hazard, reactivity with water, or polymerization. (219)

52. Class 1A flammable liquids have flash points below 73°F (22.8°C) and boiling points below 100°F (37.8°C).
Class IB flammable liquids have flash points below 73°F (22.8°C) and boiling points at or above 100°F (37.8°C).
Class IC flammable liquids have flash points at or above 73°F (22.8°C) and below 100°F (37.8°C). (219)
53. Class II combustible liquids have flash points at or above 100°F (37.8°C) and below 140°F (60°C).
Class IIIA combustible liquids have flash points at or above 140°F (60°C) and below 200°F (93.4°C).
Class IIIB combustible liquids have flash points at or above 200°F (93.4°C). (219)
54. Flash point refers to the minimum temperature at which a liquid fuel gives off sufficient vapors to form an ignitable mixture with the air near the surface. The fire point refers to the temperature at which a liquid fuel will burn continuously. (220)
55. The boiling point of a liquid is the temperature at which the vapor pressure of the liquid is equal to the external pressure applied to it. When this state of equilibrium exists, boiling occurs. The bubbles produced during boiling are bubbles of vapor that have formed within the liquid and are rising to the surface, where they can escape into the atmosphere. (220)
56. The specific gravity of a flammable or combustible liquid refers to the ratio of the weight of the liquid to an equal volume of water. Water is assigned a value of one. Liquids with specific gravities of less than one are therefore lighter than water and will float on water. Liquids with a specific gravity greater than one will cause water to float on their surface. (220)
57. The flammable and explosive limits of flammable or combustible liquids are the upper and lower concentrations of the vapor that will produce a flame at a given pressure and temperature. These limits are expressed as a percent of the vapors in the mixture with an oxidizer. (220)
58. The lowest concentration of vapors in an oxidant that will ignite is known as the lower explosive limit, or LEL. Mixtures below the LEL are said to be too lean to burn. The highest concentration of vapors in an oxidant that will ignite is known as the upper explosive limit, or UEL. Vapor concentrations above this point are said to be too rich to burn. Variations in temperature will affect explosive limits: when the temperature increases, the range will increase and when the temperature decreases, the range will decrease. (220)
59. When the temperature of a flammable or combustible liquid is raised, more vapors are emitted from the liquid. If the liquid is in a closed container, the pressure inside the container will increase. If the temperature rise is significant, the resulting pressure rise inside the container may be sufficient to rupture the container, often with explosive force. Such explosions are known as Boiling Liquid Expanding Vapor Explosions (BLEVEs). (220)
60. Compressed gases are those materials, at normal temperature, that exist as gases when pressurized within a container. In contrast, liquefied gases, at normal temperatures, exist in both liquid and gaseous state when pressurized in a container. (221)

61. Vapor density is the weight of a gas compared to the weight of air and is used to evaluate the relative weights of gases. Air is assigned a vapor density of one. Gases with vapor densities less than one will rise and can be expected to concentrate near the ceiling or form vapor clouds before they dissipate. Gases with vapor densities greater than one will descend and can be expected to concentrate near the floor and dissipate laterally. (222)

62. Charles' Law — If the volume of a gas is kept constant and the temperature is raised, the pressure will increase in direct proportion to the increase in temperature. This relationship is given by the formula: $P^1 T^1 = P^2 T^2$
    where P^1 = original pressure
    T^1 = original temperature
    P^2 = final pressure
    T^2 = final temperature (222)

63. Boyle's Law — The volume of gas will vary inversely with the applied pressure, if the gas is confined. This relationship can be shown by the formula: $P^1 V^1 = P^2 V^2$
    where P^1 = original pressure
    V^1 = original volume
    P^2 = final pressure
    V^2 = final volume (222)

64. A. The inherent hazard of the particular gas, which may be intensified when it is in liquid form.
    B. The tremendous liquid-to-vapor ratio.
    C. The extremely low temperatures (severe freeze burns). (222)

65. A. Pressure relief valve — a device that opens well below any pressure that would threaten the integrity of the tank.
    B. Frangible disk — ruptures if the pressure rise is excessive or if the pressure relief valve malfunctions.
    C. Safety vent in the insulation space — guards against leakage from the inner vessel. (223)

66. Corrosives are those chemicals that cause visible destruction or irreversible harm to skin tissue. Liquid corrosives that are leaking will also have a severe corrosion rate on steel. Corrosives may also be strong oxidizers; however, they are classified as corrosives because of their hazardous effect when someone inhales, ingests, or touches them. Examples of corrosives include inorganic acids (such as hydrochloric acid, nitric acid, sulfuric acid, hydrofluoric acid, and perchloric acid), halogens (such as bromine, iodine, fluorine, and chlorine), and several strong bases (such as sodium hydroxide, potassium hydroxide, calcium oxide, calcium hypochlorite, hydraxine, and hydrogen peroxide). (224)

67. Some of these materials, known as pyrophorics, will spontaneously ignite when exposed to air. Others may ignite or explode when exposed to small quantities of water. During such a reaction, the mass quantities of heat that are produced may lead to self-ignition or to the ignition of nearby combustibles. (224)

68. Unstable materials are those materials that are capable of undergoing chemical changes or decomposition in the presence of a catalyst or without a catalyst. These materials may spontaneously decompose, explode, polymerize, or react, often with violent results. Some of the more common unstable materials include the follow-

ing: acetaldehyde, ethylene oxide, hydrogen cyanide, benzoyl peroxide, nitromethane, ethyl acrylate, and iospropyl ether. (224)

69. A. Absorption
    B. Ingestion
    C. Injection
    D. Inhalation (225)

70. TLV is an acronym for Threshold Limit Value. This value is the concentration of a given toxic material that generally may be tolerated without ill effects. These values are important because they may serve as guides for fire inspectors in determining the maximum allowable concentration of a substance to which an individual may be repeatedly exposed without harmful effects. The inspector must check for proper ventilation in these areas, along with the adequacy of exit requirements. The action of these products under fire conditions and the products of combustion will also be noteworthy. (225)

71. A. American Conference of Governmental Industrial Hygienists (ACGIH)
    B. National Institute of Occupational Safety and Health (NIOSH). (225)

72. Acute toxicity refers to the effects caused by a single dose or exposure. Depending upon the inherent concentrations and rates of exposure, the effects may be as minor as a simple headache or as serious as death. Acute exposure can be found in any and every type of occupancy.

    Chronic toxicity refers to the effects of substances upon repeated exposure over a long period of time. Chronic exposure is most often found in industrial situations where toxic substances are part of a daily or regular process. (225)

73. LC_{50} refers to the concentration in the air of a given substance that killed 50% or more of the test animals when they inhaled or absorbed the vapors, fumes, or mists of the substance. (225)

74. LD_{50} refers to the ingested dose of a given substance that was lethal to 50% or more of the animals tested when they swallowed or ate the substance. (225)

75. A. Alpha Particles — Alpha radiation has the least amount of penetrability. It can be stopped by a sheet of paper. Outside the body, this type of radiation is relatively harmless. If dust containing alpha particles is inhaled or ingested it may cause severe sickness or death.
    B. Beta Particles — Beta radiation is more penetrating; beta particles can usually be stopped with a thin piece of sheet metal.
    C. Gamma Particles — Gamma particles have much greater penetration properties than alpha or beta particles and generally must be stopped by some type of lead shield. (226)

76. Thermoplastic materials have a tendency to melt and flow during a fire situation, thereby presenting an additional way for flames to spread. Thermoset materials tend to retain their shape when exposed to a fire. (226)

77. An explosive is any material or mixture that will undergo an extremely fast self-propagation reaction when subjected to some type of energy. This reaction produces heat and creates a sudden buildup of gas. The release of the gas pressure produces the explosive force. Explosive materials include explosives, water gels, and detonators. (227)

78. A. Primary or initiating high explosives are easily detonated by applying small amounts of heat, mechanical shock, or pressure. Their chief function is to initiate detonations in secondary high explosives. The major ingredients in primary explosives include but are not limited to lead azide, lead styphnate, and mercury fulminate. Electric blasting caps and detonating cord delay connectors are both examples of primary high explosives. (227)

    B. Secondary high explosives are much less sensitive to heat and mechanical shock but are considerably more powerful than primary explosives. Secondary explosives are usually detonated by use of primary explosives. Products such as TNT, nitroglycerin, and dynamite are considered to be secondary high explosives and can be found in commercial blasting and military operations. (227)

    C. Low explosives or propellants usually operate by deflagration (rapid burning) rather than by detonation. (Detonation is defined as the introduction of a combustion zone into an unreacted explosive medium.) Major propellants include such materials as solid rocket fuels, black powder, and smokeless powder. Under the proper conditions, some low explosives may detonate. (227)

79. The following are correct: Institute of Makers of Explosives (I.M.E.), New York, NY; Federal Bureau of Investigation, Bomb Data Center; International Association of Bomb Technicians and Investigators; E.I. DuPoint de Nemours, Wilmington, Delaware; Motorola Telecommunications; U.S. Army-Explosives Ordinance Disposal (E.O.D.); Bureau of Mines, U.S. Department of Interior; and Bureau of Alcohol, Tobacco, and Firearms, U.S. Department of the Treasury. (229)

80. Combustible metals include virtually all metals since almost all metals will burn under the right conditions. How easily they ignite depends upon the physical state of the metal. Finely divided particles, molten metal, or fine thin sections tend to ignite much more easily than those in more solid forms. In addition, powdered or flaked metals such as aluminum or magnesium can be explosive under certain conditions.

    The most commonly encountered combustible metals include the following: magnesium, titanium, sodium, lithium, potassium, hafnium, calcium, zinc, and sodium potassium alloys. (229)

81. The following are correct: hazards such as electric arcs, lights, friction sparks, static sparks, high pressure steam pipes, smoking materials, and open flames are all potential ignition sources and must be strictly controlled or eliminated. (230)

82. NFPA 70, *National Electrical Code*, and it should be rated for service in Class II, Division 1, or Class II, Division 2 locations. (230)

83. The following are correct: chemical composition of the fiber, the fabric finish, the weight of the fabric, the tightness of the weave, and any flame-retardant treatments. (231)

Chapter 10 Answers

TRUE/FALSE

1. True (239)
2. True (239)
3. False (240)
4. True (240)
5. False (240)
6. True (242)
7. True (242-243)
8. True (243)
9. True (244)
10. False (245)
11. False (246)
12. True (246)
13. True (246)
14. True (250)
15. True (251)
16. False (251)
17. False (251)
18. True (252)
19. True (252)
20. True (252)
21. False (253)
22. True (253)
23. True (256)
24. False (258)
25. True (259)
26. True (259)
27. True (259)
28. False (259)
29. True (259)
30. False (261)
31. True (261)
32. False (266)
33. True (267)
34. False (267)
35. True (267-268)
36. True (269)

MULTIPLE CHOICE

37. C (240)
38. C (240)
39. D (240)
40. B (240)
41. A (241)
42. A (241)
43. C (241)
44. A (241)
45. A (241)
46. B (242)
47. B (242)
48. C (243)
49. A (243-244)
50. A (244)
51. A (244)
52. D (246)
53. B (246)
54. C (249)
55. C (249)
56. C (250)
57. B (252)
58. A (252)
59. B (258)
60. B (258-259)
61. D (260)
62. A (260)
63. C (269)
64. B (270)
65. B (270)

SHORT ANSWER

66. A. Eliminating or excluding sources of ignition such as electrical, mechanical or frictional sparks; static electricity; open flames; hot surfaces; and incompatible materials.
    B. Excluding air (oxygen).
    C. Storing liquids in closed containers or systems.
    D. Ventilating to prevent the accumulation of vapors within the flammable range.
    E. Maintaining an atmosphere of inert gas instead of air (air will support combustion). (239)

67. A. Atmospheric tanks are designed for pressures of 0 to 0.5 psi (0 kPa to 3.5 kPa).
    B. Low-pressure storage tanks for pressures of 0.5 to 15 psi (3.5 kPa to 103 kPa).
    C. Pressure vessels for pressures greater than 15 psi (103 kPa). (240)
68. These tanks include those that are arranged in an irregular fashion or in rows of three or more, tanks that contain Class I or Class II liquids, and tanks that are in the drainage route of Class I or Class II liquids. (241)
69. In addition to normal venting, emergency venting is required for most aboveground tanks to prevent a Boiling Liquid Expanding Vapor Explosion (BLEVE). (241)
70. A. The opening pressure.
    B. The pressure at which the valve reaches the full open position.
    C. The accompanying flow capacity in cubic feet per hour (cubic meters per hour). (242)
71. A. Besides emergency relief provisions, all tanks or tank areas storing Class I, II, or IIIA liquids must have dikes or some form of drainage to prevent any leaks or accidental discharges from endangering nearby facilities, property, or waterways.
    B. If dikes are used, the volume of the diked area should be large enough to contain the entire amount that could be released from the largest tank.
    C. The walls of the dike should be liquidtight and can be constructed of steel, concrete, solid masonry, or earth. Dikes that are made of earth and that are 3 feet (1 m) or more high must have a 2-foot (0.6 m) wide, flat section at the top. Loose combustible materials, empty or full drums, and other items must be kept out of the diked area. (242)
72. Perhaps the simplest and most economical method of detecting leaks is to be sure that inventory is stringently controlled, taking into account unavoidable losses from evaporation, product shrinkage, and improper meter calibration. (245)
73. A. They may be left in the ground permanently. In this case, the fill line, gauge opening, pump suction, and vent lines are disconnected. The underground piping must be capped. The tank is then filled with an inert, solid material.
    B. The second method for safeguarding tanks involves removing them from the ground. All liquid must be removed from the tank lines. All inlets, outlets, and underground piping must be capped. If the tanks are to be disposed of as waste, they must be cleaned and rendered vapor-free. Holes should be made in the tanks so that they will be unfit for later use. (245-246)
74. DWELLING OCCUPANCIES/BUILDINGS CONTAINING THREE OR FEWER DWELLING UNITS should not store more than 25 gallons (95 L) of Class I or Class II liquids, or 60 gallons (227 L) of Class IIIA liquids.

    ASSEMBLY OCCUPANCIES/BUILDINGS CONTAINING MORE THAN THREE DWELLING UNITS may store no more than 10 gallons (38 L) of Class I and Class II liquids, or 60 gallons (227 L) of Class IIIA liquids. All liquids must be stored in approved cabinets and safety cans.

    OFFICE, EDUCATIONAL, AND HEALTH CARE OCCUPANCIES should store only the amount of flammable or combustible liquids needed for operation, maintenance, demonstrations, or treatment. In these facilities, the containers for Class I or Class II liquids must be approved safety cans holding no more than 2 gallons (8 L).

MERCANTILE OCCUPANCIES AND RETAIL STORES storing flammable or combustible liquids in areas accessible to the general public should store no more than the amount needed for displays or operating purposes. If the quantity of liquids exceeds certain limits, the excess must be stored in a room approved for storing flammable liquids. These limits are as follows:

60 gallons (227 L) of Class IA liquids
120 gallons (454 L) of Class IB liquids
180 gallons (680 L) of Class IC liquids
240 gallons (908 L) of Class II liquids
660 gallons (2 498 L) of combustible liquids
More than 240 gallons (908 L) of any combination of flammable liquids.

Containers in display areas may not be stacked more than 3 feet (1 m) high or two containers high unless they are stored on fixed shelving. The shelving should be sturdily constructed and arranged so that the containers stored on them cannot be easily knocked off.

WAREHOUSES AND BUILDINGS USED STRICTLY FOR STORING FLAMMABLE LIQUIDS AND LOCATED NO MORE THAN 50 FEET (15 m) FROM ANOTHER BUILDING OR PROPERTY LINE should have blank, exposed walls that are constructed of noncombustible materials with a fire-resistance rating of two hours or more. (247-248).

75. Generally, no more than 120 gallons (454 L). No more than 60 gallons (227 L) of the 120 gallons (454 L) can be Class I or Class II liquids, and no more than three metal storage cabinets may be located in the same fire area unless they are 100 feet (30.5 m) or more apart. (248-249)

76. A. *Balance system* has a highly specialized nozzle that provides a tight seal around the fill neck of the vehicle's fuel tank. This special nozzle has an interlock that must be pushed into the gasoline tank fill neck before the gasoline will flow. This interlock maintains a tight seal while the gasoline is being dispensed. Because of this tight seal, flammable vapors are not released into the atmosphere. (253-254)

    B. The *vacuum assist system* uses a small vacuum generator, which keeps the vapor return hose and piping under a slight negative pressure. If the dispensing nozzle and the gasoline tank fill neck are not tightly sealed, air is drawn into the vapor return hose. This keeps vapors from being released into the atmosphere. (255)

77. A. *Interstate level:* The U.S. Department of Transportation (DOT) through a number of its divisions regulates the interstate (between different states) transportation of flammable and combustible liquids.

    B. *Intrastate level:* Individual states regulate intrastate (within the state) transportation.

    C. *Within your local jurisdiction:* Usually the fire inspector may further regulate transportation. For example, local regulations may designate routes and times of delivery for some products, close some tunnels for certain products, or require that vehicles transporting certain liquids not be left unattended during loading or unloading. (256)

78. Fire officials assume jurisdiction. Depending upon the location of the leak or suspected leak, inspectors should use common sense and good judgment. They

10

should avoid causing panic by unwarranted evacuation or publicity. If there is a strong potential hazard to life or property, and if conditions warrant evacuation, law enforcement agencies can help with evacuation procedures and assist in crowd control. Planning is essential for these types of emergencies: lack of cooperation and coordination among all parties involved could result in increased risk to life and property. (256)

79. A. Inhabited subsurface structures such as basements, subways, and tunnels.
    B. Uninhabited substructures such as sewers, utility conduits, and observation wells near tanks.
    C. Groundwater such as drawn from wells, on or in surface water, or emerging from cuts or slopes in the earth. (256)

80. The area should be evacuated immediately. Law enforcement agencies should be notified to evacuate everyone in the endangered area and to prevent any further traffic from entering the area until it is determined safe. (256)

81. The following are correct:
    Fire Department — Personnel, specialized equipment, and materials.
    Police Department — Traffic and crowd control, evacuation, property protection, and investigation.
    Civil Preparedness — Communications, crowd control, evacuation, and radiological services.
    Public Works — Sand and other containment material, construction equipment, personnel, and maps of natural watershed areas; can also terminate utility service.
    Public Health — Water, air, soil monitoring, and poison control information.
    Building Department — Consultants on manufacturing locations. (257)

82. The following are correct:
    National Guard — Communications, crowd control, evacuation, transportation, radiological services, and helicopters.
    State Police and Sheriffs — Crowd and traffic control, accident investigation, evacuation, property protection, and communications.
    Public Health — Monitoring and testing of water, air, and soil for contamination treatment or injured personnel, access to hospitals, ambulances, and poison control centers.
    Environmental Protection — Access to cleanup contractors and to chemists, biologists, and other scientists with specialized knowledge of hazardous materials.
    Agriculture — Soil and water testing, knowledge of pesticides and fertilizers.
    Fire Marshal, Fire Academy and Universities — Training and advice in hazardous materials response and suppression, and use of specialized response equipment. (257)

83. The next step is to determine the source of the leak and to prevent any further liquid from escaping. (257)

84. The following are correct: gasoline service stations, automotive garages or agencies, airports, marinas, heating oil distributors, chemical companies, fleet operators such as taxicab companies, dairies, trucking companies, municipal garages, and any abandoned flammable or combustible liquid tanks. (257)

85. The following are correct:
    Notice the area around the fill pipes where the liquid is transferred. Note if the area is discolored or saturated, concrete is stained, or asphalt is disintegrated. Any of these can indicate repeated spills that may accumulate underground.
    Notice if the area aboveground shows signs of overfilling.
    Check pumping equipment for leaks. Use a combustible gas indicator when checking service station pumps. Open the cover of the unit just far enough to insert the probe. Also check the hose and the nozzle.
    Notice floor and street drain areas. Note if waste liquids have been dumped there.
    Look for signs of dumping waste liquids into any streams or bodies of water (flammable and combustible liquids are lighter than water and will float on the water's surface; furthermore, the contaminate will usually display an oily pattern of colors on the surface of water).
    Check for dead vegetation in the area that might indicate spillage or dumping.
    Use a combustible gas indicator and check underground cavities such as sewers, utility conduit, and telephone manholes.
    Check for any nearby steep cuts, excavations, or natural slopes for signs of liquid coming through the soil. (257-258)

86. A. Excessive pressures caused by the expansion of gases when they are heated.
    B. Actual combustion of the gases within the cylinder.
    C. Structural failure of the container caused by flame impingement on the container.
    D. Mechanical damage to the container, such as collision with another object. (260)

87. The following are correct: electrical arcs, hot surfaces, open flames, as well as operations involving cutting, welding, grinding, and use of impact tools. All electrical fixtures within the hazard area must be explosion proof. Lift trucks used within the hazard area should be electrically powered. The electrical equipment on the trucks should be designed, constructed, and assembled for use in atmospheres containing flammable vapors. Lift trucks rated for this service will have the symbol EX stamped on the unit. (260-261)

88. A. Accept only cylinders approved for use in interstate commerce for transportation of compressed or liquefied gases.
    B. Do not allow numbers or marks stamped on cylinders to be removed or changed.
    C. Do not allow cylinders to be dragged; however, they may be rolled on their bottom edge.
    D. Protect cylinders from cuts.
    E. Do not lift cylinders with an electromagnet.
    F. Do not drop cylinders or let them strike each other violently.
    G. Do not use cylinders for rollers, supports, or any purpose other than to contain gas.
    H. Do not tamper with safety devices on valves of cylinders. (261)

89. A. Failure to check cylinders on receipt for any problems.
    B. Storage and/or use of cylinders below ground level or in nonventilated or poorly ventilated areas. Leakage has resulted in flammable, toxic, corrosive, or asphyxiating atmospheres.

C. "Locking up" a connected (to cylinder) cutting torch head or instrument in a tool box cabinet. Leakage has allowed an explosive mixture to form.

D. Not understanding the properties of the gas or the type of cylinder and associated hardware being used. Forced fits, use of adapters, and incompatible metals have resulted in failure of the container.

E. Using transfer arrangements where differences in pressure and lack of check valves were not considered. Failure of the system or cross-contamination of incompatible materials has occurred.

F. Not following proper startup, shutdown, and purging procedures, resulting in hazardous mixtures of gases.

G. Turning a cylinder valve open very quickly, allowing the gas to expand and cool, and then quickly recompressing the gas, which heats it to a high temperature. Regulators and other devices have failed due to high temperature.

H. The presence of oil or grease in oxygen systems, which can cause an explosion.

I. Improperly lifting cylinders by the cap, or by using magnets or slings. Not securing cylinders properly or not using a cap. Cylinders have fallen and been damaged, resulting in failure.

J. Modifying a cylinder by welding legs, hooks, and so on. Cylinders have been weakened, resulting in failures.

K. Storing incompatible gases in the same area.

L. Storage or setup of cylinders in an area where poor housekeeping practices have allowed an accumulation of combustible materials. Cylinders have vented because they were involved in fire.

M. Neglected and old cylinders have corroded and failed, releasing their contents.

N. Using cylinders that have been abused, dented, arc struck, in a fire, have broken or bent valves, or are severely corroded. Weakened cylinders have failed during use.

O. Failing to ensure that all pressure system components are rated for the actual service pressure.

P. Failing to provide and/or maintain pressure relief devices with appropriate setting and adequate pressure relief capacity.

Q. Not wearing adequate protective clothing and equipment when transferring liquefied gases. Skin contact has caused severe burns due to cryogenic temperatures.

R. Failing to provide a separate relief device of sufficient capacity for each segment of a cryogenic system in which liquefied gas can be trapped or valved off.

S. Liquefied gas containers have failed after a fall and a ruptured disk on the inner wall and/or the safety relief on the outer container failed to operate. (**NOTE:** Liquefied gas containers are multi-walled and are not constructed as strong as high-pressure gas cylinders.)

T. Using instruments that have not been calibrated to test for explosive mixture, oxygen contents, and so on. False readings have contributed to various accidents. (262-263)

90. The *Code of Federal Regulations, Title 49 Transportation* details these regulations, including the requirements of the Department of Transportation (DOT) for transporting these gases by air, motor vehicle, rail, and to some extent, vessel. Fire inspectors should have a copy of this code available for reference. (264)

91. Step 1: Clear the building or area of all occupants.
    Step 2: Ventilate the affected portion of the building by opening windows and doors.
    Step 3: Use every practical means to eliminate ignition sources.
    Step 4: Terminate gas supply to the area.
    Step 5: Investigate other buildings in the immediate area to determine if gas is present.
    Step 6: Notify all personnel in the area (the danger of explosion and exposure hazards may require evacuation) and the gas supplier (from a telephone away from the gas area). (264-265)

92. The first objective in controlling leaks is to divert, dilute, and disperse the gas so that it does not infiltrate buildings or come into contact with people or ignition sources. The next objective is to stop the flow of gas. (265)

93. The basic technique is to evacuate the area, deny access, and cool the cylinder or container by applying large volumes of water. It is important to concentrate the streams of water on the upper portion of cylinder or tank, where the vapor space is. If cylinders cannot be cooled, firefighters should also be evacuated from the area because a rupture (BLEVE) can be expected. Compressed and liquefied gas fires are **NOT EXTINGUISHED** unless the escaping gas or liquid can be shut off because escaping gas presents an explosion hazard that is more serious than the fire hazard. (266)

94. Storage of combustible metals vary according to the applicable codes and the chemical properties of the metals. In general, storage buildings must be made of noncombustible materials and the stored metals should be separated from other combustible materials. Wet scrap and filings should be stored outside because there is always the possibility that they will generate hydrogen gas and ignite spontaneously. (266)

95. A. Combustible dusts are hazardous because of the possibility of a dust explosion. Fine particles of dust (even metal) can be easily ignited.
    B. Proper removal of combustible dust is essential to prevent explosions and fires. Vacuum cleaners and dust collection equipment remove dusts from their point of origin and deposit them in a safe location. Suction is applied at locations where dust escapes from processing machinery and the dust is conveyed to safe collection areas. Systems that convey combustible dusts should be designed so that the fans are on the clean side of the collector. (267)

96. Regulations concerning the manufacture, distribution, and storage of explosives are issued by the Bureau of Alcohol, Tobacco, and Firearms (BATF), which is part of the U.S. Department of the Treasury. Additional regulations are set forth by NFPA 495, *Manufacture, Transportation, Storage, and Use of Explosive Materials,* and may be enforced at the local level if they have been adopted as an ordinance. (268)

97. A. A Type 1 magazine is a permanent facility for the storage of explosive materials sensitive to initiation by a number 8 test blasting cap and will mass detonate. These magazines are fire resistant, weather resistant, theft resistant, and bullet resistant. Materials stored in Type 1 magazines include dynamite or nonelectric blasting caps.

B. A Type 2 magazine is a portable or mobile magazine used for outdoor or indoor storage of the same materials found in a Type 1 magazine. These facilities are fire resistant, theft resistant, weather resistant, and bullet resistant. Magazines used strictly for indoor storage need not be bullet resistant.

C. A Type 3 magazine is a portable facility for the temporary storage of explosive materials under constant attendance of a qualified employee. These facilities are bullet resistant, fire resistant, theft resistant, and weather resistant. Type 3 magazines must be secured by a five-tumbler padlock at all times.

D. A Type 4 magazine is a permanent, portable, or mobile magazine for storing explosives that will not detonate when initiated by a number 8 test blasting cap and that will not mass detonate. These facilities are fire resistant, theft resistant, and weather resistant.

E. A Type 5 magazine is a permanent, portable, or mobile magazine for storing explosive materials that will not detonate when initiated by a number 8 test blasting cap. These facilities include tanks, tank trailers, tank trucks, semitrailers, bulk trucks, and bins. These magazines are theft resistant, and outdoor magazines are also weather resistant. They must be secured with at least one case-hardened five-tumbler lock. If the magazine is vehicular, it must be immobilized when unattended. (268-269)

98. The initial responsibilities include the following: determining what materials are involved; determining the approximate amount of material; assessing hazards posed by resulting fires or spill; controlling access to the area; beginning evacuation of the surrounding area; rescuing trapped persons, if safely possible; implementing fire and spill control procedures; and preventing further damage to the environment. (271-272)

99. The following are correct:

Fire Department — Personnel trained in hazardous materials handling procedures, specialized equipment, and materials.

Police Department — Traffic and crowd control, evacuation, property protection, and investigation.

Emergency Civil Preparedness — Communications, crowd control, evacuation, and radiological services.

Public Works — Sand and other confinement material, construction equipment, personnel, and maps of streets, sewers, and natural watershed areas.

Public Health — Water, air, and soil monitoring, and poison control information.

Building Department — Consultants on manufacturing locations and structural damage.

Public Utilities — Gas, electric, water, sewer, and so on. (272)

100. The following are correct:

National Guard — Communications, crowd control, evacuation, transportation, radiological services, and helicopters.

State Police and Sheriffs — Crowd and traffic control, accident investigation, evacuation, property protection and communications. (**NOTE:** in some states, they are in charge of handling the incident.)

Public Health — Monitoring and testing of water, air, and soil for contamination, treatment of injured personnel, access to hospitals, poison control centers, toxicologists, and hygienists.

Environmental Protection — Access to chemists, biologists, and other scientists with specialized knowledge of hazardous materials, and knowledge of cleanup contractors.

Agriculture — Soil and water testing, knowledge of pesticides and fertilizers.

Fire Marshal, Fire Academy, and Universities — Training and advice in hazardous materials response and suppression, and the use of specialized response equipment.

State Sponsored Hazardous Material Response Teams — To bolster the capabilities of local responders. (272)

101. The following are correct:
Department of Transportation (DOT) — Responsibility for regulating air, rail, ship, highway, and pipeline transportation. Of its various agencies, the following are especially important to emergency response:

Materials Transportation Bureau (MTB) — Ensures uniform implementation of movement of hazardous materials by highway, rail, water, and air.
Federal Highway Administration (FHWA) — Highway safety, under the supervision of FHWA, is carried out by the Bureau of Motor Carrier Safety (BMCS). The BMCS serves to enforce proper loading, packaging, labeling, handling, and transportation of hazardous materials.
Federal Railroad Administration (FRA) — Oversees all railway activities in the United States. Officials from the FRA inspect hazardous materials, track, equipment, signals, train controls, and operations.

National Response Center — Site emergencies involving significant chemical releases should be coordinated with federal response organizations. The federal government has established a National Contingency Plan (NCP) to promote the coordination and direction of federal and state response systems, and to encourage the development of local government and private capabilities to handle emergencies involving chemical releases.

United States Coast Guard (USCG) — All waterways, ports, and shipping by water are the responsibility of the USCG. Anyone loading, discharging, storing, or transporting hazardous materials must obtain the appropriate permit from the USCG. The USCG also provides information on the chemical and physical properties of hazardous materials through its Chemical Hazards Response Information System (CHRIS). The system includes a four-volume manual, a regional contingency plan, the Hazard Assessment Computer System (HACS), and a response team. The four-volume set is as follows:

Volume 1: *A Condensed Guide to Chemical Hazards*
Volume 2: *The Hazardous Chemical Data Manual*
Volume 3: *The Hazard Assessment Handbook*
Volume 4: *Response Methods Handbook*

National Transportation Safety Board (NTSB) — The sole function of the NTSB is to conduct investigations and safety studies on accidents involving all forms of transportation. The NTSB is independent of the DOT and reports directly to the Executive Branch.

10

Environmental Protection Agency (EPA) — Water and air quality, solid waste, and pesticides are the primary concerns of the EPA. The EPA has the Oil and Hazardous Materials Technical Assistance Data System (OHMTADS) which includes chemical, biological, toxicological, and commercial data on more than 1,000 chemicals.

Department of Energy (DOE) — The DOE, under the Federal Radiological Monitoring and Assistance Plan (FRMAP), assists with planning and responses involving radioactive materials.

Nuclear Regulatory Commission (NRC) — The primary purpose of the NRC is to license and regulate radioactive materials. NRC allows DOT to regulate the transportation of radioactive materials, but the DOT and the NRC together have established regulations controlling packaging, labeling, handling, loading, and storing of radioactive materials. (272-274)

Case Study 1 Answers

1

1.1 Experienced inspectors should realize that when building management refuses inspection there usually is something to hide.

Proper action would be to make a second call requesting permission for inspection. If once again refused, building management should be advised that legal measures (obtaining a warrant) would be pursued, if necessary, to gain entry for inspection.

1.2 The first step should be (during the afternoon inspection) to determine if the limitation of 175 people is justifiable, that is, was the calculation of the allowable occupancy correct?

If the calculation is correct, requirement for *immediate* limitation of occupancy to 175 should be presented to management, based upon imminent danger to the building occupants. This is a situation that is easily correctable and should not warrant a two-week grace period unless required by law.

Fire inspectors should be discouraged from making "off-duty unofficial inspections." The inspector has no authority in such situations; furthermore, personal liability problems may be increased.

1.3 After the fire, the courts will decide who is responsible. Both the municipality and the inspector should expect to be named as possible responsible parties because they permitted a known hazard to continue in existence after discovery.

Proper procedure in this case, if permitted under the law, would have been to instruct the management to immediately correct the problem. This order should have been followed up that evening (as an official inspection). If the occupancy was still overloaded, the facility should have been closed. Assistance from the local law enforcement agency may have been required.

Case Study 2 Answers

2

2.1 Prior to the inspection, community laws and ordinances pertaining to such activities must be reviewed, particularly with respect to which codes and standards can be enforced. Once these are identified, the pertinent sections of these documents must be reviewed. It would make the inspection more efficient if a checklist of important things to look for was created.

2.2 The response to this situation always depends upon existing laws and ordinances within a community. Effective fire codes within a jurisdiction should provide the owner with no other option than compliance in this obviously dangerous situation. It should be politely but firmly emphasized to the owner that his/her options are closure or compliance. Of course, written documentation of the violation and citations are imperative.

2

2.3 Documentation must include detailed descriptions of the situation at the plant, ordinances and codes violated, and the recommended corrective action.

Documented evidence that the above information was provided to plant management.

You must be prepared to be abused by the opposing attorney, but your demeanor must be professional and controlled at all times. Anger, sarcasm, vulgarity, etc. are out of place. Rely upon the advice of the city attorney when possible.

2.4 Operation E.D.I.T.H. published by the NFPA, and home escape plans furnished by other departments will be of assistance. Promote quick escape, good communications, and safety.

3

Case Study 3 Answers

3.1 I. THE COMBUSTION PROCESS

- A. Sources of Heat Energy
  1. Chemical
  2. Electrical
  3. Mechanical
  4. Nuclear
- B. The Fire Triangle — (Use an Illustration)
  1. Oxygen/Heat/Fuel
- C. The Fire Tetrahedron — (Use an Illustration)
  1. Fire Triangle w/Chemical Chain Reaction
- D. Phases of Fire
  1. Incipient
  2. Free Burning
     - a. Steady State
     - b. Clear Burning
  3. Hot Smoldering
- E. Heat Transfer
  1. Conduction (Use an Illustration)
  2. Convection (Use an Illustration)
  3. Radiation (Use an Illustration)

II. FIRE HAZARDS

- A. Types of Fire Hazards
  1. Common
  2. Special
- B. Levels of Hazards
  1. Low
  2. Ordinary
  3. High Hazard

3

3.2 The paint and body shop would contain painting, flammable liquids and welding, both of which are special hazards. The service department could also be a special hazard area due to cutting and welding of mufflers and exhaust systems, and the washing of parts with flammable liquids. In addition, the cars always contain flammable liquids. Other areas in the new facility, including the snack bar, should qualify as common hazard areas.

Case Study 4 Answers

4

4.1 The duties of the fire inspector at these functions are as follows:

- Check the files to see when the last regular fire safety inspection of the premise was made and review the recommendations that were made. If the premise is past due for inspection or there were major problems, a complete fire safety inspection should be made.
- Check with the person in charge and determine if any hazardous event or display (in terms of fire safety) will take place. If so, the inspector should receive a detailed briefing describing exactly what is proposed. The inspector can then determine if the display will be allowed or what special precautions, if any, are necessary.
- Check equipment brought in to be sure that it meets code requirements and, where appropriate, that the equipment is of an approved type.
- Check the "temporary" wiring used for the event.
- Be sure that all exits are unlocked and the exit lights are on.
- Check emergency lights to be sure they are working.
- Work with the building management to be sure that the occupancy limit is not exceeded.
- Just before the event begins, have an announcement made calling attention to the location of exits.
- Keep aisles open. Prevent people from standing or sitting in the aisles.
- If smoking is not allowed, enforce this rule.
- In case of any significant fire, transmit an immediate alarm, then direct an orderly evacuation. Make special efforts to control panic.
- Strategic fire planning should be considered for the entire area.
- Check accessibility within fairgrounds for fire apparatus.
- Also evaluate the existing fire suppression systems for their adequacy to protect the incoming event. This would include evaluation of sprinkler systems and standpipe and hose systems for their operability and adequacy.

5

Case Study 5 Answers

5.1 I. Why is construction regulation necessary?
- A. Provides reasonable safety to building occupant
- B. Property preservation and prevention of fire
- C. Safety of firefighters

II. Why are construction classifications used?
- A. For establishing height limitations
- B. For establishing area limitations
- C. For limiting use of buildings (ex: hospitals not permitted in Type V buildings)
- D. For the basis of the requirement of various fire systems

III. Identify the building code used in the local community and basic requirements of the code.
- A. Construction classifications systems
- B. Height and area limits
- C. Occupancy classification system
- D. Impact of automatic sprinkler on code requirements

5.2 I. Ratings established by nationally recognized laboratories.
- A. Underwriters Laboratories
- B. Factory Mutual

II. Ratings based upon standardized test procedures published.
- A. NFPA
- B. UL
- C. ASTM
- D. ANSI

III. Ratings are measures of relative performance in a standard test, not prediction of real life performance.

IV. Summary of most common test methods.
- A. Steiner Tunnel Test
- B. Fire Tests on Walls
- C. Fire Tests on Roofs

Case Study 6 Answers

6.1 A. The occupancy will qualify as a Class B Assembly Occupancy (Class B because it is between a 300 and 1,000 occupancy load).

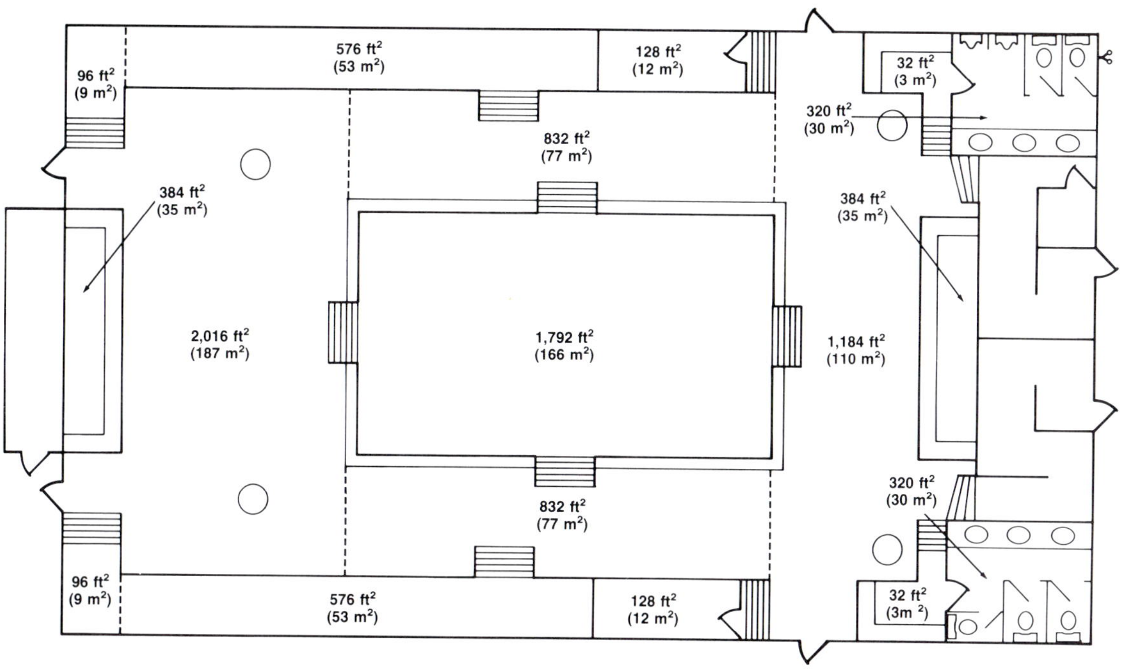

Figure 6.1

B. Occupant load should be established based upon net floor area in assembly areas. In cases where subtractable areas such as closets or restrooms are difficult to establish, gross area can be used as the worst possible circumstances. In this building:

Gross Area = (140 x 80) = 11,200 square feet; however,
(32 x 56) = 1,792 square feet is used for a dance floor.

Occupancy load calculations become:

(11,200 - 1,792) / (15 sq.ft/per person) = 627 people
1,792 / (7 sq.ft./person) = 256 people

$$\begin{array}{r} 627 \text{ people} \\ + \underline{256 \text{ people}} \\ 883 \text{ people} \end{array}$$

Metric Equivalent:
Gross Area = (43 x 24) = 1 041 m^2
(9.8 x 17) = 167 m^2 is used for a dance floor

6

Occupancy load calculations become:

$1\,041 - 167\ m^2 / 1.4\ m^2$ per person = 624 people
$167 / .6\ m^2$/person = 278

$$\begin{array}{r} 624 \text{ people} \\ +\ \underline{278 \text{ people}} \\ 902 \text{ people} \end{array}$$

NOTE: If *actual* net area were calculated, the permissible occupant load would be somewhat less than this.

Using the alternative method, the "Unit of Exit Width Method," the following results are obtained:

Since the "maze" entrance is *not* countable, the remaining 4 exits constitute 8 exit widths (48 inches, or 2 units each). Since 1 unit of level egress can accommodate 100 people, the occupant load is first calculated to be 800. However, Chapter 8 of NFPA 101 requires a "main" exit be designated and have a capacity of one-half the occupant load. Therefore, since all countable exits have a capacity of only 200 people, the calculated occupant load under this method is only 400 people (2 x 200).

C. As this occupancy exists, more than 400 people should not be permitted inside this building.

D. Adequate emergency lighting must be provided as well as proper, distinct marking of all exits. If those two items are not accomplished, consideration must be given toward prohibiting occupancy.

E. The "maze" exit at the main entrance is not acceptable because such design will contribute to confusion. In addition, NFPA 101 requires a main exit, and this main exit must be capable of accommodating 50 percent of the occupant load. For this reason, the maze should be eliminated and no less than 4½ units of exit width provided at the main entrance. (NFPA 101, 2-5 and 8-2.3.2)

F. The four freestanding fireplaces pose a problem in conjunction with what appears to be extensive use of Class C interior finish. Also, NFPA 101 prohibits the use of open flame devices in assembly occupancies. Their use in this situation should be prohibited. (NFPA 101, 31-2.3).

G. Handrails will be required. Since the stairs exceed 88 inches (2 235 mm) wide, a center rail will be required in addition to the rails along the edge. (NFPA 101, 5-2.2.6.1).

H. Special attention needs to be paid to the electrical wiring to make sure it meets all requirements of NFPA 70, and the sprinkler system should be evaluated to determine if the design and installation complies with NFPA 13.

I. The best feature is that the building is protected by automatic sprinklers. The worst feature is that little regard has been given to complying with NFPA 101. Instead of considering whether the permissible occupant load should be increased, the authority having jurisdiction should be considering whether it should be allowed to continue in operation.

Case Study 7 Answers

7

7.1 A. Industrial Occupancy with High Hazards.

B. Location and types of extinguishers required.

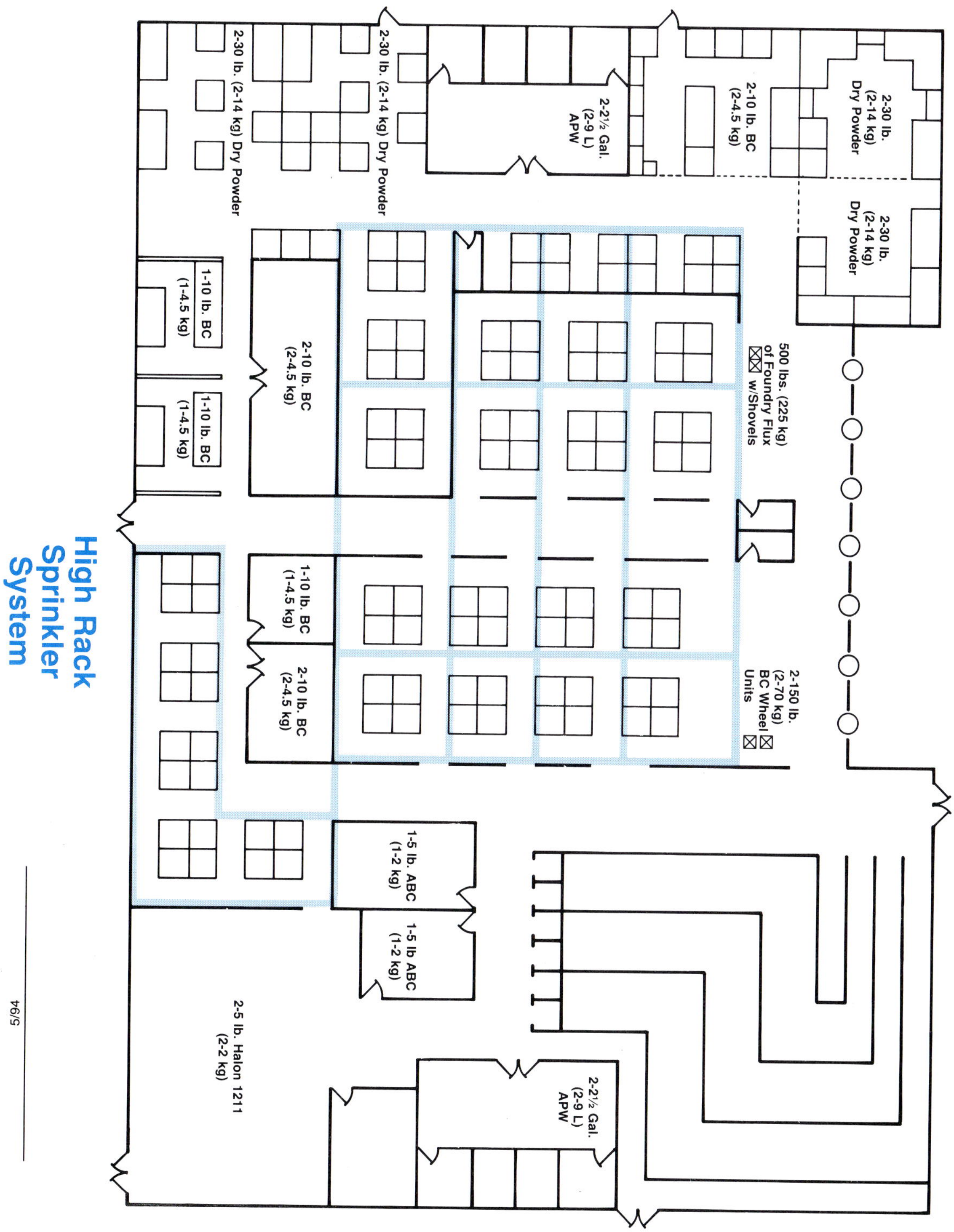

5/94

8

Case Study 8 Answers

8.1 A. The pressure is the same at all hydrant locations.

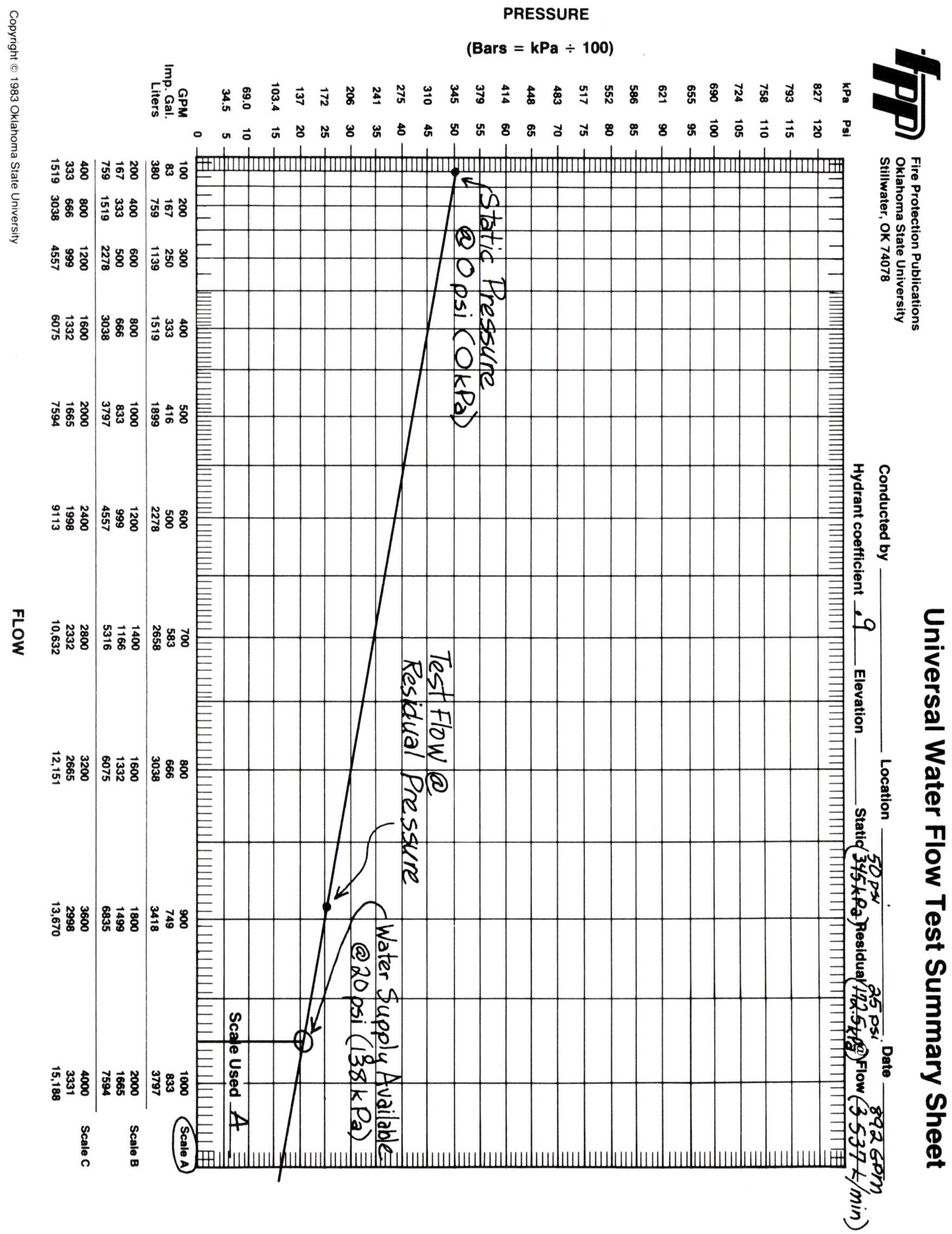

8

B. Based on the available information, the roadways and driveways appear to be wide enough. Very little information on the base or construction of the roadways, driveways, or parking lots is given; however, we can probably safely assume that the driveways will be strong enough since the company plans to bring tractor-trailers around to the loading dock on the pavement. However, parking lots are notorious for being "thin skinned." This area should be examined further. Also, information needs to be provided on the arrangement of vehicles in the parking lots to determine whether emergency vehicles will be able to maneuver within them during peak loads.

Case Study 9 Answers

9

9.1 PART ONE

A. NFPA 1: 1-3.4 and 1-7.2

B. This could be a Labor Department problem; although, if you have reason to believe that the occupancy is a fire hazard (NFPA 1-8.1) appropriate action could be taken.

C. Make an appointment with the manager requesting the inspection during normal business hours. Do not expose the caller. Notify other interested agencies.

9

PART TWO - Chart 9.1

CHART 9.1 — Chemicals used in REHAZMAT Inc.

Chemical	Health	Flam	React	Extra	State	Rm #	St#
Ammonia	3	1	0	___	Liq	111	14
Acetic Acid	2	2	1	___	Liq	116	12
Amyl Nitrate	2	2	0	oxy	Liq	105	11
Bromopropyne	4	3	4	___	Liq	205	13
Hydrogen Peroxide ›52%	2	0	3	oxy	Liq	214	14
Isopropyl Alcohol	1	3	0	___	Liq	204	24
Hydrochloric Acid	3	0	0	___	Liq	112	23
Sulfuric Acid	3	0	2	W	Liq	109	10
Turpentine	1	3	0	___	Liq	204	15
Chloroform	2	0	0	___	Liq	204	22
Diethyl Ether	2	4	1	___	Liq	108	25
Perchloric Acid	3	0	3	W	Liq	112	26
Nitric Acid	3	0	0	oxy	Liq	116	27
Phosphorus	3	3	4	___	Sol	216	29
Picric Acid	2	4	4	___	Sol	116	30
Sodium Nitrate	1	0	0	oxy	Sol	218	31
Aluminum Chloride	3	0	2	W	Sol	218	32
Aluminum	0	1	1	___	Sol	103	9
Lithium	1	1	2	W	Sol	109	8
Zinc	0	1	1	___	Sol	102	7
Zirconium	1	4	1	___	Sol	102	17
Sodium	3	1	2	W	Sol	104	18
Magnesium	0	1	2	W	Sol	104	20
Potassium	3	1	2	W	Sol	104	19
Chlorine	3	0	0	oxy	Gas	202	1
Butane	1	4	0	___	Gas	111	2
Acetylene	1	4	3	___	Gas	110	3
Formaldehyde	2	4	0	___	Gas	110	4
Cyanogen	4	4	2	___	Gas	205	5
Ethene	1	4	2	___	Gas	203	6

PART THREE

Refer to NFPA 49 to determine the hazards associated with this group of chemicals.

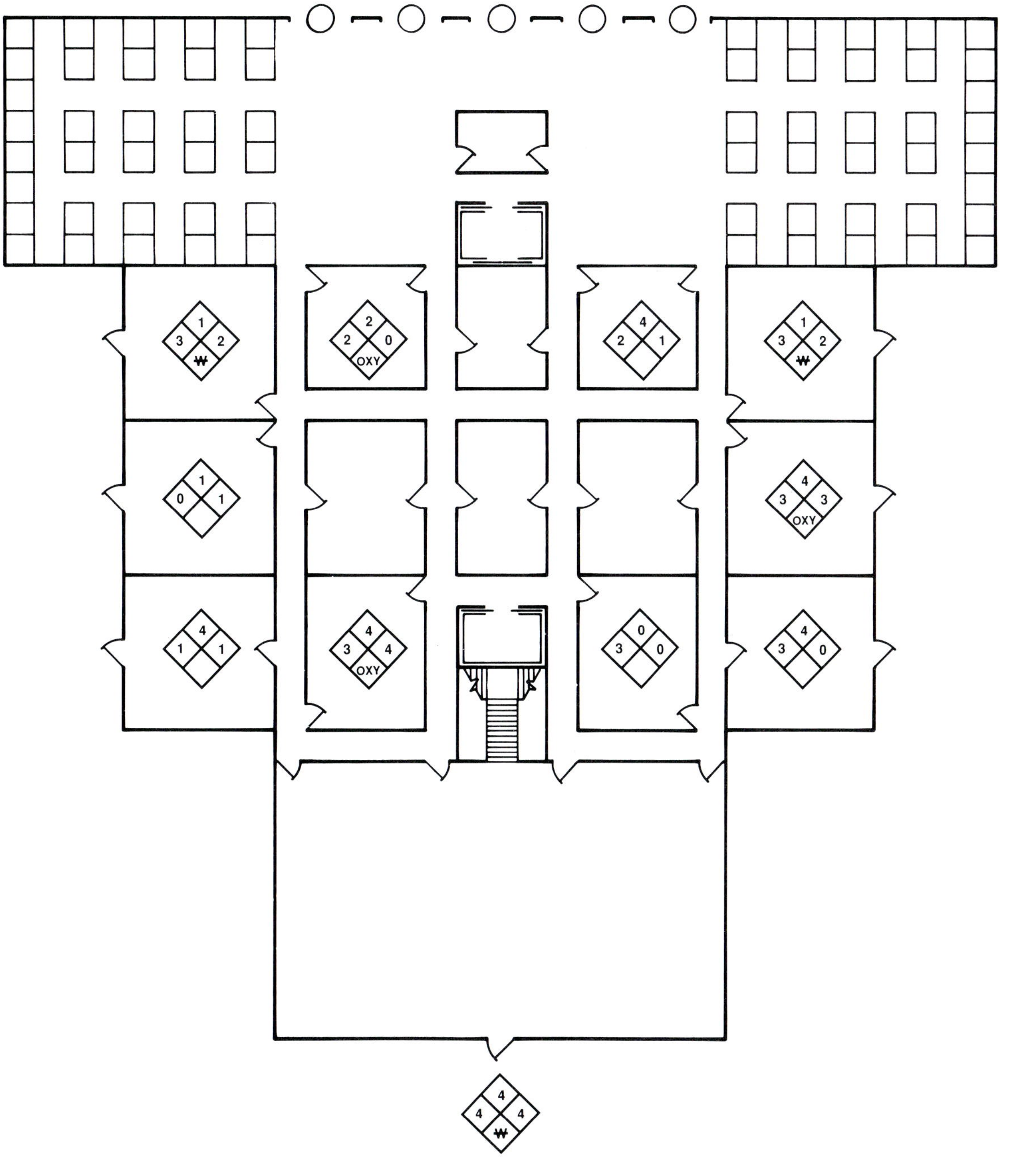

Figure 9.1 Ground Floor.

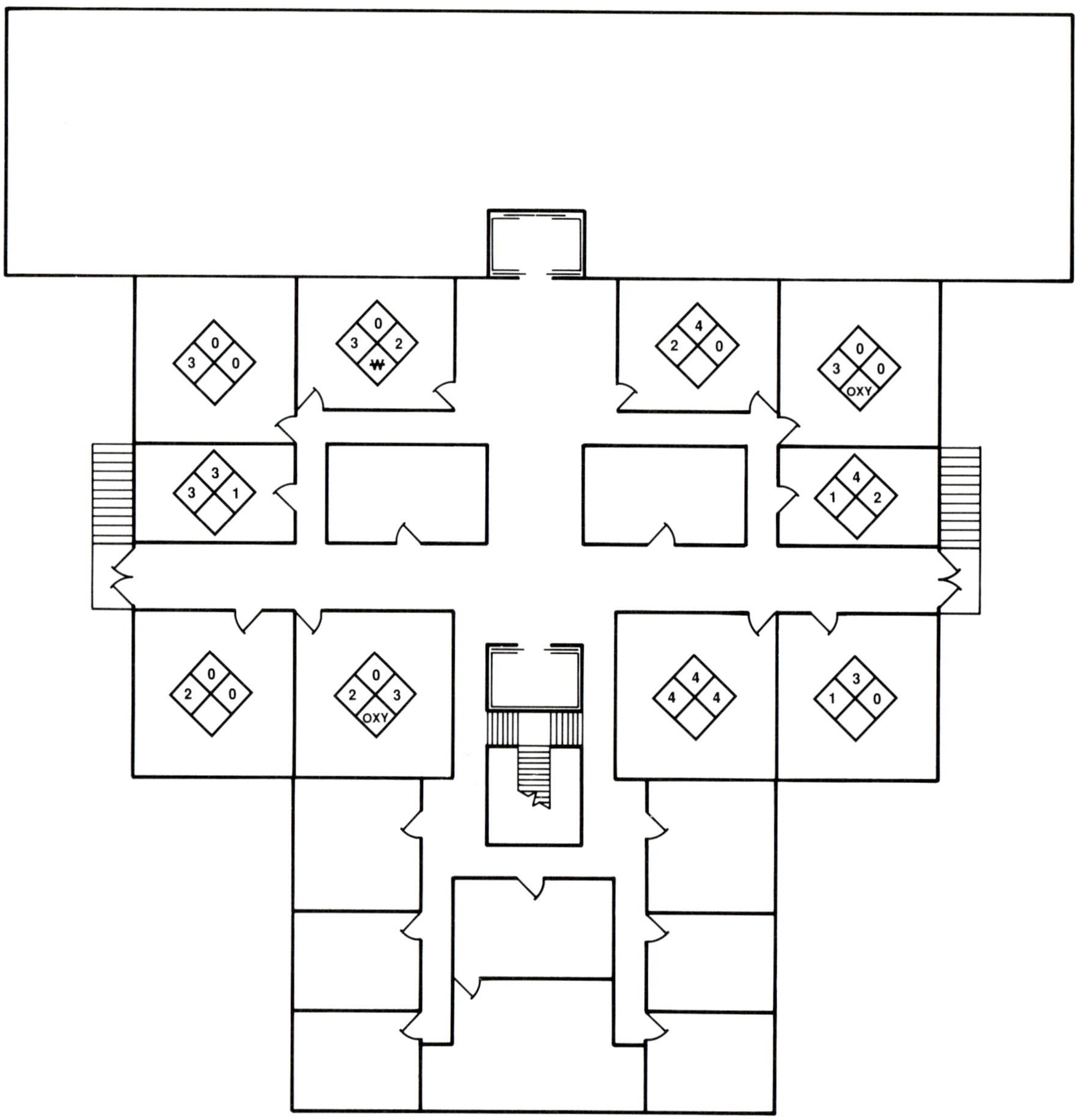

Figure 9.1 Second Floor.

Case Study 10 Answers

10

10.1 PART ONE

Refer to NFPA 49 to determine the common storage and shipping containers associated with this group of chemicals.

PART TWO

Below is a partial list of possible problems, there could be others.

- Room 217 is above Room 104 — Potassium reacts violently with Carbon Tetrachloride (if leakage should occur and flows through floor).
- Second floor is sprinklered. Rooms 104 and 109 are nonwater areas. If sprinkler system is activated, rooms 104 and 109 would suffer water damage. Violent reaction would occur and possible explosion would result.
- Room 205 contains Cyanogen. It is heavier than air. If leakage occurs, flammable gas would travel down atrium and collect throughout ground floor — Possible explosion.
- Room 110 contains Chlorine and Acetylene. If these two chemicals mix, Acetylene Chloride (a spontaneous explosive) is formed.
- Room 205 — Cyanogen is heavier than air. If leakage occurs, fumes could travel down the atrium into rooms 116 or 112 (both rooms contain acids). Reacts to produce highly toxic fumes.
- If fire should occur in Rooms 108, 110, or 111 (all extremely flammable), Rooms 201, 203, or 205, respectively, are directly above and are also extremely flammable (3 or 4 ratings) and could pose an additional hazard.
- Room 116 — The Picric Acid could form a highly sensitive explosive compound with Zinc in Room 102. Advise manager.
- Room 116 — Acetic Acid is dangerous if it comes in contact with Nitric Acid. Separate the two chemicals into different rooms.
- Room 110 — Acetylene is lighter than air. If leakage occurs, gas would travel up through atrium and find an ignition source.
- Room 109 — Sulfuric Acid should not be in the same lab as Lithium.
- Room 109 — Protected by Halon 1301. Lithium should not be exposed to halogenated hydrocarbons.
- Room 104/109 — Contents should be on the same side of the building to protect those chemicals best from any type of moisture.
- Room 116/214 — Acetic Acid is dangerous if it comes in contact with oxidizing materials (hydrogen peroxide).
- Room 218 — The Aluminum Chloride is located in the sprinklered part of the building.
- Room 108 — The Diethyl Ether is located next to the elevator. If the elevator motors are installed on bottom of the building, ether vapor could travel to the elevator motors and ignite. Ensure the motors are installed above this level.

- Room 202/203 – The vapors of these two chemicals could mix causing a spontaneous explosion.
- Chemical odors in building suggest improper ventilation or uncontained chemicals. Check venting system and containment systems.

PART THREE

This model example of a standard field trip report suggests how to organize information under five main headings: Summary, Assignment Details, Accomplishments, Problems, and Follow-up Action. Headings may be omitted from very short reports.

Summary

A short opening statement used to introduce the body of the report. It should include needed background information, accomplishments, deficiencies, and highlights; basically any significant outcome.

Assignment Details

State the purpose of the trip and include specific information that the reader may want to know. If the information is too involved or complex to write as a single paragraph, use subheadings such as:

Purpose of Trip
Specific Background
Project No./Authority
Personnel Involved
Date(s) of Trip

Accomplishments

Describe all work that was completed. The standard method of presentation is chronological unless more than one project or inspection is involved, in which case describe each project separately (but still maintain a chronological order for each project). Keep it short: do not describe routine work at great length if it ran smoothly.

Problems

Describe problems in detail, discussing problems encountered and how they should be or are being corrected. The information might be used as legal documentation in the future, it must be specific. Whenever possible, refer to codes used within the jurisdiction, or work instructions, references, or specifications. Attach them to your report if you deem necessary.

Follow-up Action

This section of the report ties up any loose ends by telling readers what still remains to be done. Any violations or unfinished work should be mentioned. Even though it may have been mentioned in one of the other headings, it is appropriate to restate the problem. Identify what needs to be done, indicate how and when it should be done, and include names of those whose responsibility it now becomes.

IFSTA MANUALS AND FPP PRODUCTS

For a current catalog describing these and other products, call or write your local IFSTA distributor or Fire Protection Publications, IFSTA Headquarters, Oklahoma State University, Stillwater, OK 74078-0118. Phone: 1-800-654-4055

FIRE DEPARTMENT AERIAL APPARATUS

includes information on the driver/operator's qualifications; vehicle operation; types of aerial apparatus; positioning, stabilizing, and operating aerial devices; tactics for aerial devices; and maintaining, testing, and purchasing aerial apparatus. Detailed appendices describe specific manufacturers' aerial devices. 1st Edition (1991), 386 pages, addresses NFPA 1002.

STUDY GUIDE FOR AERIAL APPARATUS

The companion study guide in question and answer format. 1991, 140 pages.

AIRCRAFT RESCUE AND FIRE FIGHTING

comprehensively covers commercial, military, and general aviation. All the information you need is in one place. Subjects covered include: personal protective equipment, apparatus and equipment, extinguishing agents, engines and systems, fire fighting procedures, hazardous materials, and fire prevention. Over 240 photographs and two-color illustrations. It also contains a glossary and review questions with answers. 3rd Edition (1992), 247 pages, addresses NFPA 1003.

BUILDING CONSTRUCTION RELATED TO THE FIRE SERVICE

helps firefighters become aware of the many construction designs and features of buildings found in a typical first alarm district and how these designs serve or hinder the suppression effort. Subjects include construction principles, assemblies and their resistance to fire, building services, door and window assemblies, and special types of structures. 1st Edition (1986), 166 pages, addresses NFPA 1001 and NFPA 1031, levels I & II.

CHIEF OFFICER

lists, explains, and illustrates the skills necessary to plan and maintain an efficient and cost-effective fire department. The combination of an ever-increasing fire problem, spiraling personnel and equipment costs, and the development of new technologies and methods for decision making requires far more than expertise in fire suppression. Today's chief officer must possess the ability to plan and administrate as well as have political expertise. 1st Edition (1985), 211 pages, addresses NFPA 1021, level VI.

SELF-INSTRUCTION FOR CHIEF OFFICER

The companion study guide in question and answer format. 1986, 142 pages.

FIRE DEPARTMENT COMPANY OFFICER

focuses on the basic principles of fire department organization, working relationships, and personnel management. For the firefighter aspiring to become a company officer, or a company officer wishing to improve management skills, this manual helps develop and improve the necessary traits to effectively manage the fire company. 2nd Edition (1990), 278 pages, addresses NFPA 1021, levels I, II, & III.

COMPANY OFFICER STUDY GUIDE

The companion study guide in question and answer format. Includes problem applications and case studies. 1991, 243 pages.

ESSENTIALS OF FIRE FIGHTING

is the "bible" on basic firefighter skills and is used throughout the world. The easy-to-read format is enhanced by 1,600 photographs and illustrations. Step-by-step instructions are provided for many fire fighting tasks. Topics covered include: personal protective equipment, building construction, firefighter safety, fire behavior, portable extinguishers, SCBA, ropes and knots, rescue, forcible entry, ventilation, communications, water supplies, fire streams, hose, fire cause determination, public fire education and prevention, fire suppression techniques, ladders, salvage and overhaul, and automatic sprinkler systems. 3rd Edition (1992), 590 pages, addresses NFPA 1001.

STUDY GUIDE FOR 3rd EDITION OF ESSENTIALS OF FIRE FIGHTING

The companion learning tool for the new 3rd edition of the manual. It contains questions and answers to help you learn the important information in the book. 1992, 322 pages.

PRINCIPLES OF EXTRICATION

leads you step-by-step through the procedures for disentangling victims from cars, buses, trains, farm equipment, and industrial situations. Fully illustrated with color diagrams and more than 500 photographs. It includes rescue company organization, protective clothing, and evaluating resources. Review questions with answers at the end of each chapter. 1st Edition (1990), 365 pages.

FIRE CAUSE DETERMINATION

gives you the information necessary to make on-scene fire cause determinations. You will know when to call for a trained investigator, and you will be able to help the investigator. It includes a profile of firesetters, finding origin and cause, documenting evidence, interviewing witnesses, and courtroom demeanor. 1st Edition (1982), 159 pages, addresses NFPA 1021, Fire Officer I, and NFPA 1031, levels I & II.

FIRE SERVICE FIRST RESPONDER

provides the information needed to evaluate and treat patients with serious injuries or illnesses. It familiarizes the reader with a wide variety of medical equipment and supplies. **First Responder** applies to safety, security, fire brigade, and law enforcement personnel, as well as fire service personnel, who are required to administer emergency medical care. 1st Edition (1987), 340 pages, addresses NFPA 1001, levels I & II, and DOT First Responder.

FORCIBLE ENTRY

reflects the growing concern for the reduction of property damage as well as firefighter safety. This comprehensive manual contains technical information about forcible entry tactics, tools, and methods, as well as door, window, and wall construction. Tactics discuss the degree of danger to the structure and leaving the building secure after entry. Includes a section on locks and through-the-lock entry. Review questions and answers at the end of each chapter. 7th Edition (1987), 270 pages, helpful for NFPA 1001.

GROUND COVER FIRE FIGHTING PRACTICES

explains the dramatic difference between structural fire fighting and wildland fire fighting. Ground cover fires include fires in weeds, grass, field crops, and brush. It discusses the apparatus, equipment, and extinguishing agents used to combat wildland fires. Outdoor fire behavior and how fuels, weather, and topography affect fire spread are explained. The text also covers personnel safety, management, and suppression methods. It contains a glossary, sample fire operation plan, fire control organization system, fire origin and cause determination, and water expansion pump systems. 2nd Edition (1982), 152 pages.

FIRE SERVICE GROUND LADDER PRACTICES

is a "how to" manual for learning how to handle, raise, and climb ground ladders; it also details maintenance and service testing. Basic information is presented with a variety of methods that allow the readers to select the best method for their locale. The chapter on Special Uses includes: ladders as a stretcher, a slide, a float drag, a water chute, and more. The manual contains a glossary, review questions and answers, and a sample testing and repair form. 8th Edition (1984), 388 pages, addresses NFPA 1001.

HAZARDOUS MATERIALS FOR FIRST RESPONDERS

provides basic information on hazardous materials with sections on site management and decontamination. It includes a description of various types of materials, their characteristics, and containers. The manual covers the effects of weather, topography, and environment on the behavior of hazardous materials and control efforts. Pre-incident planning and post-incident analysis are covered. 1st Edition (1988), 357 pages, addresses NFPA 472, 29 CFR 1910.120 and NFPA 1001.

STUDY GUIDE FOR HAZARDOUS MATERIALS FOR FIRST RESPONDERS

The companion study guide in question and answer format also includes case studies that simulate incidents. 1989, 208 pages.

HAZARDOUS MATERIALS: MANAGING THE INCIDENT

takes you beyond the basic information found in **Hazardous Materials for First Responders**. Directed to the leader/commander, this manual sets forth basic practices clearly and comprehensively. Charts, tables, and checklists guide you through the organization and planning stages to decontamination. This text, along with the accompanying workbook and instructor's guide, provides a comprehensive learning package. 1st Edition (1988), 206 pages, helpful for NFPA 1021.

STUDENT WORKBOOK FOR HAZARDOUS MATERIALS: MANAGING THE INCIDENT

provides questions and answers to enhance the student's comprehension and retention. 1988, 176 pages.

INSTRUCTOR'S GUIDE FOR HAZARDOUS MATERIALS: MANAGING THE INCIDENT

provides lessons based on each chapter, adult learning tips, and appendices of references and suggested audio visuals. 1988, 142 pages.

HAZ MAT RESPONSE TEAM LEAK AND SPILL GUIDE

contains articles by Michael Hildebrand reprinted from *Speaking of Fire*'s popular Hazardous Materials Nuts and Bolts series. Two additional articles from *Speaking of Fire* and the hazardous material incident SOP from the Chicago Fire Department are also included. 1st Edition (1984), 57 pages.

EMERGENCY OPERATIONS IN HIGH-RACK STORAGE

is a concise summary of emergency operations in the high-rack storage area of a warehouse. It explains how to develop a pre-emergency plan, what equipment will be necessary to implement the plan, type and amount of training personnel will need to handle an emergency, and interfacing with various agencies. Includes consideration questions, points not to be overlooked, and trial scenarios. 1st Edition (1981), 97 pages.

HOSE PRACTICES

reflects the latest information on modern fire hose and couplings. It is the most comprehensive single source about hose and its use. The manual details basic methods of handling hose, including large diameter hose. It is fully illustrated with photographs showing loads, evolutions, and techniques. This complete and practical book explains the national standards for hose and couplings. 7th Edition (1988), 245 pages, addresses NFPA 1001.

FIRE PROTECTION HYDRAULICS AND WATER SUPPLY ANALYSIS

covers the quantity and pressure of water needed to provide adequate fire protection, the ability of existing water supply systems to provide fire protection, the adequacy of a water supply for a sprinkler system, and alternatives for deficient water supply systems. 1st Edition (1990), 340 pages.

INCIDENT COMMAND SYSTEM (ICS)

was developed by a multiagency task force. Using this system, fire, police, and other government groups can operate together effectively under a single command. The system is modular and can be used to meet the requirements of both day-to-day and large-incident operations. It is the approved basic command system taught at the National Fire Academy. 1st Edition (1983), 220 pages, helpful for NFPA 1021.

INDUSTRIAL FIRE PROTECTION

is designed for the person charged with the responsibility of developing, implementing, and coordinating fire protection. A "must read" for fire service personnel who will coordinate with industry/business for pre-incident planning. The text includes guidelines for establishing a company policy, organization and planning for the emergency, establishing a fire prevention plan, incipient fire fighting tactics, an overview of interior structural fire fighting, and fixed fire fighting systems. 1st Edition (1982), 207 pages, written for 29 CFR 1910, Subpart L, and helpful for NFPA 1021 and NFPA 1031.

FIRE INSPECTION AND CODE ENFORCEMENT

provides a comprehensive, state-of-the-art reference and training manual for both uniformed and civilian inspectors. It is a comprehensive guide to the principles and techniques of inspection. Text includes information on how fire travels, electrical hazards, and fire resistance requirements. It covers storage, handling, and use of hazardous materials; fire protection systems; and building construction for fire and life safety. 5th Edition (1987), 316 pages, addresses NFPA 1001 and NFPA 1031, levels I & II.

STUDY GUIDE FOR FIRE INSPECTION AND CODE ENFORCEMENT

The companion study guide in question and answer format with case studies. 1989, 272 pages.

FIRE SERVICE INSTRUCTOR

explains the characteristics of a good instructor, shows you how to determine training requirements, and teach to the level of your class. It discusses the types, principles, and procedures of teaching and learning, and covers the use of effective training aids and devices. The purpose and principles of testing as well as test construction are covered. Included are chapters on safety, legal considerations, and computers. 5th Edition (1990), 326 pages, addresses NFPA 1041, levels I & II.

LEADERSHIP IN THE FIRE SERVICE

was created from the series of lectures given by Robert F. Hamm to assist in leadership development. It provides the foundation for getting along with others, explains how to gain the confidence of your personnel, and covers what is expected of an officer. Included is information on supervision, evaluations, delegating, and teaching. Some of the topics include: the successful leader today, a look into the past may reveal the future, and self-analysis for officers. 1st Edition (1967), 132 pages.

FIRE SERVICE ORIENTATION AND TERMINOLOGY

Fire Service Orientation and Indoctrination has been revised. It has a new name and a new look. Keeping the best of the old — traditions, history, and organization — this new manual provides a complete dictionary of fire service terms. To be used in conjunction with **Essentials of Fire Fighting** and the other IFSTA manuals. 3rd Edition (1993), addresses NFPA 1001.

PRIVATE FIRE PROTECTION AND DETECTION

provides a means by which fires may be prevented or attacked in their incipient phase and/or controlled until the fire brigade or public fire protection can arrive. This second edition covers information on automatic sprinkler systems, hose standpipe systems, fixed fire pump installations, portable fire extinguishers, fixed special agent extinguishing systems, and fire alarm and detection systems. Information on the design, operation, maintenance, and inspection of these systems and equipment is provided. 2nd Edition (1994).

PUBLIC FIRE EDUCATION

provides valuable information for ending public apathy and ignorance about fire. This manual gives you the knowledge to plan and implement fire prevention campaigns. It shows you how to tailor the individual programs to your audience as well as the time of year or specific problems. It includes working with the media, resource exchange, and smoke detectors. 1st Edition (1979), 169 pages, helpful for NFPA 1021 and 1031.

FIRE DEPARTMENT PUMPING APPARATUS

is the Driver/Operator's encyclopedia on operating fire pumps and pumping apparatus. It covers pumpers, tankers (tenders), brush apparatus, and aerials with pumps. This comprehensive volume explains safe driving techniques, getting maximum efficiency from the pump, and basic water supply. It includes specification writing, apparatus testing, and extensive appendices of pump manufacturers. 7th Edition (1989), 374 pages, addresses NFPA 1002.

STUDY GUIDE FOR PUMPING APPARATUS

The companion study guide in question and answer format. 1990, 100 pages.

FIRE SERVICE RESCUE PRACTICES

is a comprehensive training text for firefighters and fire brigade members that expands proficiency in moving and removing victims from hazardous situations. This extensively illustrated manual includes rescuer safety, effects of rescue work on victims, rescue from hazardous atmospheres, trenching, and outdoor searches. 5th Edition (1981), 262 pages, addresses NFPA 1001.

RESIDENTIAL SPRINKLERS A PRIMER

outlines United States residential fire experience, system components, engineering requirements, and issues concerning automatic and fixed residential sprinkler systems. Written by Gary Courtney and Scott Kerwood and reprinted from *Speaking of Fire*. An excellent reference source for any fire service library and an excellent supplement to **Private Fire Protection.** 1st Edition (1986), 16 pages.

FIRE DEPARTMENT OCCUPATIONAL SAFETY

addresses the basic responsibilities and qualifications for a safety officer and the minimum requirements and procedures for a safety and health program. Included in this manual is an overview of establishing and implementing a safety program, physical fitness and health considerations, safety in training, fire station safety, tool and equipment safety and maintenance, personal protective equipment, en- route hazards and response, emergency scene safety, and special hazards. 2nd Edition (1991), 366 pages, addresses NFPA 1500, 1501.

SALVAGE AND OVERHAUL

covers planning salvage operations, equipment selection and care, as well as describing methods and techniques for using salvage equipment to minimize fire damage caused by water, smoke, heat, and debris. The overhaul section includes methods for finding hidden fire, protection of fire cause evidence, safety during overhaul operations, and restoration of property and fire protection systems after a fire. 7th Edition (1985), 225 pages, addresses NFPA 1001.

SELF-CONTAINED BREATHING APPARATUS

contains all the basics of SCBA use, care, testing, and operation. Special attention is given to safety and training. The chapter on Emergency Conditions Breathing has been completely revised to incorporate safer emergency methods that can be used with newer models of SCBA. Also included are appendices describing regulatory agencies and donning and doffing procedures for nine types of SCBA. The manual has been thoroughly updated to cover NFPA, OSHA, ANSI, and NIOSH regulations and standards as they pertain to SCBA. 2nd Edition (1991), 360 pages, addresses NFPA 1001.

STUDY GUIDE FOR SELF-CONTAINED BREATHING APPARATUS

The companion study guide in question and answer format. 1991, 131 pages.

FIRE STREAM PRACTICES

brings you an all new approach to calculating friction loss. This carefully written text covers the physics of fire and water; the characteristics, requirements, and principles of good streams; and fire fighting foams. **Streams** includes formulas for the application of fire fighting hydraulics, as well as actions and reactions created by applying streams under a variety of circumstances. The friction loss equations and answers are included, and review questions are located at the end of each chapter. 7th Edition (1989), 464 pages, addresses NFPA 1001 and NFPA 1002.

GASOLINE TANK TRUCK EMERGENCIES

provides emergency response personnel with background information, general procedures, and response guidelines to be followed when responding to and operating at incidents involving MC-306/DOT 406 cargo tank trucks. Specific topics include: incident management procedures, site safety considerations, methods of product transfer, and vehicle uprighting considerations. 1st Edition (1992), 51 pages, addresses NFPA 472.

FIRE SERVICE VENTILATION

presents the principles and practices of ventilation. The manual describes and illustrates the safe operations related to ventilation, products of combustion, elements and situations that influence the ventilation process, ventilation methods and procedures, and tools and mechanized equipment used in ventilation. The manual includes chapter reviews, a glossary, and applicable safety considerations. 7th Edition (1994), addresses NFPA 1001.

FIRE SERVICE PRACTICES FOR VOLUNTEER AND SMALL COMMUNITY FIRE DEPARTMENTS

presents those training practices that are most consistent with the activities of smaller fire departments. Consideration is given to the limitations of small community fire department resources. Techniques for performing basic skills are explained, accompanied by detailed illustrations and photographs. 6th Edition (1984), 311 pages.

WATER SUPPLIES FOR FIRE PROTECTION

acquaints you with the principles, requirements, and standards used to provide water for fire fighting. Rural water supplies as well as fixed systems are discussed. Abundant photographs, illustrations, tables, and diagrams make this the most complete text available. It includes requirements for size and carrying capacity of mains, hydrant specifications, maintenance procedures conducted by the fire department, and relevant maps and record-keeping procedures. Review questions at the end of each chapter. 4th Edition (1988), 268 pages, addresses NFPA 1001, NFPA 1002, and NFPA 1031, levels I & II.

CURRICULUM PACKAGES

COMPANY OFFICER

A competency-based teaching package with 17 lessons as well as classroom and practical activities to teach the student the information and skills needed to qualify for the position of Company Officer. Corresponds to **Fire Department Company Officer**, 2nd Edition.

The Package includes the Company Officer Instructor's Guide (the how, what, and when to teach); the Student Guide (a workbook for group instruction); and 143 full-color overhead transparencies.

ESSENTIALS CURRICULUM PACKAGE

A competency-based teaching package with 19 chapters and 22 lessons as well as classroom and practical activities to teach the student the information and skills needed to qualify for the position of Fire Fighter I or II. Corresponds to **Essentials of Fire Fighting**, 3rd Edition.

The Package includes the Essentials Instructor's Guide (the how, what, and when to teach); the Student Guide (a workbook for group instruction); and 445 full-color overhead transparencies.

LEADERSHIP

A complete teaching package that assist the instructor in teaching leadership and motivational skills at the Company Officer level. Each lesson gives an outline of the subject matter to be covered, approximate time required to teach the material, specific learning objectives, and references for the instructor's preparation. Sources for suggested films and videotapes are included.

TRANSLATIONS

LO ESENCIAL EN EL COMBATE DE INCENDIOS

is a direct translation of **Essentials of Fire Fighting**, 2nd edition. Please contact your distributor or FPP for shipping charges to addresses outside U.S. and Canada. 444 pages.

PRACTICAS Y TEORIA PARA BOMBEROS

is a direct translation of **Fire Service Practices for Volunteer and Small Community Fire Departments**, 6th edition. Please contact your distributor or FPP for shipping charges to addresses outside U.S. and Canada. 347 pages.

OTHER ITEMS

TRAINING AIDS

Fire Protection Publications carries a complete line of videos, overhead transparencies, and slides. Call for a current catalog.

NEWSLETTER

The nationally acclaimed and award-winning newsletter, *Speaking of Fire*, is published quarterly and available to you free. Call today for your free subscription.